George Gilfillan

Modern Christian heroes

A gallery of protesting and reforming men, including Cromwell, Milton

George Gilfillan

Modern Christian heroes
A gallery of protesting and reforming men, including Cromwell, Milton

ISBN/EAN: 9783337196479

Printed in Europe, USA, Canada, Australia, Japan

Cover: Foto ©Lupo / pixelio.de

More available books at **www.hansebooks.com**

MODERN CHRISTIAN HEROES:

A GALLERY

OF

PROTESTING AND REFORMING MEN,

INCLUDING

CROMWELL, MILTON, THE PURITANS, COVENANTERS, FIRST SECEDERS, METHODISTS, &c.

BY

REV. GEORGE GILFILLAN,

Author of "Bards of the Bible," "Night, a Poem," &c., &c.

LONDON:
ELLIOT STOCK, 62 PATERNOSTER ROW.
EDINBURGH: JOHN MENZIES & CO., 2 HANOVER STREET.
GLASGOW: T ADAMSON, 165 COWCADDENS STREET.
1869.

PREFACE.

—o—

IN the Introductory Chapter the author has given an outline of the general plan he has pursued in the present little book, and intends to pursue in the sequel.

The book consists of a series of lectures which were delivered two successive seasons to very large miscellaneous audiences on Sabbath Evenings in his own chapel in Dundee. He mentions this to explain the general style of the composition, which is not didactic or specially researching, but popular. He has gone over the salient points—the *summa fastigia rerum*—and striven rather to give a broad clear outline than to go into minute details, or to present the results of any new investigation of facts. Yet he trusts that few inaccuracies of much importance will be found.

His great aim throughout has been candour and catholicity of judgment. Occasionally, in condemning the acts of the stronger party, he may have erred by allowing his feelings to hurry him into extravagance. This may be in some measure excused on account of the fact that, apart from his own temperament, he is of the Covenanting and Seceding race, and much as he differs from some of their views, he glories in the relationship. He aims at being eclectic, but has yet to learn that indifferentism and eclecticism are the same thing.

While something of the perfervid blood of his country may be found in the *spirit* of these pages, the *views* of things will be found to approach those of the Broad Church School more than is yet common in Scotland. None of the men, indeed, assuming that name, does he call master, not even Arnold, the "father of them all;" and from many of the opinions of their present leaders he considerably differs. But he largely honours the object which they seek, which is to deliver Christianity from its mummy swathings and encumbrances, to make it a power in the present instead of a mere tradition of the past, to get its kernel to survive the husk, its spirit to outsoar the letter, and to bring it more into *rapport* with the literature, philosophy, and progressive tendencies of the age. He feels that if "the Word of the Lord" is "to endure for ever," it must be not by its remaining apart upon some lofty eminence, and uttering its thunderous oracles, but by coming down and mingling with and seeking to colour and to consecrate the energies which are at work in the vale. He believes that it is high time for Christians to abandon many of the outposts, some of which have been driven in and others shattered, and to concentrate their energies in the defence of the citadel, the leading and central truth. And should it be said that it, too, may by and by be in danger, he replies—"No; since while the outposts are of men, the central truth in our religion is of God; and therefore it cannot be shaken, but must remain."

There is at present in London a club newly formed, which is certainly one of the signs of the times. It is called, he understands, "The Metropolitan Club," and its object is the freest discussion of the great philosophical and religious questions of the day. It is to include representatives of all sections of thought, and a Tennyson and a Huxley, a Maurice and a Martineau, a Dean Stanley and an Archbishop Manning, are to be among its members. He hails such an institute with hope and gladness. He will be intensely disappointed if it do not issue in good, and if Scotland and its Evangelicalism do not furnish some members and thousands of sympathisers with it. It is on a much smaller scale certainly than Pope Pio Nono's new "Council of Trent;" but even as Burke's "Reflections" was a real and effectual "Reply" to the French Revolution, and a book was the means of modifying the will of a great nation; so he trusts that this select vestry of master spirits, and the works to issue from it, may be of service in checking the reaction of mediæval imposture on the one hand, and of destroying some of the beggarly elements of a doting Protestantism on the other.

DUNDEE, 5*th October*, 1869.

CONTENTS.

	PAGE
PREFACE,	5

CHAPTER I.
INTRODUCTORY,	9

CHAPTER II.
OLIVER CROMWELL—
Part I.	25
" II.	48

CHAPTER III.
JOHN MILTON,	81

CHAPTER IV.
THE PURITANS—
Part I.—OWEN AND HOWE,	119
" II.—BAXTER AND BUNYAN,	135

CHAPTER V.
THE SCOTTISH COVENANTERS—
Part I.	149
" II.	183
" III.	208

CHAPTER VI.
THE SECESSION AND RELIEF CHURCHES IN THEIR CRADLE—
Part I.	233
" II.	247

CHAPTER VII.

	PAGE
RISE OF METHODISM—	
Part I.—WESLEY,	264
,, II.—WHITFIELD,	278

CHAPTER VIII.

NATURE AND EXTENT OF LIBERTY OF CONSCIENCE, 297

MODERN CHRISTIAN HEROES.

―――o―――

CHAPTER I.

INTRODUCTORY.

WHEN comparing the men of the present to those of the past there are, as in other matters, two extremes. There are those who, on the one hand, look upon the men of the past as something more than mortal. Standing on the distant eminence, and illuminated by the sunshine of fancy, they seem, as did the troops to young Norval,

"A host gigantic clad in glorious arms!"

Their every attitude is graceful, their every action is infallible, their every word is inspired. People now are little men, and these, oh! these were the men, and wisdom lived, died, and was buried along with them. Others, again, look on their ancestors with supreme and sovereign contempt, and if they do not, with our modern Anthropologists, class them with apes, they are far enough from identifying them with angels; they were, they think, dull, decent, commonplace characters, awfully narrow, and woefully ignorant—fathers to us in name, children in reality, giants in distant perspective, dwarfs upon the nearer view. Here the truth lies between, or, rather, the truth is something different from, and superior to both these extreme views; and we may express it thus—There were giants in those days: there are giants in our days, too,—every age has had its giants, although some have excelled others alike in the number and the loftiness of their progeny, and others, somewhat deficient, perhaps, in outstanding and overtopping celebrities, have made up for it by the general diffusion of knowledge and intellect throughout the mass of the community. Our intention, accordingly, is to fill this new gallery with Protesting and Reforming heroes, not only from the Past, but from our own times.

Our reasons for selecting such a subject, and our intended method of treating it, shall form the subject of a few introductory remarks. We live in a time when hero-worship abounds. With many it has become a part of their religion; with some, it is the whole. And as smokeless altars in this new worship, there are arising, in all directions, here magnificent monuments to the great departed, and there brilliant volumes or ardent odes in their praise. Like all new sects, this has carried its belief and adoration to extremes. It has sought for and found heroes on the gallows, on the highway, in the brothel, and in the robber's cave; and such names as Robin Hood, Rob Roy, Mahomet, Mirabeau, and Marat, attract nearly as much homage as those of William Tell, Sir William Wallace, Martin Luther, or Oliver Cromwell. Now, that there is a truth and value in a modified hero-worship is at once conceded. It is natural for us to look up to those who are taller than ourselves, to admire feats of agility and strength, to laugh at the jests of the witty, to love the beautiful, to bow to the strong, and to reverence the holy.

Hero-worship is at once a necessity of our intellect, and an irresistible instinct of our heart; it is at once a duty and a delight; it is related to the very highest feelings we possess—those, namely, with which we regard God himself—and, although practised in this age more systematically, and carried, perhaps, to greater extravagance by some than in former days, it has always more or less characterised the human race, and, unlike many primeval feelings, has not yielded to, but rather been strengthened by culture and civilisation. We do not, therefore, wish hero-worship suppressed: the wish were idle. We wish it purified and exalted; we wish it set upon proper objects, and carried on in a proper spirit; we wish to sever it from idolatry, and connect it with religion. And for this purpose we propose to open up a gallery where every picture shall be that not only of a hero, but a Christian hero—of one distinguished not more by intellectual power, genius, or learning, than by moral worth, noble aspirations, Christian beliefs, and, at the same time, by liberal and progressive tendencies, and by a protesting mission.

There is, our readers will have noticed, one peculiarity in our selection of heroes. We have called them reforming and protesting men, and have thus linked them together as by a chain of martyrdom and fire. We have a notion that in all ages it has been much the same. The Christian hero, even before Christ—for we need hardly say that there were many true Christian heroes before Christ—was a protesting, wrestling, reforming, fighting, martyr-like man. And it is to that class that the apostle who wrote the Epistle to the Hebrews alludes so glowingly—to those who through faith wrought righteousness, subdued kingdoms, stopped the mouths of lions, and were tortured not accepting deliverance, thereby showing that these men not only protested, but suffered for their protest. When Christ himself came, he followed the example of his forerunner. John the Baptist—viz., in the commencement of his ministry, by preaching the gospel and doctrine of repentance—in other words, by denouncing and protesting against the evils of his age. Since then, his protest has been repeated and continued—first of all by his disciples, many of whom were honoured by the martyr's crown, and afterwards by the nobler of the Fathers of the Church, and by that whole army of Confessors who were sacrificed to the fury of the Pagan Power, because they would not conform to the idolatries of worship and superstitions of practice which then prevailed. During the dark ages, on the other hand, when the intellect of Europe was eclipsed, and its belief succumbed under the yoke of Popery, there was little or no protest; on the contrary, there prevailed a dead and prostrate submission, through which the Bulls of the Vatican were heard

"To bellow through the vast and boundless deep,"

like the thunder o'er the sleeping angels in the burning marle of old. But by and bye, now by Wickliff in England, and now by John Huss and Jerome of Prague abroad, the power of protest was again exerted, and the voice of protest again rose. Nor did the one slumber, nor the other sink into silence, till Luther appeared—

"The solitary monk that shook the world,"

and shook it chiefly by the energy, the vehemence, and the

perseverance of his protest. Need we say that in his time arose the glorious name of *Protestant*—a name that has been for 300 years a terror to Popish despotism, and which, in its wider, future meaning, shall be a terror to every form of arbitrary power, civil or sacred, throughout the world.

Since then, the protest has continued, although it has sometimes changed its form and its watchword. In Luther's age and country, it was entirely a religious protest against the usurpations and corruptions of the Church of Rome. In Scotland, again, it had more of political character, and included resistance to the arbitrary power of a Court as well as the exactions and tyrannical sway of a Church. In the next age, it assumed the shape of the great Puritanic Protest, culminating in the great Puritanic Revolt, when Monarchy and Episcopacy fell. In Scotland about the same time, the spirit of protest blossomed into the scarlet and blue colours of the Covenant, and was embodied in the Solemn League —a document of which few now entirely approve, but which did noble service in its day, and was, for the time being, the charter of our political and religious liberties. In the next, or eighteenth century, we find it in the form of Methodism in England, protesting against the dead religious indifference of that age, and in Scotland in the form of the Seceder and Relief Movement against the yoke of State Patronage. More lately we have had it in the Voluntary Question, contending against the connection between Church and State. And at present it is fast assuming the aspect of protest against whatever unduly stereotypes religious opinion, and tyrannises over the consciences of enlightened and progressive Christian men.

As to the mode in which we propose to deal with our heroes, we are not, first of all, to speak of them in terms of idolatrous reverence. This were absurd and wrong in any case, but especially so in reference to men who gave themselves out in general as Iconoclasts, idol-breakers; to turn *them* into idols were unspeakably ridiculous. And yet this has been extensively done. Many even still look upon our Reformers, Puritans, Covenanters, and First Seceders, as absolutely perfect—perfect in life, perfect in spirit, and perfect in doctrine. We shall not homologate any such extravagant notions, but show the men as they were—men of like passions with ourselves—paint their faults as well as their virtues, show the errors and limitations of their views as well as the portion of truth which they contained, and bring out the points in which they are inferior to the present day, as well as those in which they had the advantage. At the same time, we would desire to do this in a candid and reverent spirit. We would touch the faults of those noble men of the past with a tender and filial hand. We would imitate rather Japheth and Shem than Ham in the treatment of even what we might regard as crimes in our revered ancestors, and rather spread the mantle of apology than point the finger of scorn. And that mantle we would find in their early age, their deficient knowledge, their strong prejudices, and the scales remaining on their eyes, from a bad and blind religion, which combined in some measure to impair their vision. Again, we would desire to treat them all in the spirit of genuine catholicism. There shall appear in this gallery men of the most diverse temperaments and habits, circumstances and creeds, ages and ranks; yet it is our duty, and shall be our endeavour, to look at them all in the large lights of the common humanity, the common spirit of courage and earnestness, and the common Christianity which belonged to them all. We may and we do have our favourites among these heroic men. There are some with whom intellectual and religiously we have more sympathy than with others; but we shall endeavour to prevent that partiality from leading us either to exaggerate their merits, extenuate their errors, or depreciate others too much in comparison with them. And most of all we would desire in the course of this little book to show the "increasing purpose" which runs through the testimony of these protesting men; how, as the ages have rolled on, their protest has become less narrow, more enlightened, less that of party, and more that of principle, and has run parallel, in short, to the spirit of the respective periods when it has been given—now obeying and now overruling each successive stream of tendency.

We have decided to omit at present the Reformers—partly owing to the fact of Principal Tulloch's able work about them being so popular and so recent; otherwise we would have led off with Luther the lion-hearted, who stands up like one of the pillars of Hercules dividing two continents or worlds from each other, rough, gigantic, earnest—to men passionate and proud, to God pious and humble as a child, the mailed hand of the Reformation; then have passed to Calvin, the Head of the movement, learned, serene, lofty, and icy as one of his own Alps; and then have come to Knox, the "Reformer of a kingdom," as Milton calls him, and bearing a striking resemblance to the kingdom he reformed, "the land of the mountain and the flood;" like the mountain stern and unmovable, and like the flood impetuous and passionate, yet clear, pure, and powerful. We intend, as it is, to begin with the Puritans, and to speak, first, of the Puritan as Statesman and Soldier, or Cromwell; secondly, of the Puritan as Poet and Literary man, or Milton; and thirdly, of the Puritan as Divine and Christian Orator, or Bunyan, Baxter, Owen, and Howe. We shall then take a glimpse at the old Covenanters, Samuel Rutherford and the rest, with their honest, sometimes mistaken earnestness, and their wild but wondrous outpouring of mind and heart. Then we shall speak of the First Seceders—the Erskines, Gillespies, and others of that stalwart type who lifted up a noble, though not at the time a far-seen banner, in a cold and corrupt age. Then we mean to do what some of the First Seceders did not—justice to Whitfield and Wesley, and their energetic, varied, and most successful labours. We may glance too at the fathers of the Voluntary Movement in England and Scotland. And then we propose to wind up with a view of the great class of original Christian thinkers and eloquent protesters who have distinguished this age: the profound and solitary Foster; the impetuous and broad-minded Chalmers, rather a conflagration than a man, who rather burned than breathed for 67 years; the impassioned, short-lived, gifted Edward Irving—a nobler Herod eaten of worms, the worms of ecclesiastical bigots and cold-hearted Pharisees; Arnold of Rugby, the teacher of the young mind of England, the Greatheart of the Christian pilgrimage of these days; and, besides some others, the martyred, magnificent Robertson of Brighton, who is yet speaking from the dust in his posthumous writings, and, like Samson, has done more execution in his death than during his short and much-embittered existence.

We cannot conclude this introductory essay without saying a few words on a subject which may be said to underlie the whole of our projected series—namely, the important obligations of the present to the past. There are, indeed, moods in which we are tempted to think that the present has been very little benefited and instructed by the past. How little, we often cry, has the experience of the past taught us after all! From its "red rain" of innumerable ages what a scanty harvest has grown! How barren has been its bloodshed! How empty of real warning or instruction have been its mistakes! How partial, interrupted, and reactionary has been its progress! How oft has the whirlwind been reaped from the sown wind, and the disappointed reaper been forced to exclaim, finding no ears in his hand, and no sheaves in his bosom, "It hath no stalk—the bud thereof shall yield no meal; if so be it yield, strangers shall swallow it up!" What promises of high individual excellence, or of national advancement, have been blasted in the very leaves of their spring! How many "Lost Leaders," to use the title of one of Robert Browning's best poems, there have been! How many men, born out of due time, have been of little service to ages which were too early and discerned them not! How little of the past is surely known to us! How much of it is utterly buried, or, what is worse, so partially revealed as to leave a confused and false impression of the real character of events! What a fragmentary, interlined, and blotted palimpsest the history of the past is! What partisans, bigots, one-eyed judges, or wholesale executioners, historians for the most part have been, and how insecure, consequently, has been their guidance! How little, often, has been the real, solid, lasting residuum of revolutions, reformations, and religious excitements! Sometimes, what an uncertain pendulum, each oscillation an age, has the motion of society been! How at other times it has resembled a railway train rushing impetuously on to be blown to pieces by the mere fury of its own motion, or to come into ghastly collision with some contradictory and equally impetuous movement! How often, as Macaulay shows, one dreadful calamity has to be expelled by another, like the Plague by the Fire of London—like the stupefaction of the later years of the Roman Empire, by the invasion of the Goths, and the thousand years of barbarism which succeeded! And when we look to the main evils which have destroyed and degraded society, we shall find them all extant, as if they were the immovable clouds of a picture; war still drinking its oceans of blood, and craving more to quench its thirst, like a volcano in rain; despotism concentrating its iron ridges, multiplying its myrmidons, and surrounding its throne by diplomacies fathomless as hell; ignorance, intolerance, intemperance, licentiousness, bigotry, and every species of fraud, falsehood, folly and sin revelling in power, established by law, sanctioned by custom, mistaken oft for religion, and sustained by the increase of population itself, as if by a fertile and ever-enlarging spring. And when we look to the nature of man, whence these evils mainly flow, we shall find it, as a whole, unchanged, still "casting ominous conjecture on the whole success," still outrunning every remedy, undermining every useful institution, and producing endlessly new and marvellously ramified varieties of evil. Yes! and when we look at Christianity itself, the Divine scheme of deliverance, we find that it has been 2000 years on the earth, and that, although still mighty, it is no longer young, and that, owing to various causes, it is not exerting the genuine, unforced, and deep-seated influence on that world which is not its own, nor even on that church which it calls its own, to which it is entitled by its age, its pretensions, its beneficent character, and the records of its past triumphs. There is not a thinking, Christian man who does not at times entertain and tremble at such thoughts as these!

But although we have now stated the truth, we have not stated the whole truth, and that not only may there be another side to the picture, but there may be some way of accounting, although not perfectly, for its darkness. We should remember that the authentic history of the human race does not extend farther back than 6000 years, which is a mere drop in the bucket compared to the myriads and millions of ages during which man may continue to exist. We should remember that man is not only a weak but a depraved being, and that the wonder should be not that he has advanced so slowly, but that he has advanced at all. His has been the cramped and cumbered motion of one in fetters. We should remember that the revelations given him by God have been, no doubt for good and sufficient reasons, all more or less imperfect, both as to the extent of the sphere they have reached, and as to the clearness of the light they have shed. We have, after all, been working and walking in twilight, although a divine twilight, and the morning twilight to a coming day. We should remember that that very principle of free-will, which accounts for man's perversity, is also the grand element of his advance; he is, as often happens, at once weak and strong in the same point, or, at least, on the same plane. We should remember that the progress of truth and love has been often retarded by the scrupulousness and fastidiousness of their votaries as to the means to be used in advancing them; they have not willingly drawn the sword, and never save in self-defence; and they have been slow to fight the cause of God by pious frauds, falsehoods, and other weapons of the devil; whereas delusions, despotisms, and impostures of every kind have been true to themselves, and become popular by methods of propagation as degrading as their doctrines. We should remember that in proportion to the future grandeur and permanence of the reign of good, there required probably to be an enormous length of time during which its foundations were to be firmly laid, and its eternal throne securely set upon its own base. We should remember that these reactions of evil at present manifest in the world may be convulsionary, and that strong reactions in weak systems are the sure symptoms of approaching death. And we should remember, in fine, the Scripture hope substantiating the human instinct of a "good time coming," of the cause of righteousness, and peace, and love being yet gloriously and finally triumphant. Such explanations, imperfect as they are, should cheer us, especially when connected with the many distinct and great obligations which the present owes to the past. Among these we do not class dogmas, some of which have become incredible, while others are seen to be hasty and imperfect generalisations, like half-filled ears of corn, creeds and confessions crumbling away most of them in the lapse of time and progress of enquiry, like sandcliffs with many scattered grains of gold, however, in them, which no solution or disintegration can destroy—old customs, opinions, or ecclesiastical organisations. But we owe to the past far better things, involving more lasting obligations than these, such as certain great principles of which the past was the seedfield, and which now stand up before us in clear certainty and solid magnitude, such as the Fatherhood of God, the Unity of Man, the Supremacy of the Moral Law, the Value of Liberty, and the importance of the Religious Element—principles which have all of them, indeed, been doubted, but the doubts have no more affected them in their broad and fixed proportions than shadows of rare and thin clouds in the burning sky of Egypt affect the vast Pyramids over which they seem to tremble as they hurry by; great institutions such as Magna Charta, the Habeas Corpus Act, and Trial by Jury; certain great public examples of heroism and self-sacrifice, such as the Primitive Martyr Age, the Puritanic Protest, and the noble act of conscientious surrender of pulpits in 1662; a high and hitherto unparalleled literature, and the history of certain noble and heroic men. A word on the two last of these obligations.

We owe to the past a great and as yet unparalleled literature. The older books came forth like suns; the modern books like planets. The former, fresh from the great aboriginal light and glory; the latter, formed by a slower process, and warmed by a feebler ray. Whatever the causes of the superiority of ancient literature to modern, there can be no doubt of the fact. The last two centuries have been far more cultivated than any preceding ages, and yet have produced no works to be compared to the old masterpieces, which bear the relationship to the present that the stars do to the fires burning low, though beautiful, on the October hearth. The claims of the Bible, considered in a merely literary point of view, are admitted on all hands to be paramount—in lofty poetry, in impassioned eloquence, in pathos, simplicity and grandeur, it stands alone: alone, and yet not very far beneath its transcendent peak, there are the epics of Homer, the tragedies of Eschylus, and, in a later day, the Divina Commedia of Dante, the Paradise Lost of Milton, and the all-embracing dramas of Shakespeare. Truly, when we contemplate such works as these, we are compelled to feel (as Emerson said to us about the Old Steeple of Dundee) that they seem made by a different race of beings. Far be it from us to depreciate modern literature, but there is nothing amid all the splendid variety of its produtions, nothing in the passion of Byron, in the abundance and naturalness of Scott, in the mystical beauty of Coleridge and Shelley, in the exquisite polish and sea-shell-like intonations of Tennyson, in the magnificent exuberance of Bailey, or the brilliance of Bulwer, that can bear comparison with the better works of the past; and we would rather, for our part, have written Milton's Comus, than all the poetry which has appeared in Britain during the last twenty years, and rather have produced the Pilgrim's Progress of the brave old Nonconformist, John Bunyan, than all the webs of fiction which have come from the teeming brains of such prolific silkworms of the novel as Charles Dickens, Wilkie Collins, or William M. Thackeray. The beauties of the olden books have been tested by time; their glory is as mellow as the light of an Indian summer; their talk to us is like conversation carried on from a mountain peak, commanding, aërial, far-withdrawn, like the voice of spirits; and we say of them, in the language of one who, of all the moderns, has come nearest in severe simplicity and original insight to the ancients, viz., Wordsworth—

> "Blessings be with them, and eternal praise,
> The Poets, who on earth have made us heirs
> Of truth and pure delight by heavenly rays."

But we owe, in fine, to the past a high and noble race of men whom but to name is to canonise. Such are the patriarchs, the prophets, and the Divine Man of Galilee; such are the sages of Greece and the warriors of Rome; such is that grand group of Puritanic men we mean to in part portray—Owen, and Baxter, and Howe, and Vane, and Selden, and Milton—in the midst of whom we see a countenance of more rugged grandeur, a more dauntless determination, and more piercing insight than any of them all—a face whose iron lines tell of a thousand nights of prayer, and of a hundred days of battle—of grave suffering and sorrow, and of graver victory and success—of agony bravely borne, and of triumph manfully welcomed—a face proclaiming its owner "every inch a king," although no crown is ever to rest upon his head: it is the granite countenance of glorious Old Noll. These are the men, and still they have representatives, who redeem the sad and scandalous history of humanity hitherto;

these are the men who dwindle into insignificance the common rabble of kings, and statesmen, and popular favourites; these are the men who prove that there is a divinity at work in man, throwing up, ever and anon, such Alps of humanity even as the plastic power of nature piles up its far-seen pinnacles and blazing volcanoes, its Etnas and its Mount Everests; and these are the men who, as pledges and prophetic specimens of a better era, when man shall emphatically become man, excite in our breasts the most ardent trust in the future prospects of the human family.

CHAPTER II.

OLIVER CROMWELL.—PART I.

BEFORE coming to Cromwell, a glance must be permitted us at the circumstances which preceded and served to develop the Puritanic type of hero. After much difficulty, although with the shedding of very little blood, with the exception of course of Queen Mary's Smithfield martyrs, the Reformation was at last established in England. With the accession of Queen Elizabeth, Popery in its ranker forms and more arrogant pretensions was abolished. But although externally Popery was no more, yet internally there remained much of its spirit. The Queen, instead of the Pope, became the Head of the English Church; but her power was as arbitrary, and was often as cruelly used, as his had been. The bishops were her creatures—made by her, supported by her, and compelled to obey and almost worship her. Episcopacy itself was felt by many to be a heavy yoke. The principles of Presbyterianism had been learned by some of the exiles, who had been driven to Geneva by persecution, and they did not forget them when they returned home. The English service was not so simple as that of Geneva had been. A good deal of the Popish pomp and ceremony remained. Kneeling at the Lord's Supper and the use of the ring at marriage were some of the relics of Popery which were suffered to exist, and which greatly scandalised many devout Protestants. Civil freedom, too, even in its republican shape, was much prized by many who had been abroad, and who, when they came back to England, found themselves the vassals of a diluted despotism, not the less disagreeable that it was connected with the government of a woman however able and distinguished. The seeds, in short, of Puritanism were sown in Queen Elizabeth's reign, although the energy of her character, the wisdom of her counsellors, and the fear into which the whole country was plunged by the machinations of Papists and the Spanish Armada, and which served to unite it into one, prevented them from growing fully till the reign of James and especially of Charles I. In the reign, indeed, of the former, the great Puritanic contest began, and the peculiarity of James's reign lay in the struggle between royal prerogative and popular freedom. The proceedings of Parliament were characterised by a spirit of boldness and pertinacious resistance never before manifested, while the speeches and acts of the King were marked by an obstinate and stupid attachment to those privileges which absolute kings extorted from their subjects in former ages of darkness and despotism. The boldness of the Commons and the bigotry of the King led to incessant disagreement and discontent, and finally, under Charles I., to open rupture, revolution, and bloodshed. Charles I. tried to rule without a Parliament, because Parliament disliked his favourites as sycophants, distrusted him as a crafty despot, hated his Queen as a foreigner and as a Papist, and refused to grant him supplies of money. He was at last compelled to call one—to raise a devil he was unable to lay; and on the 13th of April there met what was called the Long Parliament, which did not dissolve till it made the most thorough-going changes in the government, impeached and beheaded King Charles's favourite statesman and archbishop, Strafford and Laud, abolished the Star Chamber—the instrument of his oppression—overturned Prelacy and, in fine, waged war against the king himself—a war which terminated in the death of Charles upon the block at Whitehall.

Let us look next with equal brevity at the parties and the leading men who were involved in that great civil war, which made the middle of the seventeenth century illustrious. The Cavaliers or King's friends were by no means a despicable class. There were, indeed, many of them not a little debauched; others were fond of showy dress, long curling locks, gilded rapiers, and so forth; and some of them were fierce to cruelty, loyal to superstition, and religious to bigotry. But they were, on the whole, brave and high-bred men, of a good station in life, and full of the spirit of ancient chivalry; burning, according to their light, with zeal for their country and devoted attachment to their King, although their light was too often discoloured by the mists of semi-Popish dogmas in religion, and they themselves weakened by the paralysing absurdities of passive obedience and non-resistance in politics. They were not a despicable class who, under Prince Rupert, fought so bravely at Marston Moor, Naseby, and many another field of severe contest, whose charge, indeed, in its fiery energy and speed, formed the model for that of the French cavalry in after days, and whose roll-call of worthies contains such names as Rupert himself, the gallant general; Lord Falkland, the blameless and amiable character; Lord Clarendon, the astute politician and picturesque and sagacious historian; Archbishop Usher, that great luminary of the Irish Church; and Strafford, or Wentworth, a man whose crimes may and ought to be condemned, but who was admitted even by his enemies to have possessed ability as great as his ambition, and a courage so unflinching, that Milton might have had him in his eye when describing Satan, the Sultan of Pandemonium, bearing the pains unshrinkingly for the sake of the pre-eminence of his burning throne!

But ah! the Puritans, with all their faults, were a far nobler race of men than the Cavaliers. The latter read the words, "Fear the King and God;" the former, "Fear God, and know no other fear." The Cavaliers were rapid in their charges, but their fire and fury soon expended themselves and expired. The Puritans were firm and patient as the old rocks: they knew how to die, but they did not know how to be defeated. The Cavaliers were, on the whole, sprightly but shallow thinkers,—they looked only at the outside of things; the Puritans had gazed, or sought to gaze, into the deepest and darkest secrets of God. The Cavaliers were Jews outwardly—loving the pomp of Jewish service and the beauty of external holiness, the sound of organs, and the smell of incense and of oil; but of the rugged inspiration of the Jewish mind, and the austere consecration of the Jewish morals, they had little conception. The Puritans still seemed worshipping before the Mount that burned; and in singing the Song of Moses and the Lamb, it was the former burden which they sung with most sympathy and power. They preferred the Joshua of the Old to the Jesus of the

New Testament. They were Israelites to the backbone, and resembled those Gadites who were with David in his desert fortress of old, that could handle shield and buckler—men that had the faces of lions, and who were swift as the roes upon the mountains. The Cavaliers were vain, rather than proud,—full of graceful courtesies and elegant accomplishments. The Puritans were proud, and, as Macaulay has it, "on wise men and orators, on nobles and on priests, they looked down with disdain; for they looked on themselves as wise, with a more profound intelligence and eloquent in a more sublime language—nobles by the right of an earlier creation, and priests by the imposition of a mightier hand." And as the two classes were diverse, so were the men that sprung from them, and the Puritans have given us instead of a Laud and an Usher, a John Howe and a Richard Baxter; instead of a Lord Falkland, a John Hampden; instead of an Abraham Cowley, a John Milton; and instead of a Clarendon and Charles First, an Oliver Cromwell.

After all that has been written about Cromwell, his life is still a desideratum. Guizot has too few sympathies with his creed or character; Carlyle, too many with his character, but too little with his creed; Dr Vaughan is heavy and lumbering; Godwin had not enough religion; Noble, Henry Cromwell, &c., are now obsolete; D'Aubigné gives a feeble, meagre, rosewater outline of his career. Nor can we wonder at the comparative failure of most of his biographers, when we consider the extreme complexity and extraordinary combination of the qualities which distinguished him. A writer, too antithetically, but with some truth, describes him as by turns sincere and a hypocrite, a religionist and a zealous worldling, a man of gravity and a buffoon, a preacher and a punster, a clown and a gentleman; stately and familiar, slovenly and precise, an orator and without words to express himself, cautious and yet enterprising, ardent and yet methodical, ready and yet invariably politic. He has been extraordinary both in his own history and in the history of his fame. From a brewer's son, if not a brewer himself, he became the Lord Protector of England—the terror of France and Spain, the bulwark of Protestantism, and the feared and hated of the Pope and every Catholic power in the world. From (as many have believed) a dissipated gambler in his youth, he became a great Christian man and ruler. And so, from the extreme disgust entertained for his memory, not only by Papists, High Churchmen, and extreme Conservatives, but by moderate Whigs, he has risen into all but universal esteem. Burke even in his day speaks of Cromwell as a "great bad man;" but now men of orthodox sentiments admire him for his Calvinism, the heterodox for his regard to liberty of conscience, the hero worshipper for his energy of character, the republican for his putting Charles I. to death, and the Orangeman for his crushing and butchering the Roman Catholics. Only a few Puseyites express occasionally a little stale and stupid spite at his name, because he despised such mummeries as they are trying to re-introduce into the Church, and was neither descended from nor gave birth to a line of kings; but in this they are not wiser than a beef-eater we once spoke to in the Tower of London. He was showing the crowns of the various monarchs who had reigned in England. We asked why Cromwell's was not there, and he replied, "O sir, he was not royal." Royal! No, not in the sense of the beef-eater; but if manhood, courage, conduct, genius, knowledge of human nature, and reverence for God, constitute a man fitted to govern, then he who possessed them all and more must have been a true king of men, and the Edwards, Henrys, and Charleses look small and second-rate compared to Old Noll.

Without attempting to supply what we have just called a desideratum—a full life of Oliver Cromwell—we propose a a rapid sketch of his career. Oliver Cromwell was not, after all, a plebeian. He was descended from an old and highly honourable family. His father, Robert Cromwell, was the second son of a knight, and his elder brother, Oliver's uncle, was himself a knight. Cromwell's father being, however, a second brother, and not possessed of a very great patrimony, he seems to have eked it out by establishing a brewery in Huntingdon. In that town, at all events, Oliver Cromwell was born on the 25th of April, 1599. His mother's name was Elizabeth Williams, and she also was sprung from a good and ancient house in Wales. Young Cromwell was first entrusted to the educational care of the Rev. Mr. Long, of Huntingdon, but was soon removed to the Free Grammar School of that place, which was taught by Dr. Beard, described as a very learned and sensible person. At school young Cromwell showed a good deal of the versatility which distinguished him in after years, the boy being father of the man. He had now fits of learning, it is said, and was a hard student for a week or two, and now an idler or truant for a season, and sometimes he took the lead in robbing orchards and scaling dovecotes, as spirited boys will sometimes do. A curious story is told of his meeting Charles I., whom he afterwards beheaded, when they were children of nearly the same age, at Hinchinbrook House, the seat of Sir Oliver Cromwell, his uncle, which Charles, then Duke of York, visited on his way from Scotland to London, and that the two boys quarrelled, and that Oliver, being the stronger of the two, beat little Charles. This probably, however, is only one of those myths which gather round the young days of all celebrated men. Another more stirring story of a different kind is told as having been narrated by Cromwell in after life. Lying one night, when a boy, in his bed, he saw a gigantic figure, which came and opened the curtains of his bed, and told him he should be the greatest person in the kingdom—but did not use the word "king." From the Grammar School in his own town he passed to Cambridge University, and was entered in Sydney Sussex College in April 23rd, 1616. Here, it is said, he made little proficiency in his studies, but pursued an erratic life, being famous, as Christopher North also was, at the University in youth, for football, cricket, cudgelling, wrestling, and other violent and manly sports—to which some say that he added a bad habit of gambling, and the pursuit of other vices. His father died in 1617, and it seems probably about that time he quitted Cambridge, and was soon afterwards sent by his mother to Lincoln's Inn, London, where, however, if we believe his enemies, instead of studying the law, he learned and practised the follies of the town. Returning to his native place, Huntingdon, he, under the watchful care of his mother, seems to have turned over a new leaf—became first remorseful, then regular, and, in fine, pious,—attended public worship constantly, dismissed his evil companions, and, to complete and seal his reformation, when he was only twenty-one years of age, he married, on August 22nd, 1620, Elizabeth Bourchier, daughter of Sir James Bourchier, of Fitsted, Essex. By her he had nine children, of whom only five survived him. For sixteen years after his marriage he resided either at his native town, or at St. Ives, in the same county—engaged, it would appear, in agricultural labours, being what is now called a gentleman farmer, besides a brewer, and while supporting an excellent character, and, indeed, distinguished by eminent piety, was gradually accumulating a modest fortune. Who that saw the plain dressed husbandman perhaps binding after his reapers, or watching the ripening of the fields, and the thickening of the farm-yard, or chaffering in the market-place about the price of malt, would have dreamed that here was the future monarch of Britain? But even then he was cherishing within himself a lofty ambition. Milton says of him, " Though noted for nothing so much as the culture of pure religion and integrity of life, he had enlarged his hope, relying upon God and a great soul in a quiet bosom, for any the most exalted times." But if this hope should have slipped out in words now and then, we doubt not, visionary, madman, presumptuous fool would have been the least contemptuous terms applied to him by his neighbours. No man was ever a hero to his valet. And seldom has a man been a hero to his country neighbours. Yet, if they did not recognise the genius and powerful intellect of the man, they did his probity, moral worth, and patriotism, and hence they elected him the member of Parliament for Huntingdon, which met March 17th, 1627, when he was only 28 years of age. This was the third Parliament called by Charles I. It met in a sufficiently determined humour, and began immediately to discuss the grievances of the country, to appoint committees for their consideration, and to refuse supplies of money to the king till they were redressed. For more than a year Cromwell sat a silent senator in the house, saying little or nothing, but observing and meditating much. In 1628 he informed the house "what countenance the Bishop of Winchester did give to some persons who preached at Charing Cross flat Popery," and mentioned the persons by name, and spoke besides of a notorious papist, or something very near it, by name Maynwaring, having been preferred by that Bishop's means to a rich living. If these, he said, be the steps to Church preferment, what may we expect next? Cromwell never became a graceful or eloquent speaker, and at first he must have been exceedingly awkward. He stuttered and stammered, his sentences were often very confused, and sometimes he broke down altogether; but there was always strong sense and manliness in what he uttered; and those who have seen his portrait must be aware that the power, sagacity, and resolution which spoke in his noble rugged countenance were such as no assembly could refuse to respect and to listen to whatever came from it. In Parliament he remained till the King, about the twelve months after it met, dissolved it in a pet, because it meddled with the conduct of his favourite, the Duke of Buckingham, and tried for some time to govern without Parliaments altogether. Cromwell returned quietly to his native county, and resumed the labours of the farm, residing sometimes at Huntingdon, sometimes in what is now the bustling and prosperous town of St. Ives, which a well-known rhyme has made familiar to everybody, and sometimes at the Isle of Ely, a country all through flat, fenny, and destitute of fine scenery, but where he felt that his lot for a season was cast, and where he made himself busy and useful, not only in farming and brewing matters, but in parochial business. To the Isle of Ely he went because his maternal uncle, Sir Thomas Stewart, had left him his estates there. Of his doings and purposes while residing in that place we have only one or two incidents. Brooding constantly among the fens on the wrongs of his country, on the slavery of the royal yoke, on the ecclesiastical tyranny of Laud, who had just issued the famous Book of Sports, commanding all manner of games and diversions to be pursued on the Lord's-day, and enjoining ministers to read the same from the pulpit, Cromwell began to weary of England, and to meditate emigration to America. New England was held by the settlers there by patent from the King. Numbers of the people, and many ministers too, sold their estates and set sail for that province, in order to escape from religious bondage, and push their fortunes in a new country. At length the Court became jealous of losing so many subjects, and issued a proclamation forbidding any more to leave without a royal license. This proclamation was evaded, and there came an order in Council, commanding the Lord Treasurer to stop eight ships, then in the Thames, prepared to go to New England, and to bring back to land all passengers and provisions intended for the voyage. This was done, and in one of the vessels were embarked the great John Hampden, Cromwell's cousin, and Oliver himself. They were like Garibaldi when arrested at Asilunga, very reluctant to submit, but they could not help themselves, and were reserved for a noble work at home. Charles must have often afterwards regretted that he had not rather sent a special fleet to convey his two most formidable enemies to the backwoods, and got rid of them thus for ever. And if this had happened we might now have been living very stupid and contented Episcopalians, or perhaps Papists, under the yoke of Charles VII. or James VIII. But it was otherwise ordered, and Cromwell went growling back like a wild boar to his fens and flats once more.

But a few years afterwards he came out from them again, and raised such a dire pother and din as to frighten Charles I. himself. The Earl of Bedford had engaged, along with some other gentlemen, to drain a portion of the immense marshes or fens found in that region, and turn them into fruitful fields. But Charles, for some reason or other, found fault with the drainage, and sought to wrest from Bedford the recovered lands, when Cromwell arose, grappled with the general oppressor, met, argued with, and triumphantly confuted the Commissioners he had sent to Huntingdon, aroused the universal feeling of the country in behalf of the original undertakers, became an object of admiration for his spirited resistance to prerogatived tyranny in his own and all the neighbouring counties; and, long after, the grateful recollection of his conduct in this affair procured for him the appellation of "The Lord of the Fens."

Eleven years passed away, and Charles, requiring money for his war with the insurgent Scots, and unable to procure it otherwise, was compelled to call a Parliament, which met on the 13th April, 1640. Cromwell was elected member for Cambridge, owing, no doubt, to the great popularity he had acquired by his conduct as to the drainage of the fens. This Parliament, however, did not please Charles—it was not the supple slave to his will he expected. It debated with great boldness, whether the question of supplies or of grievances should take the precedency; and hence, after sitting twenty-three days, he angrily dissolved it. He was forced, however, by his necessities, to summon another, which met on the 3rd of November, the same year, and which, as most are aware, did not dissolve in a hurry. The Long Parliament, destined to play a part so important in the kingdom, was now met, and Cromwell was elected one of its members, sitting again for Cambridge. Never did a nobler galaxy of patriots meet in any Parliament than in this. There were such men as Selden, the most learned scholar of his time; the noble and disinterested Hampden; the fearless Pym; the hardy Holles; the enthusiastic St. John; and the chivalrous Lord Falkland. But none of them was destined to exert an influence so deep, or to gain a name so illustrious as yonder ill-dressed, red-nosed, stuttering, awkward-looking, middle-aged farmer from the fens—Oliver Cromwell. Let us hear him described by an eye-witness, a Royalist contemporary, Sir Philip Warwick: "I came into the house one morning, and perceived a gentleman speaking, whom I knew not, very ordinarily apparelled for this; a plain cloth suit, which seemed to have been made by an ill country-tailor; his linen was plain, and not very clean, and I remember a speck or two of blood upon his little band, which was not much larger than his collar; his hat was without a hat band, his stature was of a good size, his sword stuck close to his side, his countenance swollen and reddish, his voice sharp and untuneable, and his eloquence full of fervour." He adds that he was very much hearkened unto, and says that afterwards, when he saw him in his power, and better dressed, that he appeared of a great and majestic deportment and comely presence.

The Long Parliament, once met, commenced immediately its work of opposition to the King and his evil counsellors. It reversed the sentences passed against Hampden, and others of the popular party—impeached and afterwards beheaded Earl Strafford and Archbishop Laud—succeeded in placing Ministers of State of popular principles in the royal counsels, and sent Commissioners down to the various counties to deface and demolish images and altars, pictures and crucifixes, and all other relics of Popish worship throughout the land. The Star Chamber too, and the High Commissioners' Court, both odious instruments of royal oppression, were abolished. While Charles was absent in Scotland, they prepared, too, a remonstrance, recounting and denouncing all the evils of his Government and the calamities of his reign. At this, when he returned, he was excessively irritated, and proceeded to impeach five members of the house, including Hampden and Pym, and even came in person to the Commons, attended by a large body guard, to seize upon the obnoxious persons, but found them gone, and was compelled to depart, very much disappointed. The next day, going into the lobby to lay his complaint before the Common Council, and to order them to produce the five members who had fled there, he was saluted by the populace, as his carriage drove along, by cries of "Privileges of Parliament;" and one of the crowd, more daring than the rest, approached close to his coach, and exclaimed, "To your tents, O Israel;"—the cry of the rebellious Hebrews when they abandoned Rehoboam. In short, all things were ripe for the civil war. Charles left his Palace and London for the midland counties; his Queen went over to the Continent; and after the Commons had voted the assembling of an army, to be confided to the command of the Earl of Essex, the King on the 25th of August, 1642, erected his standard at Nottingham, and it was observed by those studious of omens that a tempestuous wind overturned the standard the same evening it was erected—just as a little before the Russian war, which proved the ruin of Napoleon, and at a ball in celebration of his marriage with Maria Louise, the ball-room took fire, the great chandelier fell with a tremendous crash, and hundreds of the most elegant men and beautiful women in Paris were burnt to ashes—a young Princess covered with diamonds, rushing out half consumed from among the blazing rafters and calling frantically for her children,—an awful omen, many imagined, of the calamities which came upon France.

Of the contest when it commenced, Cromwell was soon revealed to be the genius and master-spirit. And here certainly is a matter of astonishment. Napoleon was educated and trained a soldier, a man of war from his youth; Cromwell, up to his 43rd year, was a peaceful husbandman and politician, and yet, in a short time, he took a rank in warfare among the very ablest and most successful generals that ever lived. He began, ere ever war was proclaimed, to exert himself in behalf of the Parliament by distributing arms in the town of Cambridge, which he represented, raising a troop of horse out of that county and Huntingdonshire, seizing the magazine of arms in Cambridge Castle for the use of the Parliament, crushing all attempts in these midland counties to raise armies for the King's cause, and, above all, surrounding himself with troops of horsemen, who, for courage and strength, conjoined with piety and respectable character, became the wonder of the country, and the terror of the Cavaliers.

Charles commenced the war under many disadvantages. The Parliament was incomparably more powerful, possessing more numerous forces and all the places of strength in the kingdom, besides the favour of the best of the nation. Yet such was the courage of his troops, and the prestige connected with the presence of the King himself, that the first battle, fought at Edgehill on the 24th October, 1642, was claimed by the Royalists as a victory. Cromwell's eagle eye saw the reason of this at once, and told his friend John Hampden, "Your troops are most of them old, decayed serving men and tapsters, and such kind of fellows; while those of the King are gentlemen's younger sons, persons of quality. Do you think the spirits of such base and mean fellows will be ever able to encounter men that have honour, and spirit, and resolution in them? Truly you must get men of a spirit that will go on as far as gentlemen will go, or else you will be beaten still." And Cromwell found that spirit in religion. He raised up men that had the fear of God in them, and made some conscience of what they did, and these men (John Bunyan was one of them), he tells us, after a little, were never beaten. It was something like what it was in the late American war, where at first the rude and mercenary soldiers of the North had no chance with the terrible barefooted and ragged gentlemen of the South, rushing on with wild yells of defiance, and carrying all before them, till the latter years of the war, when the West sent its backwoodsmen, burning with a belated Puritanism, and as hard as the wood and the iron of their own axes, and they decided the contest.

Various engagements succeeded Edgehill, and in most of them Charles's troops continued to have the advantage—the intervals between the battles being filled up by attempts at amicable adjustment, which, however, came to nothing. At Chalgrave Field, Bucks, June 18th, 1643, on which day the soldiers of the Parliament sustained a defeat, John Hampden perished—Hampden, who had resisted the exactions of the Government about the ship money so manfully. He was a man of sterling honesty and invincible resolution, and some imagine that, had he lived, he would have saved the State, and the Monarch too. We do not think, however, he had the powers of his relative Cromwell, or could have played such a prominent part. Man is immortal till his work be done, and Hampden's work was done, as he rode out of Chalgrave Field, that June evening, with drooping head, and hand laxly holding his bridle rein, to die. Cromwell, now Colonel Cromwell, that same month, made his first military hit, near Gainsborough. The Lincolnshire men, who fought for the Parliament, had been completely routed by Cavendish, the Cavalier General, when Cromwell, along with Ireton, who afterwards married his eldest daughter, Bridget, came suddenly up, restored the battle, and drove Cavendish and his men into a bog, where most of them were destroyed. This exploit turned the eyes of the whole army on Cromwell, and they began to feel that here was the man for the hour—the master of the situation, and so, by-and-bye, he abundantly proved himself. Other successes followed. In one fight Cromwell's men, advancing to the watchword, "Truth and Peace," and singing psalms, gained a decisive victory. He had a horse killed under him, and was nearly slain himself. Then followed the famous junction of the Scotch and English forces—the Scotch, under Lord Leven, crossing the Tweed to meet the Parliamentary army, and both binding themselves under the bond of that immortal "Solemn League and Covenant," which proved such a distinguished landmark in the history of our country, and led to such momentous results. It is interesting to know that, although Cromwell became a fierce enemy to the Covenanters afterwards, his name, as plain Oliver Cromwell, is one of the signatures at the Covenant—just as it is a fact that Daniel O'Connell, who was so hated by the thankless Chartists, wrote the Charter with his own hand, as he told them at a large public meeting in London. This junction, itself enough to secure the destruction of the Royalists, was followed by the great battle of Marston Moor. This battle took place in consequence of the Royalists, under the Marquis of Newcastle, being besieged in York, and the gallant Prince Rupert having sought to raise the siege. This he effected; but, not content with this, he rushed, with his usual impetuosity, after the retreating foe, who were compelled to stop at Marston Moor and give battle to Rupert. At first the Parliamentarians were successful; but Rupert rallied and gave one of those tremendous charges which have become proverbial in warfare, and have never been paralleled, unless by those of Napoleon's Old Guard, or of Stonewall Jackson in the recent American struggle. His soldiers, mounted on fiery steeds, and armed to the teeth, rushed on with the unity and fury of a whirlwind, their horses devouring the ground in fierceness and rage, and their swords flashing like lightning amid the tempest; scattered the Scottish chivalry of the Covenant, scattered the troops of Fairfax, scattered and beat all but Cromwell, and the remnant of 300 who were with him. This little band not only stood firm itself against the shock, but became a rallying point to the fugitives who turned back, aided by a troop of Scots under General Leslie, (that very General, afterwards beaten at Dunbar,) and commanded by Cromwell, assumed the offensive, and fell resistlessly on the scattered and divided bodies of the enemy, totally dispersed them, pursued them to the gates of York, captured all their artillery and baggage, and in a few days after entered the city in triumph. The Earl of Manchester, and some of the Scotch troops had been routed by Rupert, and were in full retreat to Scotland, when they were arrested by horsemen, who rode to report that they had gained a complete victory. The year closed with a battle at Newbury (where, if Cromwell had had his way, the war would have been finished, but in which the Earl of Manchester allowed the King to escape), and with some abortive attempts at negotiation.

Cromwell was still secondary, but was determined to be first in the Army, and in the State. For this purpose, it is said, he planned a measure, entitled "The Self-denying Ordinance," by which it was arranged that all the members of Parliament holding whether civil or military offices, should resign them in behalf of others better qualified for the duties. In this way the Earl of Essex had to resign his office as leader of the armies. It fell to Sir Thomas Fairfax, who, feeling himself incapable of performing its duties, got Cromwell exempted from the ordinance he had himself planned, and appointed the principal commander ostensibly under, but in reality above him. Woe now to Charles and to the Cavaliers, for their enemy was come down among them, having great wrath and all power! No more delay or half measures, for whether the whole scheme had been matured in his own mind, or whether he was the mere slave of circumstances, certain it was that the object of his ambition was attained. He was at length supreme in command. A man of iron energy had now the army to guide and manage, and it became a mere question of time that he should succeed. Nor had he long to wait, for, on the 14th of June, 1645, the battle of Naseby was fought, and proved decisive and final. Let us glance at this for a moment. The King is with his troops in person, and commands the main body. Sir Marmaduke Langdale has the left wing, and Prince Rupert the right. Opposite to them is the Parliamentary army—

the main body commanded by Fairfax and Shipton; Ireton, Cromwell's son-in-law, has the left, and Cromwell the right wing. Rupert is, as usual, the first to begin the attack. He dashes his fierce troops like a spring-tide upon Ireton, who offers a brave resistance; but after having been pierced through the thigh with a pike, wounded in the face with a halberd, and his horse shot under him, he is at last made a prisoner, and his division of the army routed. But Rupert, though he could gain, could not use a victory well. Instead of turning his victorious troops upon the main battle, he allowed them to employ themselves in plundering the baggage on the rear. Meanwhile the main bodies had charged mutually and with extraordinary fierceness and resolution, often retreating, and then rallying, falling to a hand-to-hand conflict with their swords, and even assailing each other with the butt-ends of their muskets. Cromwell had attacked the King's left wing almost at the same moment that Rupert had charged that of the Parliament, and had driven it like chaff before the wind. But *he* did not pause in his impetuous career, *he* did not allow his soldiers to amuse themselves with the baggage, but fell with full swing on the first line of the reserve, then upon the second, then upon the main body, and, as it is said, "with fine force he quite charged through the three bodies, and beat them irrevocably from the ground. Returning with unabated speed, he met the victorious right wing and Rupert returning from his too forward progress, and gave them a signal discomfiture—thus folding up the fortunes of the day, driving the King back upon Leicester, and finishing, to all intents and purposes, the civil war." No wonder though these Cavaliers, who fought at Marston Moor, and especially Naseby, and witnessed Cromwell's prodigies of valour there, ever afterwards regarded him with hatred and horror, considering him less as a man than as a destroying angel, or perhaps rather a sorcerer who had bought from the great enemy the power of trampling them as mire. In vain they sought to laugh at their destroyer—at his rude manners, his red nose, his nasal twang, his canting psalm-singing troops—their laughter died away into a quaver of consternation, and was lost in the groans of despair, the hysterical gurglings of fear, and the shrieks and supplications of death.

Sometime after, Charles, driven from Oxford, which had been his headquarters, took refuge with the Scotch at Newark, but was, in May, 1646, surrendered by them to the Parliament—in plain English, sold. Parliament was now triumphant, and was disposed, having mounted on the ladder, to spurn it away, having risen by the army, to disband it. This, however, Cromwell would not submit to, and he and Ireton, and other leading Independents, managed the soldiers as they chose, and were suspected of having urged them to seize upon the person of the King, which was done accordingly by Cornet Joyce, who took him, then residing at Holmby House, and brought him off with them—he, nothing loath, wishing to play one party against another, and make his own out of their controversies and quarrels. Cromwell's influence, meanwhile, grew every hour, notwithstanding the hatred of the King's party, the envy of the Presbyterians, and the suspicion of the Republicans, who were afraid he was himself aiming at the monarchy; and hence, as Wales and Scotland were both up in arms in the King's behalf, to Cromwell was entrusted the task of subduing these two turbulent countries. It was high time, for not only were these two countries risen up, but, in Kent, in the North of Scotland, in Ireland, and even in London, men were arming to do battle for Charles. And now came another opportunity for one of those supernaturally swift and daring feats of arms in which Cromwell and Napoleon surpassed all men. At the head of five regiments he departed for Wales, and promised that Pembroke Castle, the centre of the Royalist movement there, would be in his power in a fortnight. But tidings from the North troubled him. On the 8th of July the Scottish Royal army crossed the border. Three days after, Pembroke Castle surrendered, and on the very next day Cromwell hastened northward. Writing to his friends at Derby House, he said, "Send me some shoes for my tired soldiers; they have a long march to take." With these ill-shod, ill-clad soldiers he traversed England from west to east, and then from south to north, with the rapidity of lightning, and suddenly the cavalry sent back word to the Duke of Hamilton, who commanded the Scotch army, that Cromwell was approaching. Terrible news—terrible name. Like what it was in the American war when the murmur ran, "Jackson's coming,"—like what it was in Italy when the cry arose, "Garibaldi with his red shirt is near,"—like what Scott in Marmion describes of James IV. rushing upon the English at Flodden-field—

> "At times a warning trumpet blown,
> At times a stifled hum,
> Told England from his mountain throne
> King James did rushing come."

"Cromwell's coming," cried the cavalry. "Impossible," replied the Duke, "he has not had time to come." But the outposts are already engaged with the advanced guard of the Parliamentarian General. Here he is. He defeats the Royalists; he dashes upon the Scotch, whom he found near the river Ribble, routs them thoroughly, crosses the river with them, follows them close as they flee, comes up with them in a defile near Warrington, and compels them to surrender. Thus in a fortnight's campaign the whole northern army is swept away. Cromwell marches to Edinburgh, where he meets with a magnificent reception—the Presbyterians themselves being obliged to bow before the conquering hero, who had just cut their own army to pieces.

Charles came back from the Isle of Wight to Windsor, but he came back to die. The Commons, under the terror of the army determined to bring him to trial, and to refuse all measures of peace.

OLIVER CROMWELL, PART 2.

We come now to speak of the daring deed by which Cromwell and his party sealed and wound up the civil war—the death on the public scaffold of Charles I.

It was, indeed, a daring action. Kings had often fallen before, but fallen in battle, or fallen, perhaps, in obscure midnight murder, in prison, or by the hands of assassins. But now, for the first time in the history of civilised Europe, a king has to be arraigned, tried, condemned, and beheaded in the sight of all men and angels too ; for surely a spectacle so august and terrible must have attracted the eyes and awakened the profoundest interest of superior intelligences.

Preparations for this great catastrophe had been going on for some time. Parliament had been inclined to come to terms with the King; and on the 5th of December, 1648, it decided, by a majority of 129 to 83, that the King's letter formed a basis of peace. Next day, two regiments of soldiers were posted round Westminster Hall, and Colonel Pride, with a list of names in his hand, prevented the entrance of 41 of the most determined Royalist and Presbyterian members; others were committed to the Tower, or frightened off into the country. This was called Pride's Purge. It was ominous for the King's cause that the very day the last of his supporters left the Commons, Cromwell returned victorious from Scotland, and resumed his seat in the House. He was received with acclamation. Old St. Stephen's felt, as he entered, that here was the real king of the country arrived, while the Royalists trembled at his entrance. He, himself, was modest and unassuming. "God is my witness," he said, "that I know nothing of what has been doing in this House; but the work is in hand, and now we must carry it through." Charles, meanwhile, had been removed to Windsor, and was treated more like a king than a captive—very differently from the mean and contemptible style in which the Hero of Italy was lately served in his bondage, for which, and many other things, there shall come a day of reckoning, if there be justice on earth, and a God in heaven. Charles dined in one of his own palaces, under a canopy, as had been his wont in happier days. The cup was offered to him by a kneeling cup-bearer, and all the ceremonial of State was observed. But while there was a canopy seen to the naked eye, an axe appeared to the eye of vision suspended over his head. A canopy in Windsor, but there was a dark thunder-cloud collecting over London and Whitehall.

It was now openly proposed, in the purged Parliament, that Charles should be brought to trial on a charge of high treason against the people, and as the cause of all the blood that had been shed. This sounds strange even yet, but how much more in the day when Monarchy was hedged in by a supposed Divine right—when to rebel against or kill a king was held the same as to rebel against or aim at the dethronement of God himself. Cromwell even felt this an awful conjuncture, and for a time he hesitated, saying to the Speaker—" Sir, if any man whatsoever have carried on this design (of deposing the king and disinheriting his posterity), or if any man gave thee such a design, he must be the greatest traitor and rebel in the world. But since the Providence of God has cast this upon us, I cannot but submit to Providence; though I am not yet prepared to give you my advice." It seemed as if all the four winds were now striving upon the great sea of Cromwell's profound bosom, and the struggle threatened to tear it in pieces.

For Charles and against his trial there were ranged the Episcopalians to a man, the English Presbyterians, the Scottish Church, and, through their ambassadors, the foreign Princes—all protesting, on various grounds, against the deed. On the other side was the Parliament urged on, and backed by the army, who seem as if they had sworn a deep oath that Charles must die—that he who had troubled Israel should be troubled himself. Between these frowning forces stood Cromwell, whose influence was great enough to have turned the scale, and who did, in reality, turn it against the King. After various consultations and debates, the Commons at last determined to proceed with his trial, and appointed 150 Commissioners—a number reduced afterwards to 135—to form a High Court of Justiciary for his trial. This number included peers, judges, baronets, aldermen, lawyers—all the important men of their party in the army, in the city, and in the Commons. The President appointed was John Bradshaw, an advocate of note—a cousin of Milton's, and a man of severe and stern character—honest, and true as steel, and rather gentle than otherwise in manners and speech. Besides this, the Commons passed strong resolutions declaring the People the Source of all Power, and themselves the sole executors; declaring the King guilty of high treason in making war against his people; and ordered the Great Seal of England to be broken in pieces, and another to be engraven, bearing, on the one side, the arms of England and Ireland, and, on the other, the words, "In the first year of Freedom, by God's blessing restored."

Up to this, as we saw, the King in Windsor had been treated with great respect, and even etiquette. But suddenly all this ceased—the dishes were brought in uncovered by the soldiers, none knelt to him, the canopy was removed. He felt this bitterly as degrading him, and asked, "Is there anything more contemptible than a despised Prince?"—and, to avoid it, he took his meals in his own room. He felt, in his prophetic soul, that something terrible was at hand, and on Friday, the 19th January, it came in the shape of a troop of horse and a coach and six, to convey him to London and St James's Palace. Next day, about noon, the High Court met in the Painted Chamber to arrange matters for the trial. They had scarcely finished prayers, when it was announced that the King, carried in a sedan-chair between two ranks of soldiers, was at hand. Cromwell ran to the window, but immediately returned white as the wall, and cried, " Masters, he is come, and now we are to do that great work that the nation will be full of. Therefore, I desire you, let us resolve here what answer we shall give the King when he comes before us, for the first question he will ask of us will be by what authority and commission do we try him." There is silence for a little; but speedily one of the Court, Henry Martin by name, rose up and said, " In the name of the Commons and Parliament assembled, and all the good people of England." No objection was made, and they proceeded to Westminster Hall, the Lord President Bradshaw at their head, with the sword and mace carried before him, preceded by sixteen officers armed with partisans. The Court took their places on chairs of common velvet and seats covered with scarlet cloth, and at the two extremities were the men at arms. Then the outer door opened, and the crowd rushed in. The Act of the Commons authorising the tribunal was now read. The names of the members were called—sixty-nine were present; and then said Bradshaw, " Mr Sergeant, bring in the prisoner."

Amidst solemn, breathless silence, King Charles enters—in the centre of a guard of Colonel Hacket and thirty-two officers. He is as yet in the prime of life, not fifty years of age, yet looking much older from the traces of anxiety, suffering, battle, and imprisonment. His hair had been originally a richly curled auburn, but is now thickly mingled with grey. His stature is tall and his carriage graceful, dignified, and a little haughty. Even in early youth physiognomists observed in his countenance a shade of anticipated melancholy, prognosticating some dreadful end; but now it is stern in expression, and fixed with severity, rather than deference on his judges. He wears a hat with a plume, has the peaked beard which painters always assign him, and his countenance altogether is more in anger than in sorrow. A chair of crimson velvet is prepared for him at the bar. He advances, casts a long and stern look at his tribunal, seats himself in the chair, without taking his hat off; suddenly rises again, looks behind him at the guard placed at the left, and at the crowded spectators on the right of the hall; once more darts his eyes at his judges; and then amid universal silence, sits down. Bradshaw instantly rises, and, with deep, trumpet-like tones, says—" Charles Stuart, King of England, the Commons of England, in Parliament assembled, taking notice of the effusion of blood in the land, whereof you are guilty, have resolved to bring you to a trial and judgment, and for this cause the tribunal is erected. The charges now will be read by the Attorney-General." Here a curious and distressing scene occurred. Cook, the Attorney-General, rose to speak. "Silence!" said the King, touching him with his gold-headed cane on the shoulder. Cook turned round, surprised and angry. The head of the King's cane dropped off; he looked as if he expected some one to pick it up. None of the servants would do it. A strong expression of anger and chagrin crossed the royal features; the King seemed to feel now, for the first time, that he was dethroned—he had to stoop and pick it up himself and sit down, while the Attorney-General proceeded to read the charges brought against him as a despot and levier of war against his own subjects, and closed by demanding that justice should be done upon him as a "tyrant, traitor, and murderer." We see at the utterance of these last three words, a stern smile of contempt crossing the King's lips; but he said nothing while the reading had been going on. He had looked sometimes at the judges, sometimes at the multitude; once he had risen, turned right round from his judges to observe the faces of the people, and then coolly sat down again. When asked to plead, he, as had been expected, denies the authority of the Court. He asks, "Where are the Lords, and where is the King?" He challenges their authority as no more lawful than that of highwaymen. Bradshaw abruptly closes the sederunt, and this being Saturday, he adjourns the Court to Monday. As Charles retires he points to the sword placed on the table with his cane, and says, "I do not fear that." In going down stairs, a few cry out, "Justice," but more shout, "God save the King; God save your Majesty!"

On Monday, 22nd January, the trial is renewed—the whole day being spent in discussions between the King and his judges, as to the legality of the proceedings. At the close, the King appeals to the people present, who again cry out as he departs, with an almost unanimous shout, "God save the King!" Next day, the 23rd, the same scenes are repeated, the King still refusing to plead, the Court determined in its purpose, and the people crying, "God save the King!" As the King is leaving this day, a soldier of the guard cries aloud, "Sire, God bless you!" An officer strikes him with his cane. "Sir," said the King, "the punishment is too great for the offence." Next day and the next, being the 24th and 25th days of the month, his judges, anxious to bring the matter to a point—the more that Foreign Courts, especially the Dutch, are pouring in strong remonstrances—resolve to examine witnesses against him; but in the absence of the King, and at the close of the 25th, almost without discussion, they vote his condemnation as a tyrant, traitor, murderer, and enemy to the country, and a committee was appointed to draw up the sentence. On the 26th the form of the sentence was determined with closed doors. On the 27th, they met to pronounce it. When the roll was called, the name of General Fairfax was called; and a voice from the gallery exclaimed, "He has too much wit to be here." It turned out to be a woman's, and was, indeed, that of Lady Fairfax. Sixty-seven members were present. When the King entered the hall, a terrible shout arose among the soldiers of "Execution! Sentence! Justice!" which their commander sought to increase rather than check; but the people remained profoundly silent. Charles requests delay, and expresses a desire, as he had done before, to be heard by the Lords and Commons in the Painted Chambers, or any Chamber they might appoint. These requests are sternly refused, and the Clerk reads the Sentence, concluding—

"For all which treason and crimes this Court doth adjudge that he, Charles Stuart, as a tyrant, traitor, murderer, and public enemy, shall be put to death by severing his head from his body." The President adds: "The sentence now read and published is the act, sentence, judgment, and resolution of the whole Court." They all stand up to give them point, and their rising all at once is as the sound of thunder heard remote, which speedily, however, subsides into silence. The unhappy King requests to be heard, but is told that he cannot be heard after sentence, and, after some vain and convulsive efforts to gain a hearing, he is forced away by the guards. And as he descends, while some of the people are crying out, "God save the King!" and others, "Oliver Cromwell is a traitor!" and while Bradshaw is saying that the King has been answering for crimes alleged against him in the name of the people of England, the same woman's voice which had spoken out before is heard exclaiming, "It's a lie: not one half of them —where are they or their contents?" The soldiers, on the other hand, are heaping on him the grossest insults; some throwing their lighted pipes in his way, and others blowing the smoke of their tobacco in his face—Charles the while retaining a high and haughty serenity, and saying, "Poor souls! for a shilling they would do the same to their commanders." Thus ends what we must call the disgraceful trial of Charles I.

We spare some affecting scenes in the Palace between Charles and his family, to whom, while he had been a despot and a tool of Popish intrigues to his people, he had been a true and most affectionate father, and ask our readers to accompany us to the front of Whitehall, on Monday, the 30th of January, 1649. But first note that on the previous day the High Court had met and appointed the execution to take place between the hours of ten and five on the 30th. But when it became necessary to sign the fatal order, it was with difficulty the Commissioners could be got together—some of them keeping out of the way, and others refusing to affix their names. First of all, however, Bradshaw put down his name, then followed Thomas Grey, Lord Gorby, and then came Oliver Cromwell. Here a singular incident took place. When Henry Martin was afterwards tried for regicide, a servant of his said that, entering the Painted Chamber where the judges were signing the warrant, he saw Cromwell, before he inscribed his name, marking Martin with his pen in the full, and Martin returning the joke by marking Cromwell in like manner! This has been brought forth as an evidence of heartlessness in Cromwell. We think, on the contrary, it was a piece of hysterical horror, and that his great soul, reluctant to the deed which, nevertheless, he thought must be done, was reduced to the necessity of concealing its distress, its secret anguish, by a species of buffoonery and trick—just as Danton, on his trial, and immediately before or after making one of the grandest appeals ever made for life, is recorded to have gathered up little pieces of paper from the floor, rolled them up, and flung them as peas at the heads of the judges. Thoroughly earnest in the matter no doubt Cromwell was. He had come to the conclusion that Charles must die, after much searching of heart, and after fasting and prayer. It was on a night, the whole of which he had spent in these exercises, that it was borne in upon his mind that the deed, terrible though it must be, was his duty; and so persuaded was he of this that he sent a messenger at one in the morning to the inn where his cousin John Cromwell, who had come from Holland, sent by the Prince of Orange to try and save the King's life, to tell him that his mind was made up, and that God had revealed his will to him on the matter. Henceforth he hesitated no longer, and when, on the morning of the execution, they were met to draw out the order to the executioner, Cromwell said to Huncks—"Colonel, it is you that must write and sign it." Huncks obstinately refused. "What a stubborn grumbler," said Cromwell; "I am ashamed of you. The ship is now coming into the harbour, and will you strike sail before you come to anchor?" Huncks persisted in his refusal. Cromwell, muttering between his teeth, sat down and wrote out the order himself. The document originally signed is yet extant, and, while some of the names are written so hurriedly and timidly that they can scarcely be read, there is no mistaking the bold characters of Oliver Cromwell, which stands third upon the list.

And now had dawned on Charles his fatal last morning. After four hours' profound slumber he rose, saying, "I have a great work to do this day; I must get up immediately." Herbert, his lord-in-waiting, began to comb his hair, but more carelessly than usual. "I pray you," said the King, "though my head be not long to remain on my shoulders, take the same pains with it as usual. Let me be as trim as possible to-day; this is my second marriage day, for before night I hope to be espoused to my blessed Jesus." As he was dressing, he asked for a shirt more than usual. "The season is so sharp," he said, "as may make me shake,

which some observers would imagine proceeds from fear.
I would have no such imputation. I fear not death.
Death is not terrible to me. I bless God I am prepared."
This reminds us of what happened to Bailly, one of the
men of the French Revolution, on the scaffold. "You
tremble, Bailly," said one of his enemies, insultingly.
"Yes," replied he, "but it is only with cold." At daybreak
the Bishop, Juxon by name, arrived, and began the service,
reading the 27th chapter of Matthew, describing the death
of Christ, when the King asked him if he had chosen the
chapter as applicable to his case. "Not so," replied the
Bishop, "it is the proper lesson for the day, as the calendar
indicates." This deeply affected Charles, and he continued
his prayers with increased fervour. At last a knock is heard
at the door, at first faint, at length somewhat louder, though
gentle. Ah! it is the knock of death; it is Colonel Hacker,
announcing that it is time to go to Whitehall. At the third
knock the doors opened, and Charles calmly comes forth.
On he walks, that cold January morning, from St. James's
to Whitehall, between troops of soldiers, the banners flying,
and the drums beating; the Bishop on his right, and on his
left, uncovered, Colonel Tomlinson, captain of the guard;
his countenance serene, his eye beaming, his step firm,
walking even faster than the troops, and blaming their
slowness. Arrived at Whitehall, he ascended the stairs with
a light step, passed onwards through the great galleries into
his bedroom, where he was left alone with the Bishop, who
was preparing to administer the Sacrament. Here he knelt,
received the communion, and then rose with cheerfulness.
He took some refreshment in case, on the scaffold, any

faintness, produced by long fasting, should be imputed to fear. It was now one o'clock. Again Hacker's knock is heard at the door, and Juxon and Herbert fall on their knees. "Rise, my old friend," said Charles, holding out his hand to the Bishop. Hacker knocks again. Charles orders the door to be opened. "Go on," he cried, "I follow you." He passes through the banqueting hall, which is filled with soldiers, but not with soldiers alone, but with men and women, who have rushed in at the peril of their lives, and are praying and blessing the King. At the end of the hall, an opening made in the wall led straight to the scaffold, which was hung with black, two men dressed as sailors, and wearing masks, standing beside the axe. The King stepped out, his head erect, and looking around for the people, prepared to address them; but the troops occupied the whole space, and the multitude stood too far off to hear, although they might see distinctly. He is obliged, therefore, to address the few words he had prepared, and which were devoted to a brief defence of himself, and a proclamation of his fixed and final belief in the divine right of kings, and in the nothingness of the people in reference to rule, to those immediately beside him. While he was speaking some one touched the axe. He turned round hastily, and said, "Do not spoil the axe; it would hurt me more." The most profound silence prevailed. Not a rustle in the banners, not a clash in the arms, not a sigh among the people—their very eyelashes dare hardly twinkle till the Monarch of England is no more. He put on a silk cap, and coolly said to the executioner, "Is my hair," his long and still beautiful hair, "in the way?" "I beg your Majesty to put it under your cap," said the man, bowing. With the help of the Bishop, he did so. Then he said, "I have on my side a good cause, and a merciful God." Juxon replied, "Yes, sire, there is but one stage more; it is full of trouble and anguish, but it is short, and consider it will carry you a great way—it will carry you from earth to heaven." The King replied, "I go from a corruptible to an incorruptible crown, where I shall have no trouble to fear." He took off his cloak and George, and gave the latter to Juxon, saying, "*Remember*," though what he meant was never known. He then took off his coat, and put on his cloak again, and looking at the block said to the executioner, "Place it so it may be firm." "It is firm, sire." The king replied, "I will say a short prayer, and when I hold out my hands—then;" he muttered a few words to himself, raised his eyes to heaven, knelt down and laid his head upon the block. The executioner touched his hair to put it still further under his cloak; the King thought he was going to strike. "Wait for the signal," he cried. "I shall wait for it, sire, with the good pleasure of your Majesty." In a minute the King held out his hand, the executioner struck, the head fell off at a blow. He held it up to the people, its long brindled tresses dyed with blood, and said, "This is the head of a traitor." And now the feeling, which had been sternly suppressed, burst out, and then broke forth from the multitude a long, deep groan, blended with cries of rage and the voice of weeping, and many rushing forward, dipt their handkerchiefs in the streaming blood. When the mob had dispersed, the scaffold been cleared, the body taken away and inclosed in the coffin, Cromwell desired to see it, looked at it steadfastly, raised the head, and said, "This is a well built frame, and promised a long life." Seven days afterwards a funeral procession is seen moving westwards in the direction of Windsor; six horses, covered with black cloth, draw the hearse, four mourning coaches follow filled with some of the King's servants; it is the funeral cortege of Charles I., and the next day being the 8th of February, the Duke of Richmond, the Marquis of Hertford, the Earls of Southampton and Lindsay, and Bishop Juxon, arrived at Windsor to assist at the funeral. On the coffin they have engraved those words only:

CHARLES REX.
1648.

As they are removing the body from the interior of the Castle to St George's Chapel, where it is to lie, and where Henry VIII. was buried, the weather, hitherto clear and serene, changes all at once, and a thick shower of snow descends, entirely covering the black pall, and in this his servants thought they read an emblem and proof of his innocence, as if Nature itself had covered his ashes with a robe of purity and peace. No funeral service was permitted to be read over his body—it went down into the dust in silence. All left the chapel; the Governor locked the door, and Charles Stuart was left alone. His grave was opened in 1813 in the presence of some members of the Royal Family, and his body found in perfect preservation.

About six months after King Charles's death, Cromwell

was appointed the Parliament's Lord Lieutenant for Ireland, and Commander-in-Chief of the army for that country, which, for eight years, had been a scene of blood and anarchy. It is said that when he appeared in the House after he received his commission, he seemed full of irresolution and timidity. And we do not wonder at it. It might at first have shaken even Cromwell's iron nerve to be sent to subdue Ireland, a country which has baffled the efforts of every legislator, statesman, and soldier, if not to conquer, yet to pacify permanently, and to render, even in an average manner, civilised and contented. An eminent statesman is said to have wished that Ireland would but go down for two good hours in the sea, and come up again without any inhabitants. Others have declared it, as Dr. Croly used always to say, to be a ruined country. Some have called it the bedlam of Europe. And it remains to be seen what the recent measures and those still in the future will make of the strange country. To Ireland, however, in spite of his reluctance and irresolution, Cromwell must now go, and on the 15th August, 1619, he reached Dublin. On the 30th August he took the field, and in the course of nine days he had obtained a greater footing in the island, and inspired greater terror, than had been done by all the Protestant party, armies, and generals put together, since the commencement of the war. When France was beset by Prussians without and traitors within, and the Republic seemed going down in utter and shameful defeat—one man, George Jacques Danton saved it, and saved it by one sentence, and what followed it. The sentence was—"We must put our enemies in fear," and what followed it was the massacre in September; and which, cruel as it was, was a crime, but no blunder—it gained its object by putting the enemy in fear; it saved France from Brunswick, connected as it was with other energetic measures of defence, of which Danton also was the soul. And probably it was upon some such principle that Cromwell treated Drogheda. After a terrible struggle, he carried the town, which was garrisoned by 3000 English soldiers, and commanded his soldiers to spare none that were in arms within it. He was obeyed to and beyond the letter—2500 were put to death; all the friars, Cromwell notices, were knocked on the head promiscuously. The carnage raged two days—women and children met the same fate as armed men; and when, five or six days after, some officers, who had been concealed, were discovered, they too were put to death. "It was," says one, "a sacrifice of 3000 Irish to the ghosts of ten thousand English who were massacred some years before." Cromwell himself says, in his despatch, "that it would tend to save the effusion of blood for the future," and this certainly was the result to some extent. Fear went before him. The curse of Cromwell became a proverb, and eventually an oath, and Cork, Ross, Tim, Dundalk, Youghall, and Kilkenny submitted, though strong places, without resistance. Wexford, however, resisted obstinately, and its inhabitants were treated like those of Drogheda. At Gouran the soldiers saved their own lives by murdering all their officers. The Bishop of Ross was hanged in his episcopal robes under the walls of a fortress his troops were defending. It was the fearful manner of fearful times.

Cromwell did all this, let it be remembered, not from a bloodthirsty disposition, but from policy. At all events, he not only put his enemies in fear, but gained his purpose. By a matchless celerity of movements, by military severities upon the contumacious, by well-timed clemency to the submissive, by keeping up agents even among the Roman Catholic clergy, by dividing the Catholic lands among his soldiers, and by the master-stroke of procuring foreign service for the disbanded soldiers of the Royalist army, thus setting them out of harm's and his way, he, in the course of nine months (the time occupied in winter quarters included), all but completed the subjugation of Ireland. On the tomb of Edward I. of England, the great enemy of Wallace, there is yet to be seen the inscription—" Here lies Edward I., the Hammer of the Scotch nation." It might have been written on the grave of Cromwell—" Here lies Oliver Cromwell, the Hammer of Ireland." Pity that he left his hammering and rough-hewing work only half done.

But his presence was soon required in England and Scotland. Charles II. had been proclaimed King in Scotland. The latter country and the Scotch were preparing to invade England. Montrose, meanwhile, had been making wild work on the Royalist side in the Highlands. The state of things was altogether alarming, and the presence of a master-mind was required. Cromwell, obeying the wishes of the Parliament, returned from Ireland, and, landing at Bristol, was received with extraordinary honours—the whole town coming out *en masse* to meet him. When he approached London, almost all the officers of the army and the members of Parliament met him at Hunslow Heath.

At Hyde Park he found the Lord Mayor and the train-bands waiting for him; and around St. James's Palace, where he was to lodge, there was one vast tumult of salutation, volleys from the cannon, and loud shouts of welcome. "What a crowd has come out to see your Lordship's triumph," said a bystander. "Just as many," replied Cromwell, "would come out to see me hanged." Ah! there spoke the genuine heart of Old Noll—the man that knew and despised human nature, the man that had read history, and remembered how soon cries of "Crucify, crucify," had been exchanged for hosannas, and that was not to be imposed upon by the plaudits of crowds any more than by the blandishments of princes.

Down into Scotland Cromwell went, and fought and gained the battle of Dunbar, where, as he saw the sun rising from the German Ocean, he pointed to it with his sword, and with the instinct of genius said, "Arise, O God, and let thine enemies be scattered," and it was so. From Dunbar he went to Edinburgh and to Glasgow, conquering and to conquer, Charles having retired to Perth, and Leslie, with the wreck of his army, to Stirling. To Perth, Cromwell then proceeded, and had just taken it, when he heard great news that Charles, with David Leslie for his Lieutenant, and at the head of 14,000 men, had, instead of fighting with him in Scotland, betaken themselves southwards, having, by a dexterous movement, given Cromwell the slip. He marched with great haste to Lancashire, where he was joined by the Earl of Derby, and others, and appeared before Shrewsbury, which town, refusing to surrender, he pushed on to Worcester, where he received the unwelcome intelligence that Cromwell was at hand. Charles had marched fast, but Cromwell marched faster. In twenty-one days he rushed from Scotland to the north-west of England, his army gathering like a snowball as it advanced, the militia rising everywhere to join him, till, when he reached Worcester, he found himself at the head of 34,000 men. Charles had previously set up his standard on the beautiful meadows between the Severn and the city, and mustered only 12,000 men, chiefly Scots. He then retreated into the city, which furnished, of course, a very strong and favourable point of defence.

Cromwell, on the morning of the 2nd day of September, commenced to attack the city on both its sides at once. The Scots made a bold resistance, and the battle raged for four or five hours "as stiff a contest," wrote Cromwell, "as I have ever seen." The troops, led by Charles in person, charged the Republicans so vigorously, that they gave way at first. Three thousand Scottish cavalry, commanded by Leslie, was under arms behind the King, who gave them orders to follow up his movements, and charge in their turn. "Oh, for an hour of Montrose," shouted the English cavaliers remembering what a daring commander he had been; Leslie remained motionless. Cromwell, meanwhile, rallied his troops, and resumed the offensive. The Royal infantry, failing in ammunition, fell back. Cromwell was everywhere present, advancing in person even to the entrenchments of Fort Royal, which covered the city on that side, summoning the commander to surrender. A volley of artillery was the reply; but the fort was soon stormed, and the garrison put to the sword. In the gates of the city the

Royalists and Republicans fought hand to hand. An ammunition waggon was overthrown, and blocked up the passage. All was confusion. Charles had to dismount from his horse, and enter Worcester on foot. The Republicans dashed through the breach after him. Charles regained his horse, and tried a rally; but in vain. "Then shoot me dead," he cried, "rather than let me live to see the consequences of this day." But the more devoted of his followers gathered in a compact body round him, cut their way through in a northerly direction, and saved his life, and all are familiar with the marvellous story of his escape afterwards.

While Charles was hiding from the search of his foes, Cromwell was making an important entrance into London, surrounded by the Speaker of the House of Commons, the President of the Council of State, the Lord Mayor, hundreds of members of Parliament, and thousands of the people rending the air with their shouts. Look at him as he moves slowly along. A certain grand dignity has gathered around him since he first appeared in Parliament —a slouching and ill-dressed senator. He is now fifty-two years old and upwards. His locks are slightly silvered with thought and care. A shade of paleness rests upon his cheek, for in Scotland he had been dangerously ill. But his face is still a face of rock, and below it there is the heart of steel, while a sage's head is the crown of the whole; and no wonder, though his air, his language, and his manners seemed transformed, if not transfigured, and that Hugh Peters, the preacher, appeared speaking at once the sentiment of the multitude, and echoing the voice of

God, as he cried aloud, "This man will be King of England yet."

The Long Parliament, which alone stood between Cromwell and real sovereignty, was now manifestly drawing near its close. It was called the Rump, being the mere fag end of its former self, and had fallen into general contempt. Cromwell took advantage of this dissatisfaction; but still forbore to take extreme measures till he was told by Colonel Ingoldsby that Parliament was passing a bill prolonging its own duration, and that no time was to be lost. Cromwell in haste left Whitehall, followed by Lambert, and five or six officers, and commanded a detachment of soldiers to march round to the House of Commons. On his arrival at Westminster, he stationed guards at the door and lobby of the house, and led another body to the outside of the door of the room, where the Assembly was met. He then entered alone, plainly dressed in black clothes, and grey worsted stockings—his usual attire when he was not in uniform. He came in without noise, but with the greatest determination expressed in his countenance, smiling, frowning not, but looking firm and calm as a marble statue. Henry Vane, a wild but noble man, was speaking fiercely in favour of the Bill. Cromwell sat down in the place of the House he usually occupied, and was joined there by his friend St. John, to whom he said in a loud whisper, "That he had come to do that which grieved him to the very soul, and that he had earnestly, with tears, prayed to God against. Nay, that he had rather be torn in pieces than do it; but there was a necessity laid upon him therein in order to the glory of God and the good of the nation." Vane was still speaking, and was urging Parliament to proceed to the last stage of the Bill, and to dispense with certain formalities which might precede its adoption. Cromwell at this beckoned on his friend Harrison, and said: "Now is the time. I must do it." "Sir," replied Harrison, "the work is very great and dangerous." "You say well," replied Cromwell, and sat still for a quarter of an hour. Vane ceased his speech. The speaker rose to put the question, when Cromwell now rose, put off his hat, and began to speak. At first his tone was rather complimentary to the Parliament as a whole; but, by-and-bye, his brow darkened, his tone changed, his gestures became violent, he reproached the members of the House with their delays, their covetousness their self-interest, their disregard of justice. "You have no heart," he cried, "to do anything for the public good; but your time is come; the Lord hath done with you; he has chosen other instruments for his work which are more worthy. It is the Lord that hath taken by the hand and set me on to do this thing." Some of the members rose to reply, but he would not suffer them to speak. "You think this is not Parliamentary language, but it is the only language you need expect from me." Wentworth at length made himself heard. "He had never heard such unbecoming language used to Parliament, and it was the more horrid as it came from their servant, and one they had highly trusted and obliged, and through their bounty made what he was." Cromwell thrust his hat on his head, sprang from his seat into the centre of the floor of the House, and shouted out, "Come, come, we have had enough of this;

I'll put an end to your prating; call them in," he said to Harrison. The door opened, and twenty or thirty soldiers entered. "I say," cried Cromwell, "I say you are no Parliament; begone, give way to honester men." He walked up the floor of the House, stamping with his foot and giving orders. The Speaker had to leave the chair. Algernon Sidney, the famous patriot, after some resistance, had to walk out of the House. Vane ventured to exclaim, "This is against common morality and honesty." "Sir Harry Vane! Sir Harry Vane!" cried Cromwell, "the Lord deliver me from Sir Harry Vane! You are a juggler; you have not common honesty yourself." Then he showered out such names at the members as they retired—"Some of you are drunkards," pointing to one Challoner; "some of you are adulterers," pointing to Sir P. Wentworth; "some of you are corrupt, unjust persons," and he looked to Whitbode and others; then turning to Henry Martin, he said, "Is a whoremaster fit to sit and govern?" Then he went up to the table where lay the Mace, and called to the soldiers, "What shall we do with this bauble?—take it away!" Allen, venturing to oppose him, he ordered him to be arrested on the spot. Then the room being empty, he seized on all the papers, ordered the doors to be shut, and returned home. Next day, he announced in the public prints that he had put a period to the Parliament. On the same day, a crowd collected at the door of the House to read a large placard put there by some Cavalier. It was as follows:—

"THIS HOUSE TO LET UNFURNISHED."

Thus was the Long Parliament dissolved.

Cromwell lost no time in issuing declarations in defence and explanation of his conduct, and, finding them not much attended to, he determined, after consulting with his officers, to call together a Parliament of his own choosing. First, however, he established a Council of State. There was some difference of opinion among his advisers as to what should be the number of their councillors; some recommending ten men, that the business might be carried on more expeditiously; others seventy, like the Jewish Sanhedrim; and others thirteen, the number of our Lord and his apostles. This latter opinion prevailed, and thirteen men were appointed, with Cromwell as their President; and they, in their turn, made a selection of 139 persons to make a Parliament—122 for England, six for Wales, five for Scotland, and six for Ireland. This New Parliament became famous under the name of Barebones Parliament, but was soon dissolved, much as the former had been. Three days after its dissolution, on the 16th of December, 1653, a procession went in great state from Whitehall to Westminster, where, in the presence of the Lords Commissioners of the Great Seal, the Judges, the Lord Mayor of London, and other dignitaries, Cromwell, clad in a simple suit of black velvet, with long boots, and a broad band of gold round his hat, was appointed, in the name of the armies of the three kingdoms, Lord Protector of the Commonwealth of England, Scotland, and Ireland. He sat down in the Chair of State, and the Lord Mayor put the sword into his hand. Returning to Whitehall between four and five in the afternoon, a triple discharge of artillery announced that he had taken up his abode in the ancient halls of Monarchy, as Lord Protector, without the name of King, but with more power than ever sovereign of England before or since enjoyed; and soon he was proclaimed as such over the whole island.

It was, however, if not a tottering, yet certainly an uneasy seat where Cromwell found himself placed. Plots against his authority and his life were constantly cropping up; but he bore a charmed life. By a union of art and energy never surpassed by king, he escaped the malice of his adversaries on all sides. Some he coaxed and wheedled. When he met George Fox, the Quaker, an enemy of his—at least somewhat disaffected—he would make him get upon his chariot, and talk him over. Others he seized in their beds, and ordered to be led to execution. One man, having incited a mutiny in a regiment against his authority, Cromwell stept up to him and, presenting his pistol, at once blew him and the mutiny out of existence. Meanwhile, he assumed all the state and dignity of a king. He issued patents, passed acts of justice and legislation, gave banquets, knighted lord mayors, received ambassadors, and gave splendid entertainments exactly as a sovereign would have done; and never did a king, either in his home or his foreign adminstration, display more justice, more wisdom, and more commanding energy than did the old brewer, Oliver Cromwell. At home, he attended to everything, to the administration of the finances, the repair and conservation of the highways, the condition of prisoners, the regulation of public amusements; the state of the Law and the state of the Church, of the Universities, and the Great Schools, all occupied his thoughts, and were all made subjects of wise administration; and, in less than nine months, from the 24th of December, 1653, to the 2nd of September, 1654, eighty-two ordinances, all bearing on the social organisation of the country, passed through the hands and under the eye of this marvellous man. His foreign policy, too, was distinguished by the utmost energy and wisdom; he effected peace with Holland, and he made both France and Spain tremble.

Calling another Parliament, but not finding it subservient to his wishes, he dissolved it, for eighteen months continued sole ruler, and, in the course of that time, he found no difficulty in procuring supplies, and suppressed a dangerous insurrection in England. He determined to confirm his power, and strike awe into his enemies, by brilliant naval achievements. He prepared two great fleets, and sent the one under the famous Blake, that thunderbolt of naval battle, to the Mediterranean, and the other, under Penn and Venables, to the West Indies. He kept for some time their destination a secret; and when, one day, a mob of the wives of the sailors who were serving on board, pursued him through the streets, inquiring whither their husbands were to be sent, Cromwell replied with a smile—"The ambassadors of France and Spain would willingly give me a million to know that." While these fleets were on their way, a new field opened up for the commanding genius of Cromwell. The Waldenses—that mountain people keeping pure religion alive amidst the Alps—after having been long subjected to harassing persecutions, were at last marked out for a general massacre. For eight days, the most terrific cruelties were inflicted upon these unfortunates. They were murdered in cold blood, hanged, burnt, their women violated, and their children hurled down precipices at the command of the Duke of Savoy. The news, when it reached England, aroused a universal burst of sympathy and anger. Milton has recorded what was the general feeling in his matchless and well-known sonnet.

Milton not only indited poetry in their behalf, but, as Cromwell's Secretary also, and in Cromwell's name, he wrote prose letters, weighty, powerful, brief, and determined, to the Duke of Savoy, Louis 14th of France, and most of the kings and states of Europe, in behalf of the persecuted people, the Covenanters of the Alps. Cromwell proclaimed a fast, too, on their account, and set on foot a national contribution, which, heading it with £2000 of his own, amounted, in all, to £40,000. His remonstrances produced considerable effect, and compelled an answer from the Duke of Savoy full of reluctant promises; and even still, in the beautiful valleys of the Vaudois, under the snow-white Alps, among the descendants of that brave and pious people, Cromwell is often spoken of with reverence and love—

> "And far and near o'er dale and hill
> Are faces that attest the same,
> And kindle like a fire new stirred,
> At mention of his name."

Meanwhile his fleets were successful in both hemispheres. Blake's cannon roared all over the Mediterranean like a thunderstorm, startling Venice, Toulon, Marseilles, and Malaga, and driving the pirates and the French privateers from the deep; and, as Cromwell said himself, making the name of Englishman as great as that of Roman was in Rome's palmy days. Penn and Venables, in the West Indies, although they failed in seizing St. Domingo, seized on Jamaica, which has since become such an important possession of the British Crown.

Cromwell had now reached the pinnacle of his greatness. His armies had completely mastered the three Kingdoms. The guns of his fleet swept every sea. All the Protestant States in Europe adored him, Spain stood in awe of him, France had become his close ally, equestrian statues of him were seen on the streets of Paris, and medals were struck in Holland to celebrate his glory and humble kings before him. The Grand Duke of Tuscany sent for his portrait to adorn the picture gallery of Florence. All this might have turned any head but his own; but so far from this being the case, he felt that the top of the pinnacle was also the top of a precipice whence he might be hurled in a moment. He was glorious, but he was alone, and had been so for eighteen months—alone, no! for not only was the Father with him, but he had at least one kindred spirit, who sat every day at the same table, as his Secretary, John Milton. Their conjunction reminds us of the sight which we saw, although in a dim atmosphere, on the 30th of January, 1868, of the two splendid planets, Jupiter and Venus, which had been for so many weeks illumining the western sky. For but one or two moments we saw them so near that the star of Jove, so beautiful and large, seemed almost touching Venus, as though an old father were kissing his favourite and lovely child. The two most magnificent of the planets had met and embraced each other: was it an emblem and pledge of that coming day when Divine power and love, majesty and mercy, shall be seen to be reconciled, and the result shall be the Millennium of the earth? but the moment passed, and the clouds hid them from our sight, and perhaps centuries may elapse ere they are so near again. But day after day, there sat opposite each other the two foremost men of the world, the man of action and the man of eloquence, the man of the sword and the man of the pen—one of the sharpest swords and one of the most powerful pens ever wielded—the hero of Worcester and Dunbar, and the author of Paradise Lost; and such a conjunction of mental luminaries there had never been before, has never been since, and may never be again. Milton had met Galileo in his dungeon; but we question if he looked with more reverence on that starry sage who had conquered the heavens by his telescope than on that noble warrior and statesman who had subdued the earth by his sword.

But the end of this great man was now drawing near, and was presaged by several sad preliminary shadows. In 1648, he lost his eldest son Oliver, whose loss, he said, went like a dagger to his heart; in 1654, he lost his mother, Elizabeth Stewart, a woman of great sense and virtue; in 1658, he lost Robert Rich, his son-in-law; and three months after, the Earl of Warwick, whom, of all the nobility, Cromwell had honoured with the most of his confidence. And a few weeks after, Lady Claypole, his favourite daughter, whom he loved with the most devoted attachment, died after very severe sufferings, compounded of her own malady, and of the utmost anxiety for her father. Ere she died, Cromwell had been frequently ill, now with gravel, now with gout, now with liver complaint, and now with want of sleep. Her death increased his uneasiness to a great degree; nevertheless, he made an effort to resume his labours, holding councils, reviewing troops, and presiding over commercial negotiations with foreign countries; but this strong man was now effectually shaken—shaken not by age, for he was not quite sixty, but by labours, anxieties, sufferings of body and of mind—the weight of a world, like the burden of Atlas, which had rested on his solitary shoulder. He was seized with fever, and, at the advice of his physicians, removed to Whitehall. At first he was convinced that he was not to die, and his favourite chaplains encouraged him in the thought, and presumptuously told God in prayer that he was bound to spare such a valuable life; but at last death fixed its seal upon his face, sent its chill into his heart, and he met it like a man and a Christian. On the 2nd of September, after a brief period of delirium, he had a lucid interval of some duration, in the course of which he put a remarkable question to his chaplains. It was if they thought saints could fall from a state of grace. They replied in the negative. Then he said, "All is safe, for I was in grace once." He then uttered a very solemn prayer, closing thus, "Pardon such as are desirous to trample upon the dust of a poor worm, for they are thy people too, and pardon the folly of this short prayer, even for Jesus

Christ's sake, Amen." As night closed in, he was first in a state of stupor, then he felt much agitated, saying to himself, in low and broken tones, "Truly God is good indeed—he is; he will not, will not leave me; I would be willing to be further serviceable to God and to his people, but my work is done." One of his attendants offered him something to drink, and besought him to try and sleep. "It is not my design," he replied, "to drink or sleep, but my design is to make haste and begone." Day dawned at last; it was the morning of his *fortunate* day, as he had often called it—the anniversary of Worcester and Dunbar—a tremendous tempest, carrying great disasters both by land and sea, had raged all night: Cromwell, who had relapsed into a state of absolute insensibility, about three in the afternoon heaved a deep sigh, almost when the storm was breathing its last; and his stern, noble spirit, as if on the weakened wings of the tempest, left earth for ever. After more than two months had passed, during six weeks of which he lay in Somerset House in state, he was buried on the 23rd November, 1658, in Westminster Abbey, with greater pomp than had ever attended the funeral of an English king.

Thus died Oliver Cromwell, the man of the seventeenth century—a man in whom we recognise a union of Roman, Hebrew, and English qualities: the faith of the Jew, the firmness of the Roman, and the homespun simplicity of the Englishman of his own age; in purpose and in powers, an armed angel on a battle day; in manners, a plain blunt corporal; the middle class-man of his time, with the merits and defects of his order, but touched with an inspiration as from heaven; whose one great faculty, inflamed and consecrated commonsense, was quite sufficient to gain all his purposes, and to supply all his defects; whose eloquence was uneven and piercing as the forked lightning, which is never so terrible as when it seems falling to pieces; whose mere determined hand held up at home, or across the waters, saved millions of money, awed despots, and encouraged freedom in every part of the world; and who gave his country a model of excellence as a man and as a ruler, simple, severe, ruggedly picturesque, stupendously original, and solitary as one of the Primitive Rocks.

CHAPTER III.

JOHN MILTON.

PURITANISM was a great, but, at first sight, rather dry fact. It was a bare, gigantic tree, without leaves and blossoms; it was an Aaron's rod unbudded. Its severe simplicity of worship; the austere grandeur of its creed; the manners of its people, so formal and reserved; their nasal twang; their round, close-cropped heads; their black and sombre dress; their long faces, and the lugubrious expression, which seemed to sigh and cry for ever about them, all tended to render them and theirs repulsive to the world at large, and to start the question, Can anything that is beautiful, bright, cheerful, gay, or imaginative, come out of such a quarter? Literature—even if literature is to issue from them, it must be of a very sad and sombre description, some melancholy history of the times, or some dull controversial treatise; if poetry, it must be some awful tragedy like the sternest of Eschylus, or the saddest of Sophocles; if theology, there no novelty of opinion will be permitted, or need be expected—nothing but a reiteration of the old tremendous doctrines of reprobation, of hell being paved with infants' skulls, of the majority of the race being damned, and so forth. The answer to all this was—John Milton. He, in his single self, proved that Puritanism, stern as it was, could bear flowers and buds; that Aaron's rod could blossom; that a literature of the loftiest and most classical kind could proceed from it; that poetry, graceful and beautiful as that of the most gifted of the Cavaliers, or as the finest effusions of Shakespeare himself, could flow from the rugged lips of a Roundhead; and that a Puritan might indulge in daring speculations, hold peculiar doctrines, shoot his soul far before his time, and not fear to proclaim that Calvin and Luther were men, and not, any more than the Pope, the infallible masters of his conscience and his faith.

Milton was born in London, one of comparatively few great men who have been born in the capital. Unquestionably, indeed, some of our greatest poets—such as Chaucer, Spenser, and Keats—have been born there. But Shakespeare, Wordsworth, Coleridge, Shelley, Thomson, Young, Burns, Tennyson, and many more have come from the provinces, where, indeed, you might have expected that poets, especially those destined to excel, whether in divine and lofty contemplation, or in description of those natural scenes which form so large a part of the materials of song, should appear. Yet perhaps the very contrast to young men wandering forth at eventide, or in the fine summer or autumn holidays, between the wilderness of brick, the kennels, the cesspools, the filthy closes, the obstructed views, and the sinks of sin and woe which are contained in the city, and the fresh air, the vernal green, the beauty-loaded orchards, the clear streams, and the "dread magnificence of heaven" bending over the country fields and hills, makes these assume an aspect lovelier and more charming than to those who see them every day, and have nothing to act as a foil and a contrast. Yet it was not a city-born, but a country-born poet who wrote the "Seasons," and who thus sings—

> "I care not, fortune, what you me deny,
>   You cannot rob me of free nature's grace :
> You cannot shut the windows of the sky,
>   Through which Aurora shows her brightening face.
> You cannot bar my constant feet to trace
>   The woods and lawns by living stream at eve."

In London, at all events, the highest man, poet, and progressive thinker of the Puritans, John Milton, was born on the 9th of December, 1608. His father's name was John, and his mother's Sarah. His father was a scrivener, a kind of writer or lawyer. Lawyers are very acute and clever men usually, but they are not usually very poetical. The poet looks to things as wholes, and to that ideal glory which hovers above them, and which his eye sees and his verse shows to others. The lawyer splits them up into parts, and looks at them in their minute details, from which the gloss and splendour have fled. But Milton's father was an uncommon specimen of the scrivener. There is an epitaph in the Howff of Dundee magnifying the wonders of Divine Providence, in making once a lawyer who was also an honest man; but there have been, we doubt not, many such exceptions to the rule, and John Milton, senior, was one of them. He had been an Oxford student in his youth, and a bigoted Papist, but was converted from Popery, and abjured its errors publicly, and, for doing so, was disinherited by his father. We honour such disinherited knights, who, for conscience' sake, give up the fairest of earthly prospects; honour them because, even when their opinions are wrong, they seem right to them, and they prove the sincerity of their belief by the sacrifices they make for them. We do not believe Shelley's creed; but, even more than his genius, do we admire his honesty which drove him out of his native university and his father's house. We think Ernest Jones talked a deal of nonsense about division of land, and was far too severe on aristocracy; but we honoured him not for his eloquence merely, but because, from conscientious attachment to his political principles, he lost favour with a rich uncle, was deprived of a good estate, and had to sustain himself by his labours at the bar. So John Milton, the elder, deserves all praise for being disinherited, although that probably obliged him to 'enter a profession for which at first he had little taste. Yet although he became a lawyer, and a diligent one too, prospering so that he was able to retire to the country in his latter days, to purchase an estate, and to give his children a liberal education, he never lost his early tastes for literature and for music—tastes which he handed down to his illustrious son. Milton's mother's name was Caston. She came from Wales, that country of mountains, splended skies, and the ancient race of Britons—who have a kind of fiery, poetic blood in their veins, like that of the Irish or the Highlanders, and whose bards at one time were distinguished for their genius, or *awen*, as they called it—although, alas! we must say now of the Welsh poetry that it is

> "Vocal no more since Cambria's fatal day,
> To high-born Hoel's harp or soft Llewellyn's lay."

Perhaps some of this wild fervour was in the blood of Milton's mother, and ran down from her into the veins of her son. In the history of genius, and of poetry too, it has been remarked that more depends upon the character and intellect of the mother than of the father. We could mention a hundred eminent men who had fathers of little, or less than little, distinction, but very few whose mothers had not something remarkable about them. One reason is that mothers are more with their children, and exert a far deeper though quieter influence upon their intellect and moral character when they have moral character and intellect of their own. Byron's mother was a fool, a passionate scold, and we attribute in part his miserable failure in life to her. On the other hand, you seldom find men who have shone equally in mind and in heart without discovering that both their parents have been excellent and superior persons—the one probably contributing the intellect, and the other the moral nature to their offspring. Such men as Johnson, Burke, Cowper, Hall, Foster, and others, are cases in point; and so we believe it was with Milton, although, as his father was a more prominent character, we find more mention of him than of her in his poetry; yet he speaks of her worth and liberality to the poor.

Both his parents loved, were proud of, and perhaps a little spoiled, their favourite son. Milton's early days, by the way, had little of that struggle which men afterwards successful have to go through. We do not know if he was the better of this. Struggles are an excellent discipline for the young, if not essential to real life. How uninteresting the course of a canal, with its sluggish uniformity, or of a lazy, low-country river, like the Cam —the sleeping river, as Hall called it—and a Highland torrent resisted at every step by some rocky obstacle against which it boldly rushes, and fiercely or gaily overcomes; here fretted into the picturesque, there dashed into the sublime, and yonder tormented into the "horribly beautiful," its power developed by contradiction, and its passion provoked by controversy. Most men, including Milton in his latter life, worthy of the name, are so indebted to, and identified with struggle, that it has become difficult to think of virtue or excellence without it; and some have even conceived of it extending, in a modified form, to a future world, and have fancied that the River of Life hereafter may be grander and diviner too, if shaded by forests, flung over cataracts, and contesting its immortal way with crags and precipices, than flowing tamely over flat and fertile meadows, and through gardens of everlasting bloom. But, be this as it may, struggle is the wise law of humanity here, and, as such, should be welcomed not only with submission, but with joy. Sometimes, it may be, struggle sours and exasperates, but more frequently it invigorates, and those on whom it produces bad effects would probably have been worse under a different training. Souredness is often strength, spoiledness is always weakness. so that, on the whole, it is a pleasing, not a painful thought, that so many pilgrims are weltering in the Slough of Despond, or climbing the Hill of Difficulty—so many following pantingly the banner on which Excelsior is inscribed, or, translating Longfellow's Latin into the manly vernacular of the Scottish poet—

> " For man is a sodger,
> And life's but a fecht."

Milton lived to feel that life was a terrible battle, but we repeat all was smooth sailing in his youth. He was taught early, and exercised carefully, by excellent tutors; but he was an apt scholar, and took in his knowledge easily as the child sucks his milk. A portrait of him survives at the age of twelve, representing a happy, beautiful boy with a neat lace-frill, black braided dress, hair close cut, hair a light auburn, and the complexion a delicate pink, or clear white and red—very different from the grim though noble face he was to wear in after years, and with which all are familiar. His first tutor was a Scotchman, one Thomas Young, a Puritan divine, who came from Luncarty, near Perth—where Hay, the ploughman, decided the battle between the Danes and the Scots, in favour of the latter by drawing his plough across the road where his countrymen were fleeing, and forcing them back to renew the fight, and was made the Earl of Errol by the king. From this parish came Thomas Young to England, and, after some of those struggles to which we have been referring, settled down near London, partly as a clergyman, and partly as a teacher. Milton was greatly indebted to him.

Young taught him Latin, Greek, Hebrew, and, above all, to entertain a keen relish for poetry, so that the child became father of the man, and Milton afterwards addressed to him a splendid copy of Latin verses, which have made his tutor's name immortal. When about fifteen years of age, Milton the poet was sent to St Paul's School, under the care of Alexander Gill. There he studied very hard, and sometimes had severe headaches, being, perhaps, the first warnings of that blindness which afterwards quenched his eyes. He sat up late, too, at night studying, a habit with many scholars, and which, if it seems to lengthen life in one sense, shortens it in another. His great delight was in reading books of poetry, especially a book entitled, Sylvester Du Bartas, a vast medley of sense and nonsense, childish platitudes, and genuine poetry, and touching on some of those grand topics which Milton's genius was afterwards to handle—the Creation of the World, the Temptation, and the Fall of Man. When ten, he began to be a poet himself—lisping in numbers, for the numbers came, although these early effusions are lost—but when fifteen, he translated the 114th and the 136th Psalms into English verse.

It is interesting to know that the first efforts of Milton's muse were inspired by the Scriptures. These were the lofty fountains to which his spirit early climbed, and from which it drank deep draughts of inspiration. There was something in the character of scriptural writing and of the scenery of the Holy Land which was peculiarly congenial to the poet's mind: that land of mystery and grandeur, which had only as yet been visited by a few English travellers, with its mountains where angels had rested, and its vales where sleeping patriarchs had seen visions of heaven, with one river flowing through it all, burdened in its every wave by high and holy associations, and emptied at last in a sea of death, where the doomed Cities of the Plain had been salted with fire; with its desert boundary on the one side surrounding the grim Sinai, which had once bowed before the footsteps and darkened in the frown of a descending God, and its magnificent mountain barrier on the other, where Lebanon looked from a throne of clouds on the half of the Asian world; washed by the Mediterranean, and inhabited by a race whose nobles were princes, who had stood before their tents in the plain, and trembled while Jehovah was thundering upon the summit; whose poets were prophets, who had derived their songs immediately from the glowing lips of the Eternal God, and whose Kings were the types and forerunners of David's Son and David's Lord, and had merged their high-descended honours like stars in the morning in His diviner glory, when

"Israel's splendid line was crowned with Deity."

To such a land and such a people Milton's kindred spirit was even in boyhood drawn by the power of mental magnetism; and although in his youth he was attracted to some degree for a season by other models, those of the classical authors of Rome and the early writers of England, in his maturer age he returned to Mount Zion, and was again seen bending over and drinking from

"Siloa's brook that flowed fast by the oracle of God."

In February, 1624, he left St. Paul's School for the University of Cambridge, where, after a little, he distinguished himself much both as a scholar and a poet. Here he wrote a fine sonnet on Shakespeare, and his still finer poem on "The Morning of Christ's Nativity." We might conceive him, at this point of his life, visited in his chamber by two Muses—both in the form of virgin maidens—one gaily and elegantly attired, her cheek tinged with the freshest bloom, her mouth radiant with the sweetest dimple, one hand carrying a volume of Shakespeare, the other holding a pen which seems to drop sentences of gold—her name is the Muse of England's poetry; the other is a more mature and matronly figure—

> "Graces in her steps, heaven in her eye,
> Her every gesture dignity and love;"

a dark but transparent veil envelopes her majestic form; her eye is raised above in rapt, ethereal contemplation, one hand holds the Hebrew volume, and the other, as it is lifted upwards, appears to "allure to brighter worlds and point the way"—her name is the Muse of sacred song. The young poet gazes in admiration at both, his heart loves more the one, his higher nature admires more the other. Which of them shall he choose? They are both so beautiful, both so divine, he cannot fix; his mind sways to and fro between them, till at last he determines for the present to propitiate both, and, deriving inspiration from the looks of the one, he indites his sonnet to Shakespeare; and, turning then to the other, at the bidding of her sweet and solemn eyes, which transport him to the far East, on that night when unto us a Child was born, a Son was given, whose name was called "Wonderful, the Mighty God, the Everlasting Father, and the Prince of Peace," he rolls out the sublime strain, which rises like the swell of an organ:—

> " No war or battle's sound
> Was heard the world around;
> The idle spear and shield were high uphung;
> The hooked chariot stood
> Unstained with hostile blood;
> The trumpet spake not to the armed throng,
> And Kings sat still with awful eye,
> As if they knew their sovran Lord was by!
>
> But peaceful was the night
> Wherein the Prince of Light
> His reign of peace upon the world began;
> The winds, with wonder whist,
> Smoothly the waters kiss'd,
> Whispering new joys to the mild ocean,
> Who now hath quite forgot to rave,
> While birds of calm sit brooding on the charmed wave."

By and by, he did not feel quite so comfortable in Christ Church College. Some say that he was whipped for contumacy. At all events, he seems to have been rusticated, as they call it, sent to the country, probably for uttering his mind too freely. His private character was always blameless. Colleges have often acted like stepmothers to their most eminent students. Samuel Johnson left Oxford without a degree, and without a pair of whole shoes. Coleridge left the university, too, degreeless, and, for a time, desperate. Shelley was expelled from his. Milton left with the ordinary degree of M.A., nor did he ever receive another. Degrees are good enough things in their way. There is a class of plodding, commonplace, but very useful men, who look forward to them as high honours, and feel satisfied when they get them, and would not probably have worked so hard had they not expected them; and there are those on whom they come, like sudden gleams of light on sandy cliffs, acquainting a world that was previously ignorant of their existence with that interesting fact. But Milton and Coleridge did not need them for fame, and had they received them, the honour would have redounded chiefly on, and been too much besides for, the university which bestowed it. With one thing Milton left his college—which does not accompany the exit of all students—a whole conscience. He had not defiled his life by college sin, nor compromised his religious opinions by college subscription.

He was now twenty-four years of age, and in the bloom of youth. He repaired to his father's country seat in Horton, near Colnebrook, in Buckinghamshire. Here he lived for six years, and, we believe, these six years were about the happiest of his life. He had plenty of time for study; the country around was fertile and richly wooded, although with few hills, and these of no height or prominence. His means were ample, his temptations few; he varied his scholarly pursuits by botanising excursions, by attending musical entertainments, by going now and then to London to see its sights, buy books, and converse with such celebrities he could meet withal; and he wrote such beautiful minor poems, as "L'Allegro," "Il Penserosa," "Lycidas," and "Comus,"—poems which, although he had never written anything else, would have for ever preserved his name as one of the sweetest and most beautiful of bards. We need not quote any parts of these. Passages from them, lines and epithets are floating through every corner of the English language, and, as we said above, we would rather have written "Comus" than all the poems which have been published in Britain during the last twenty years.

But, in 1637, his dream of country life was broken in upon by the entrance of that terrible disturber of the peace, Death. His mother died, and Milton, partly in order to remove from the scene of her sufferings, and partly in order to gratify a long-cherished desire, got liberty from his father to visit the Continent; and in 1638, attended by a single servant, he set out on his travels. We remember few finer subjects for contemplation in picture than that of Milton in his young manhood, thirty years of age, with his long auburn hair, with his beautiful Grecian face, with a mild majestic enthusiasm glowing in his eyes, with a cheek tenderly flushed by exercise and country air, of middle stature, but with a form handsomely made, erect and buoyant with hope, with a body and soul pure and uncontaminated, and bearing, like one of the ancient gods, a musical instrument in his hands, leaving the Horton solitude for the lands of romance and poetry.

He went first to Paris, where he remained for a few days, and felt less interest in seeing a city which was then the main centre of Popery, and had not long before ran red with Protestant blood, than in making the acquaintance of that great and good Dutch scholar De Groot, or Grotius, who was residing in Paris as Ambassador from the States of

Holland. Grotius had been a sufferer for conscience' sake, and had once escaped death by being packed up by his wife as a bundle of books in a large chest. He had written many works, including one on the Truth of the Christian Religion. He was an Arminian in his belief, and was probably none the less liked by Milton, who was at no time of his life a Calvinist, and was, as we may see hereafter, very much advanced in his religious views. He was a truly excellent man, although he died using the remarkable words, such was his humility, " I have spent my life in laboriously doing nothing." Grotius received the young Englishman kindly, and entertained him in a manner worthy of his abilities. From Paris he went to Nice, and thence to Genoa, and thence to Florence. This famous city had been the birth-place of the great Dante, whose poem, the Divina Comedia, and especially the part devoted to Hell, has greatly influenced Milton's own works, and is, of all modern poems, alone entitled to rank beside Paradise Lost. Milton, however, did not probably admire Dante so much now when still young as afterwards when disappointments, misfortunes, and age had at once soured and sublimated his spirit, and fitted him to sympathise with the gloomy genius of the " Man that had been in hell." In Florence there were then, as well as now, the most wonderful collection of paintings in the world—the matchless gallery of the great duke—the churches and the palaces crowded with the masterpieces of Michael Angelo, Raphael, and Leonardo Da Vinci; the collection of 400 portraits of the most celebrated painters, executed by themselves, and these the eye of Milton must have studied with the profoundest admiration, probably at this stage of his life preferring the beautiful productions of Raphael to the sterner and more terrific works of Michael Angelo. At Florence our poet met with a most distinguished reception, the literati of the place writing poems and panegyrics in his praise. And here occurred the conjunction of the two most amazing geniuses then living in the world—young Milton and old Galileo. We need not recount the history of this last extraordinary man; how, having published a work, in which he maintained that the earth turned round the sun, he was summoned to appear at Rome in the winter of 1632, and there, in the presence of a great company of cardinals, priests, and monks, he had to renounce his belief in the sight of his own eyes, and the evidence of his own telescope; and how, after having made the recantation upon his knees, he rose up, and stamped his foot, and cried, *E pur si muove*, "And yet it moves;" and how for this he was shut up for an indefinite time in the dungeons of the Inquisition, and every week for three years had to repeat the seven penitential Psalms of David. Milton says—" There it was that I found and visited the famous Galileo, grown old, a prisoner in the Inquisition for thinking on astronomy otherwise than the Dominican or Franciscan licenser thought." This is all we know with certainty of this famous interview, unless it be that it probably took place at Arcetri, near Florence, where Galileo was latterly confined, and where he died in 1642, aged seventy-eight years. He was already seventy-four, and almost totally blind, when Milton visited him.

We have elsewhere* sought to describe this remarkable meeting:—

> In dungeon's darkened light the immortals met,
> The one a youthful Abdiel, fresh in bloom,
> Hope shining in his white unwrinkled brow,
> The joy of genius sparkling in his eye;
> Love curling in the tendrils of his hair,
> And manly courage binding in his lips,
> A living sunshine in that shady place.
> The other, small of stature, pale of cheek,
> A thousand furrows like the paths of stars
> Wrinkling his brow, o'er which some thin white hairs,
> Fall straggling down with weary, aimless droop,
> His piercing eyes just setting in the night
> (Ah, Milton! 'tis a dark astrology
> Foreshadowing thy fate) of blindness deep.
>
> With what comparison shall we compare
> The meeting of the matchless sage and bard;
> Call it the transit of that Comet vast,
> Which ten years since in autumn pierced our skies.
> In shape, a scimitar, with basket hilt,
> And crossed Arcturus, spectacle sublime!
> Which no gyration of the dancing heavens
> Shall e'er in grandeur or in grace surpass.
>
> Thus met, the two at Florence, soon to part,
> The one to England bound, to fight the cause
> Of freedom, not with sword, but with a pen,
> Clear, bright and piercing as Damascus blade.
> The other to remain in darkness pent,
> Till to his eye the telescope of death
> His God applied, and lo, not night but day!

From Florence he went by Vienna to Rome—alas, no longer the Rome where Augustus reigned, and Virgil

---

* In "Night:" a Poem. Book VI.

and Horace wrote, and 5,000,000 inhabitants lived, but the degenerate Rome of the modern times; a city with only 110,000 of population, but containing some elements of great interest to Milton's mind—St. Peter's Church, newly finished and decorated, after 176 years had been expended on its building and adornment; the old Vatican, the palace of the Popes, with its vast library, the largest in the world; its halls, its porticoes, and its paintings; besides a hundred other sights which, to a stranger, and especially a stranger of the poetical temperament like Milton, must have been enchanting. But his spirit, like that of Paul of old in Athens, and that of Luther in Rome the century before Milton was there, was wholly stirred within him at the sight of the idolatries practised and the superstitions flourishing in that city—the priests and monks, and nuns and cardinals—

" Friars white and grey
With all their trumpery,"

bustling through the streets, selling their spiritual wares, and parading their lying nostrums. Milton (as we learn from his own declarations), like Mr. Fearing in Vanity Fair, who was near fighting with all the men in the fair, almost got himself into trouble by lifting up his protest against Satan in his very seat, and in spite of the old proverb, while living at Rome, he strove with the Pope. Yet in Rome as well as in Florence he found some warm friends of great eminence in their day— Holsteinus, Cardinal Barbarini, and two or three others. There, too, his exquisite musical taste was gratified by hearing the fine singers who then abounded in the Eternal

City, especially the Baroni family, containing three ladies, a family of a mother and two daughters—the mother, Adriana Baroni of Mantua, surnamed the Fair, her daughter Catherine, and her other daughter Leonora. They were reputed the finest voices that had ever been in the world. Leonora was the best of the three, and seems to have been the Jenny Lind of her age. They not only sang, but played on the lute, theorbo, and the harp. To hear the mother playing and the daughters singing, both being, besides fine musicians, most excellent, amiable, and beautiful persons, was the greatest treat of the time. Milton was a pure-minded man and would have felt disgust and loathing in many musical assemblies where, as Coleridge has it,

> " Heaves the proud harlot her distended breast,
> In intricacies of laborious song."

But to hear a lovely and virtuous female pouring out liquid and soul-felt music reminded him of angels lifting their immortal voices in the ear of God: and he addressed some little poems to Leonora singing, in one of which he says—(it is the finest compliment ever paid to woman)—"Thy very voice sounds as if God were present in thee; either God or at least some high intelligence of the deserted heavens warbles through thy throat and makes mortal hearts grow accustomed to immortal song. God is diffused through all things, but in thee alone he speaks; in all else he is silent."

From Rome he went to Naples, and how a mind like his must have admired the sight of that matchless bay, with the blue ocean melting in music on the golden strand—

"Like light dissolved in star showers thrown,"

and in the distance the great Vesuvius, edging the transcendent prospect with his triple peak and his breath of fire. At Naples he became acquainted with Manso, Marquis of Villa, a man who, in his youth, had watched over the unfortunate Tasso, the Italian poet, during the dull madness of his closing years, and who became thus a link between the author of the noblest epic in Italian, the "Jerusalem Delivered," and the author of the grandest epic in English, "Paradise Lost." Manso showed Milton much attention; took him to the fine points in the scenery; told him, no doubt, much about that strange, melancholy poet he had known in his youth; "how here Tasso had uttered such a saying, here he seemed suddenly moody, and here he had lifted up his blue eyes to heaven with that peculiar soaring look he had seen in no man else." He would tell him, too, of Tasso's imprisonment for imputed madness, but in reality because he had set his affections too high, upon Leonora, the sister of the Duke of Ferrara, and of the long years of captivity which had so tired

"The eagle spirit of a child of song,"

but which he cheered by writing his great poem on Jerusalem; and Milton's heart would burn within him as Manso thus discoursed.

Milton had intended to have gone farther south than

Naples, as far as Sicily and Greece. What a pity he did not! How he would have rejoiced to have seen

"Etna fires grow dim before the rising day;"

to have sailed up the Mediterranean; to have seen on the right hand the mountains of Africa, burying their snowy summits in the sultry sky; to have visited Greece, the country of his college visions, stood on Mars'-hill where Paul had preached, seen the vale of Tempe, Mount Athos, with its precipices piled a thousand feet over the sea, old Olympus, and best of all for him, a poet, Parnassus, the hill of song—

"Not in the frenzy of a dreamer's eye,
But soaring snow clad through his native sky
In the wild pomp of mountain majesty."

Perhaps, too, he cherished some faint hope of going eastward the length of Palestine—dear to him as a Christian, and kindling his devotion at Calvary, Tabor, the Sea of Galilee, and Lebanon. But he himself gives the reason why he did not proceed farther: "While I was desirous," he says, "to cross into Sicily and Greece, the sad news of a civil war coming from England called me back, for I considered it disgraceful that while my fellow-countrymen were fighting at home for liberty, I should be travelling abroad at ease for intellectual purposes." The news he received must have been to the effect that Scotland had broken out into rebellion against King Charles's government, and that the Puritans in the south were sympathising with it. Ere leaving Naples, he wrote an epistle in Latin verse to Manso, who presented him in turn with two cups of rich workmanship, and adorned by the representation of two scenes, one oriental and the other from classic mythology, along with a couplet, conveying an exquisite compliment. All remember the story of Pope Gregory seeing some English youths captured in the market at Rome, being struck by their beauty, and saying, "Non Angli sed Angeli," "not English, but angels." To this Manso alludes in his inscription:

"John Baptist Manso, Marquis of Villa Neapolitan, to John Milton, Englishman."

" Mind, form, grace, face, and morals are perfect, if but thy creed were also,
Then not Anglic alone, but truly Angelic thou would'st be."

Milton returned to Rome and to Florence again, where he spent some of the winter months, and went also to Bologna, Ferrara, and Venice, and thence by Verona, Milan, and the Pennine Alps to Geneva. From the top of St. Bernard he would take a last fond look of the golden plains and rivers of lovely Italy.

In Switzerland he would pass the Lake of Geneva, Lake Leman, and mark Mont Blanc in the distance, but was too early to see the Swiss scenery in perfection, which it does not reach till autumn, when the view from the side of one of the lakes upwards to the top of an Alp resembles, it is said, a ladder of bright and glorious colours, rising, the one above the other, from the blue of the lake to the yellow vineyards, and thence to the red beech trees, and thence to the grey rocks, and thence to the black pines, and thence to the white snows, and thence to the blue sky again. Milton waited a few months in Geneva, making acquaintance with some of the eminent divines there, such as Frederick Spannheim, Alexander More, and Dr. John Diodati.

From Geneva he returned homewards through France, and by the same route as before, namely, Lyons, the Rhone, and Paris. In the latter part of July or the beginning of August, 1639, he again crossed the Channel and set his feet in England. He had been away one year and three months. He made, in his account of his travels afterwards, the remarkable statement, "I again take God to witness that in all these places where so many things were considered lawful, I lived sound and untouched from all profligacy and vice; having this thought perpetually with me, that though I might escape the eyes of men I certainly could not the eyes of God."

When he came back he hired a lodging in St. Bride's Churchyard, Fleet Street, where he undertook the education of his sister's sons, John and Edward Phillips, the one ten, the other nine years of age. Finding the house in Fleet Street not large enough, he removed to Aldersgate Street, where he took a larger and more commodious house, situated at the end of an entry, and in the midst of a garden, an uncommon privilege in the London of that day. Here, in addition to his nephews, he took other pupils, and was a very strict and careful, perhaps somewhat severe teacher. He spent his leisure not now in poetry, which he gave up for a long time, but in writing books suited to the circumstances and the controversies of that age, such as a treatise on Reformation, a reply to Bishop Usher on Prelatical Episcopacy, and other treatises. He did this controversial work with great power, but did not feel quite at home in it, and he said himself that he was "led by the genial power of nature to another task," and that in this he had but, as it were, the use of his left hand. He panted to behold the "bright countenance of truth in the quiet and still air of delightful studies," but it was long ere this desire was fulfilled.

Having about this time married a Mary Powell, daughter of a country squire at Foresthill, at the close of a month, offended, it is said, at his austere manner of life, and not liking to hear his nephews crying under his rod, she left him for her father's, although some time after she returned again to his home, and, after a very affecting scene, and many tears on her part, they were reconciled. He had meanwhile, however, exposed himself to much reproach by writing some books advocating the liberty of divorce. About these there were very different opinions. The Presbyterians thought so ill of them that he was summoned to answer for them at the bar of the House of Lords, but was speedily dismissed. But he wrote shortly afterwards a far superior production—his "Areopagitica," or Defence of the Liberty of the Press—one of the noblest prose productions in the English language, in which he speaks rather with the tongues of angels than of men.

He continued afterwards to instruct a few scholars, first in Barbican, where there lived in his house besides his wife, pupils, and his own father, his father and mother-in-law, and after the death of his father and father-in-law, in a smaller dwelling in Holborn, opening backwards into Lincoln's-field. He published during this period nothing except a collection of his juvenile poems in Latin and English, and a translation of some of David's Psalms, which he did so indifferently that some critic says that Milton was never such a regicide as when he smote King David.

On the 30th of January, 1648-9, Charles the First was beheaded, and while many wept, many trembled, and many doubted, John Milton lifted up his great pen to defend what *he* deemed "England's Deed Divine." He published a treatise on the tenure of Kings and Magistrates, in which he showed that it is lawful, and hath been held so in all ages, for any who have the power to call to account a tyrant or wicked king. In gratitude for this seasonable aid Cromwell's Government appointed him their Latin Secretary, with a salary of £288 a-year, amounting in present value to more than £500. Then began what may be called the golden period of Milton's life. He had no doubt many duties to discharge—a large correspondence with foreign courts to carry on, besides books and treatises to write in defence of the Government. But his salary being adequate to his simple wants, he was enabled to dismiss his pupils, give up the drudgery of teaching, and remove to a better house in Westminster, where he continued till near the time of the Restoration. There he wrote his Defence of the People of England, a very able and eloquent book, erring, however, in its title, for most assuredly the execution of Charles the First was not the deed of the people of England but only of the army of England, and one powerful party and one extraordinary man, who swayed both as he pleased.

About this time a great calamity began slowly, but surely, to come over Milton. This was his blindness. His enemies maintained that this was brought on him by his labours in defending regicide. But it had in reality begun before then, and only came to a height in the year 1652. Calamities never come single, and the same year that he became helplessly blind his wife died in child-birth, leaving him alone, and with the care of three infant daughters. But he was still comparatively young, forty-four, his circumstances were comfortable, and his resolution was firm as a rock. In 1656, he married a second time, his wife being a Miss Woodcock, of Hackney. She lived only a year after marriage, but the union was as happy as it was short.

Blind though he was and again solitary, Milton was still revolving vast literary projects. He was proposing to write a Latin Dictionary, a Body of Divinity made out of the Bible, a History of England, and an Epic Poem. Wonderful for a blind man turned fifty! He nearly accomplished them all, too. He prepared the materials for the Dictionary, but left them in an unfinished state. He wrote the system of Divinity under the title of a Treatise on Christian Doctrine, which was lost but recovered, and printed in 1825. Part of the History remains, and the projected Epic became the Paradise Lost. Meanwhile, he was writing political and religious pamphlets, and doing all he could to prevent the nation again subjecting itself to the yoke of the Stuarts, but in vain. The Restoration came, and with it Milton's prospects were blighted. He lost his Secretaryship; he left his pleasant garden-house where foreigners came to call on him, some of whom visited England solely for the purpose of seeing him. He took refuge from danger in a friend's house in Bartholomew Close; nay, if some accounts are to be believed, he gave himself out for dead, and a mock funeral was celebrated for him. He was, it is said, a short time in custody, and two of his books which were peculiarly obnoxious to the ruling powers, his Eikonoclastes and Defensio, were burnt by the hands of the common hangman. Many in 1660 expected Milton to be crushed under the pressure of misfortunes and reverses which came upon him, but the end was not yet. He was to live other fourteen years, and in the course of that time to issue works, the grandest in idea and the most perfect in execution that England, if not the world, had ever seen.

Although the heat of persecution abated, the prospects of our poet were anything but cheering. He was poor, blind, solitary; his second wife dead—his daughters undutiful, unkind, and anxious for his death—his country was enslaved—the hopes of the Church and the world seemed blasted. We might have expected that disappointment, regret, and vexation would now complete their work. It was the greatest crisis in the history of the individual man. Napoleon survived the loss of his empire, and men call him great because he survived it. Sir Walter Scott not only survived the loss of his fortune, but he struggled manfully, amid the sympathy of the civilised world, to repair it. But Milton, amidst the loss of friends, fortune, fame, sight, safety, domestic comfort, long cherished hopes, not only survived, but stood firm as a god above the ruins of a world, and built, alone and unaided, to himself an everlasting monument. Verily, he was one of the celestial coursers who feed on no earthly food. He had "meat to eat that the world knew not of.".

As soon as he felt himself out of danger, he settled in Holborn, and afterwards in Jewin Street, Aldersgate, and resumed his old studies. In 1664 he married his third wife, Elizabeth Minshull, daughter of Sir Edward Minshull, in Cheshire. His daughters, three in number, Anne, Mary, and Deborah, read and wrote for him till the period of their respective marriages. They were taught to read, without understanding, Latin, Greek, and Hebrew to their blind father. From this slavery it is not to be wondered that they shrunk; but, besides this, they are said to have combined with his maid-servant in cheating him, and to have pawned his books. On what terms he lived with his third wife is not quite certain. A little after his marriage he is said to have been offered the Latin Secretaryship again, but declined it.

About this time commenced his intimacy with Ellwood the Quaker. This amiable and intelligent young man used to come every afternoon, except that of Sunday, and read Latin to him. Ellwood, though himself an object of persecution, found means to be serviceable to Milton. He had got a situation as tutor in a wealthy family in Chalfont, Buckinghamshire; and when the plague broke out in London in 1665, he hired there a house for the poet, who removed to Chalfont with all his family. When he arrived, he found Ellwood imprisoned in Aylesbury gaol on account of his religion. As soon, however, as he obtained his liberty, he paid Milton a visit, who put into his hands a MS., requesting him to read it and give his opinion. It was Paradise Lost! He had commenced this marvellous poem two years before the Restoration, and it had occupied him seven years: a time neither too long nor too short for the construction of such a piece of Cyclopean masonry. Had the time been longer he might have flagged, had it been shorter he might have huddled it hastily up. His purpose of writing an epic had never been relinquished, and from harsh and crabbed controversies he returned gladly to poetry. It was not composed, as might be imagined, by a slow and regular succession of effort, but at fits and snatches—the "spirit moving him at times," as it did of old his Danite hero. It is remarkable that, though the most intensely cultivated of poets, he was the most dependent on moods and moments. Now, he could only indite coarse and clumsy prose, with no rhyme and little reason, and anon "flowed free his unpremeditated verse" in a torrent of beauty, music, and power.

Milton's poem was opposed, first of all, by the licenser, who acted as a kind of accoucheur to books in those days. He found in the first book the comparison, matchless as we now think for grandeur, of Satan to the Sun.

> "His form had not yet lost
> All its original brightness, nor appeared
> Less than archangel ruined and the excess

> Of glory obscured; as when the sun, new risen,
> Looks through the horizontal misty air
> Shorn of his beams, or from behind the moon,
> In dim eclipse, disastrous twilight sheds
> On half the nations, and with *fear of change*
> Perplexes monarchs."

It was the last clause which offended the licenser, who would certainly, if he lived now, have shone as literary censor on the press of Paris or of Rome; and who, besides the needful qualifications of natural stupidity and ignorance, had perhaps some spite at Milton, as the author of the Areopagitica, in which he had treated his tribe with crushing contempt. At last, however, the book was licensed, and the copy sold to one Samuel Symmons for twenty pounds, —five pounds to be paid immediately; five pounds more when 1300 copies should be sold of the first edition; the same sum after the same number of the second edition had been exhausted; and another five pounds after the same sale of the third: the number of each edition not to exceed 1500 copies. In later times Scott's Marmion was sold for a thousand guineas,—a poem of great merit, doubtless, but infinitely inferior to Milton's work; one or two of Byron's works brought in two thousand guineas; and we have seen, the other day, some of the veriest trash the Laureate chooses to disgrace his great genius by, sold for hundreds or fifties of pounds. But readers were then scarce; poetry was even more than now a drug. Milton's name had become odious on account of his principles, and he thought probably that he had made a good bargain. We remember the late eminent Dr. John Brown, of Broughton Place, showing us in his library a copy of the first edition of Paradise Lost, a small quarto volume, with ten books; this was the original number—it was afterwards expanded to twelve; and dull as was the binding, it seemed to us a fragment of a summer's sunset, radiant with glory, blushing with fame. The poem arose like the morning upon the world, first touching the mountain peaks—the loftier minds of the age—Barrow, Andrew Marvel, Sir John Denham, the Duke of Buckingham, Bishop Atterbury, Dryden, and Addison; and then shedding its light upon the valleys, circulating through all ranks and classes of mankind, till now there is not a library in Britain or in America which can be regarded as complete, or worthy of the name library at all, if it contain not a copy of Milton's Paradise Lost. We saw it mentioned lately that copies of it were to be found in the west of Scotland about forty or fifty years after Milton's death. It was published in 1667, when the author was on the verge of sixty years of age. In two years Milton got a right to the second instalment of the price—1300 copies having been sold, not a very large sale for a book that cost only three shillings. In 1674, the second edition appeared seven years after publication; but Milton died before he received the price stipulated for this impression. The third edition was published in 1678; and on the receipt of eight pounds, the widow of the poet gave it over entire to Symmons, who sold it for twenty-five pounds to Aylmer, and from him it passed into Jacob Tonson's hands, and its subsequent history need not be traced.

When the plague was over, and the city cleansed,

Milton returned from Chalfont to London, having first, however, taken the hint from Ellwood, and begun Paradise Regained—which poem, along with Samson Agonistes, he published in 1671.

Calmly, on the whole, Milton was now going down into the vale of years. Poverty, in its worst shape at least, never entered his dwelling. Playing on his organ, he was at times supremely happy; and his blind eyes, as they twinkled, if they did not see the daylight of earth, seemed to see the light of heaven. Inspiration at certain times came mightily upon him, both by day and by night. Amidst the darkness of midnight—although, indeed, night and day were the same to him, wrapt in one cloud of blindness—more than in the day, his verse flowed freely; and he had sometimes to rouse his daughters to catch the lines which were, like waves of melody, rolling from his lips. Friends, some of them of note, looked in upon him as he sate in his house in Bunhill Fields. Dryden, afterwards the greatest poet of his day, was an occasional visitor, although Milton would not admit him to be more than a good rhymer: of course, Dryden's great works were not written till long afterwards.

But the time was now come when this great spirit was to put off his tabernacle and rise to that glorious world where his imagination had long dwelt, and his heart long been translated. Milton, too, must die like men, and fall as one of the princes. He had painted in his poem Uriel standing in the sun,—

> "His back was turned, but not his brightness hid,
> Of beaming sunny rays a golden tiar

> Circled his head; nor less his locks behind,
> Illustrious on his shoulders, fledge with wings,
> Lay waving round on some great charge employed;
> He seemed as fixed in cogitation deep."

But Uriel's creator must now soar far above the sun, and enter on those regions calm of mild and serene air, where dwell the spirits of the happy dead. His disease was gout, attended by a general decay of the vital powers. Feeling himself near his end he sent for his brother Christopher, then a bencher in the Inner Temple, to aid him in making his will. His death took place in fine keeping with his dignified and holy character, amidst the still solemnity of a Sabbath eve. It was on the 8th of November, 1674. There were attendants in the room, but they did not notice the moment of his expiration, it was so gentle and easy. Milton died as he had lived, alone.

Probably few tears were shed for him. His daughters and wife would be rather glad to be relieved of the burden of the blind, helpless, and rather testy bard, whose strength, although he was not more than sixty-six, was totally exhausted; and whose work in the world was fully done. Besides, we feel that tears and lamentations for the departure of such a man were superfluous and unbecoming. With serenity, nay joy, we should witness a man of whom the world was not worthy, and to whom the world was not dear, entering on a more congenial and lofty existence; joining the company of angels—the Gabriels, Raphaels, Abdiels, and Uriels of whom he had sung, and who were waiting over his bed to carry him to Abraham's bosom—

a majestic man-child caught up to God and to his throne.

His remains were attended to the grave by all his learned and great friends in London, not without a good many, too, of the common people, who had never read his poetry, but who knew his private worth, and had a dim, but strong, impression that it was the greatest of living men whom they were following to his last resting-place. We know not what impression was produced by the news on the callous court of Charles the Second. Perhaps some Waller was ready to sneer and speak of the old blind schoolmaster being dead, who had written a long dull poem on the fall of man, and anticipate that the book would soon perish too. Perhaps Charles, who had some appreciation of literature, would swear "Milton was a great man—odds-fish; and so he was; pity he was a Roundhead and a Regicide," and they would turn to their dice and Burgundy again and not waste another word upon the matter. The poet was buried next his father in the chancel of St. Giles, Cripplegate. The stone laid on his grave at first was speedily removed, and no monument was raised over his dust till 1793, when a marble bust from Bacon's chisel was, at the instance of the patriotic Mr Whitbread, erected on the middle aisle of the church. Fifty-six years previously his bust had been admitted into Westminster Abbey, where it still stands serene, bloodless, blind, and beautiful, representing, in its marble tranquillity and simple grandeur, the character of the man and the poet.

Milton, as a man, was of the middle size; neither lean nor corpulent; his skin fresh and fair; his eyes gray;

his features regular; his hair light brown, parted at the foretop, and hanging in curls about his shoulders. In his private habits he was extremely regular and temperate, and his days were divided on an exact and severe system. He was, in conversation, affable and easy, although his temper was severe; and he was a "good hater." His favourite enjoyment was music, and his favourite instrument the organ. Liberty and religion were the two master-passions of his soul. His personal piety has never been questioned. It was not obtrusive or ostentatious, and would not tell in what are called "religious obituaries," but was manly, enlightened, sincere, and fervid. And yet he does not seem to have been a happy man. Domestic infelicities, public affairs, and personal neglect, seem latterly to have made him sour if not savage. In fact, this earth was a sphere too narrow for him. He was "before all ages." Space was his only fitting abode, and eternity his only adequate day. Compared with other men we are reminded of the words of her of Endor—"I saw gods ascending from the earth, and one of them *is like to an old man whose face is covered with a mantle.*"

An essay of this kind hardly contains adequate space for much criticism, nor indeed is it necessary. To panegyrize Milton's works is as needless as to panegyrize the sun. Human nature is proud of them. The Paradise Lost is the greatest effort on the whole of the human mind—*man's* mountain—showing how near the intellect and genius of humanity can rise toward the measure and the stature of the divine. The proof of its permanent power lies in this, that whenever we think of hell, it is Milton's hell; of heaven, it is Milton's heaven; of angels, they are Milton's; of devils, they are Milton's; of Paradise, it is Milton's; of Death and Sin, it is as he pictured them in those strange and ghastly figures which are represented keeping the gate of Pandemonium. His book colours our conceptions of all existence, and forms a new version of the universe. The moral and religious influences of the Poem, as well as of its beautiful supplement, Paradise Regained, and the Samson Agonistes, have been immense. It has embalmed in the beauty and fragrance of poetic environment the great Christian principles and facts. It is at once a system of divinity, a code of ethics, and the best of epic poems. Not that all its doctrines are true, all its morals thoroughly according to the spirit of Christ, or that all its parts are equally excellent. It has colossal faults as well as beauties; its conceptions of the Trinity and of the plan of salvation have not pleased some of the orthodox; but the very fact of such a mind doing homage to religion and gathering its divinest inspiration from the Bible, has been of incalculable advantage; and when Milton appears in the witness-box in favour of our faith, it is as if a "giant angel" were standing there, speaking what he knew, and testifying of what he had seen.

Of his character we have already indicated our opinion repeatedly. He was a brave, true, and noble man—eminently a Protester and Contender—not called upon to do so in battle or on the block, but to do so in the study and by the pen—the pen which might, in his controversial mood, be compared to the sword of his own Michael, which

> "From the armoury of God
> Was given him, tempered so that neither keen
> Nor solid might resist its edge;"

or to the spear of his own Ithuriel, which

> "No falsehood can endure
> Touch of celestial temper, but starts up
> Discovered and surprised;"

and which, in his calmer and more constructive temper, might be likened to the rod of Moses, now dividing Red Seas, and now clearing the heavens of Goshen. Not always did he possess his pen or his soul in patience. Sometimes gall and wormwood distilled from its point, and, as Johnson says, "Hell grew darker at his frown;" but he had the true moral inspiration as well as the devouring fury of the Hebrew Prophet, and did, on the whole, well to be angry, had it even been unto death. Nobly did a kindred spirit, Wordsworth, sing of him—

> "Milton, thou shouldst be living at this hour,
> England hath need of thee; she is a fen
> Of stagnant waters—altar, sword, and pen.
> Fireside, the heroic wealth of hall and bower,
> Have forfeited their ancient English dower
> Of inward happiness. We are selfish men.
> Oh! raise us up, return to us again,
> And give us manners, virtue, freedom, power.
> Thy soul was like a star and dwelt apart;
> Thou hadst a voice whose sound was like the sea,
> Pure as the naked heavens, majestic, free.
> So didst thou travel on life's common way
> In cheerful godliness, and yet thy heart
> The lowest duties on herself didst lay."

A word in addition on Milton's religious creed. It was by no means an orthodox one. He was a Millennarian, an Arminian, a believer in the Material Nature of Deity, an Anti-Sabbatarian, and approached even to the doctrines of Destructionism and Arianism. To defend him in all or any of these peculiarities of view is not our province; but it is our firm conviction that Milton's errors did more good than harm. They converted few or none to their side; but they gave the world an impression of manly independence, of a truly Protestant spirit of private inquiry, and of downright honesty and boldness of character, which were most valuable, particularly in that age, when there was a tendency to rush from one extreme to another, from prostration before the Pope to prostration before the Westminster Assembly of Divines, and when, as Milton himself has it,

"New Presbyter was but old Priest writ large."

It is in this light that we value his Treatise on Christian Doctrine. We can hardly recommend it to our readers for its interest or its eloquence, any more than for its soundness in the faith; it is a poor, clumsy, and illogical production, without a spark of genius or an atom of ingenuity; but when we remember that it contains in a rough casket the jewel of Milton's creed, and that

" A Poet's heart was broken
To seal the truth within this volume spoken,"

we regard it with more reverence than all the piled folios of the Fathers and the Reformers combined. It was all dearly, devoutly, terribly true *to him;* it contains in it besides the more important and vital doctrines of our common Christianity, and even where he errs we are tempted sometimes to think that it is better to err with Milton than to be right with the whole Bench of Anglican Bishops, or with all the three principal General Assemblies of Scotland. Apart from this, in his views of Church and State, few now will deny that he shot far before his days, and that ours have only of late, and very tardily, come up to him.

CHAPTER IV.

THE PURITANS—OWEN, HOWE, BAXTER, AND BUNYAN.

PART I.—OWEN AND HOWE.

PURITANISM was a protest—nay, a battle; a protest recorded ultimately not in ink, but in blood; a fight which issued first in a Royal martyrdom and a Republic; and was afterwards resumed and culminated after many vicissitudes, hopes, and fears, in a glorious and final Revolution—the Revolution of 1688. Well, therefore, may we call its chief divines soldiers, since they bore the burden and brunt of the fray, and discovered all the courage of the combatant; although, of the four we have named, Bunyan alone actually drew sword and shouldered a musket in the grand old cause of civil and religious freedom.

In that age, besides the Puritans, and besides that quaternion of them we have clustered together, there were, need we say, many men of the highest intellect and the noblest character, whose works are preserved in the most precious archives of their land's language, and whose lives have come down to us laden with a fragrance that shall never perish. There was among the Cavaliers Jeremy Taylor, called truly the Shakespeare of Divines, with that marvellous fancy, wondrous, wave-like style and astonishing learning of his, whose life, though chequered and saddened, and at last cut short by family and personal misfortunes, was no doubt cheered then, as it has been glorified to men's eyes since, by that rich poetical temperament and glad piety which found beauty in everything, and saw heaven hovering over the driest details and darkest incidents of earth, like the golden pinions of the butterfly over the ruined shell of the chrysalis, or the wings of the cherubim above the dried blood of bulls and goats on the Mercy-seat. There was Isaac Barrow, cut off, alas! in the summer of life, but not till he had given the world assurance of manhood, of the strongest type, in those mathematical acquirements which qualified him to be the tutor of Sir Isaac Newton; in those controversial treatises which handle difficult and knotty themes, such as that of the Papal supremacy, with so perfect a mastery and inimitable an ease; and in those sermons which sweep over their subjects with the swiftness and might of a hurricane, and yet waft odours and scatter flowers as from a west-wind while they rush along. There was Thomas Fuller, whose works may be called the Sacred Jest Book, so quaint is the wit, and so pure and holy the moral; whose laugh is an anthem, whose smile a sacrifice; who shows in his books—called "The Holy War," "Pisgah-sight of Palestine," "Church History," and "Worthies of Great Britain"—the high purpose and devout imagination of a John Bunyan, united to the humour of a Swift and the wit of a Voltaire. We could excite risible emotions a hundred times by reciting clever clenches, puns, and gibes from Fuller's works; but at the bottom of every smile-starting jest there would be found the residuum of a serious impression: and it would be found that

"Fools who came to laugh, remained to pray."

Let us quote a specimen. "No wonder if the Papists fight for Purgatory. 'Tis said of Sicily and Egypt that they were anciently the barns and granaries of the city of Rome, but now-a-days Purgatory is the barn of the Romish Court; nay, the kitchen, hall, parlour, larder, cellar, chamber—every room of Rome. When Adonijah sued for Abishaig the Shunammite, Solomon said to his mother, 'Ask for him the kingdom.' But if once the Protestants could wring from the Papists their Purgatory —nay, then they would say, 'Ask the triple crown, cross keys, Peter's patrimony, and all.' In a word, were Purgatory taken away, the Pope himself would be in Purgatory, as not knowing which way to maintain his expensiveness." There were Bishops Pearson and Patrick, distinguished by their learning and laborious works; there was Dr. Robert South—the sharpest, keenest intellect of them all—whose words were razor edges, cutting on the one side the sanctimoniousness and stiffness of the Puritan divines, and on the other trying to shear away the beautiful but sometimes fantastic and wilful wings of the genius of Jeremy Taylor; who was not afraid to attack the living Lauderdale and Charles the Second, any more than the dead Cromwell, and who lived and died with the reputation of a good hater, an independent thinker, a solid as well as a sparkling writer, and a genuine son of the family of Ishmael—his hand against every man, and every man's hand against him. And there was John Scott, the author of the "Christian Life"—a noble production, which such men as Chalmers and Foster admired and imitated, and which many still value as a mass of strong sense and practical morality, rising ever and anon, too, into fervent and imaginative bursts of eloquence—second, some of them, in our judgment, to nothing we have ever read. Hearken to this short sentence as to the crash of a thunderbolt—"It is a necessary, unalterable, and eternal law, *that if ye will be wicked, ye must be miserable.*"

Among the Puritans, besides the four mentioned, there were other eminent names. There was the famous John Flavel, whose works—so distinguished by their richness of evangelical sentiment, their knackiness of expression, their numerous anecdotes, and their illustrations drawn from common life, which he delighted to spiritualise in every possible way—were once found, and that not very long ago, in almost every pious family in Scotland, so that the name "Flauvel," as it was pronounced, was a household word; and such books of his, as "A Saint Indeed," "A Token for Mourners," and, above all, his two volumes, on "Husbandry and Navigation Spiritualised," were counted as only less precious than the Bible or the Pilgrim's Progress. There were Samuel Shaw; Elisha Coles, author of a well-known book on "Divine Sovereignty;" Edward Polhill; Culverwell, called by some The Incomparable; William Bates, author of "The Four Last Things;" Joseph Alleine, author of a very popular and powerful work, entitled an "Alarm to the

Unconverted;" Thomas Brookes, and a host of others of much the same calibre. And there was one probably greater than all of these, Stephen Charnock, who was not an acceptable preacher, being compelled (which was uncommon in that age) to read his sermons, and, as he was short-sighted, to use an eye-glass in doing so; but whose work on the "Divine Attributes" is a great treasury of profound thought, ingenious illustration, and curious learning—a book which, were you sent ten years, and taking it with you, to a desert island, would be found at the close of that period not fully exhausted, so fineless are its riches of fancy, and so deep its strata of thought.

But we propose to deal at this time more especially with John Owen, or the Puritan divine; John Howe, or the Puritan prose poet and Platonic thinker; Richard Baxter, the Puritan orator; and John Bunyan, the Puritan dreamer.

We are all familiar with the name, and some of us with the works, of John Owen. Some, indeed, who have never read him, judge of him only by the clever caricature of him given in the words of Robert Hall, who said at one time that he was a "continent of mud," and at another that he was a "double Dutchman floundering in a continent of mud." Those, by the way, who repeat these sarcasms, do not see the incongruity of the comparisons —Owen being in one version of them the continent of mud and in another the hapless flounderer. Apart from this, it must be remembered (first) that Hall was not infallible; (secondly) that he was quite as severe upon

Edward Irving, on the author of the "Natural History of Enthusiasm," and on Coleridge himself, as he was upon Owen; (thirdly) that these criticisms occur in records of private conversation, when imprudent clever men will say clever inprudent things, to which they will not be ready to swear the next day, and which they never expected to see printed; and that (fourthly) the root of Hall's severity on Owen and others lay in his conventional and narrow taste—a taste which at once made his own writings the most faultless, and himself one of the most unreasonable and fastidious fault-finders of our times; and which, while it secured the perfection of his works as to style, has greatly lessened their power, and is rapidly wearing away their popularity. Robert Hall has written some exquisitely chaste and elegant sermons, but his writings discover no such grasp of thought, originality, or grandeur, as those of Irving, of Coleridge, or of Owen. Clumsy, no doubt, and confused sometimes, is Owen's style, and very afflicting are often his long, involved sentences, and his innumerable divisions of discourse—his eighthlies and seventeenthlies, his ninthlies and his twentiethlies; but these were the faults of his age more than of himself, and perhaps our age has gone to the other extreme, in its multiplication of sermons, in many of which you have no landmarks whatever—nothing but a boundless common, without a single dyke of distinction, or heathertuft of splendid figure, or even moleheap of stumbling absurdity, to relieve the dire monotony of level yet pretentious commonplace. And while "Owen on the Hebrews" is a heavy book and his "Display of Arminianism" a mass of confusion, and his "Work on the Spirit" very didactic and dry, his "Meditations on the Glory of Christ," his "Treatise on Spiritual-mindedness," his "Book on the 130th Psalm," and his "Sermon preached before the Long Parliament," have in them a severe grandeur of thought, a searching knowledge of human nature, and a dignity and power of language worthy of his or almost any reputation.

Owen was rather too stern a Calvinist for modern taste. He not only held the Calvinistic doctrines in their utmost severity, but he gloried in them as if they were the only vital doctrines of Christianity, and found a succulence and savour in their most sapless roots, at which many now will wonder. But those who take a wide and eclectic view of matters, and feel that after we have gathered a ray from every system that has ever been held on earth, we have approached a very short step to a perfect or even intelligible scheme of truth, and who besides say with the Laureate—

> " Our little systems pass away—
> They pass away and cease to be;
> They are but broken lights of Thee;
> And Thou, O Lord, art more than they "—

can derive good and meaning even from the terrific dogmas of the past, and conclude that although, thank God! they are not the whole truth, and are now superseded by a higher truth, yet they once contained, and in a sense contain still, a portion of truth. They magnify one side of the divine character to the utmost height, and they depress and darken one side of human nature to the lowest depth; but there is something in the divine and something in the human character answering to, and forming the germ of, their extreme theories. Above all, the men holding them were better than their creeds, although thoroughly sincere in maintaining them. Yet we cannot say that we feel precisely the same respect, or that we can make the same allowance for those who now tell us that Calvinism is still identical with Christianity, and that Calvin, as a theological teacher, was the best, if not the only true interpreter of Christ.

John Owen was descended from a race of princes in Wales, who claimed kindred with the great Caractacus of old. He seems to have early thought, like his countryman Glendower, in Shakespeare, that he was "not on the roll of common men;" and although his father was only a poor clergyman in Oxfordshire, the son formed his resolution to be like his more remote ancestry—renowned; and, as arms and ambition were not his sphere, he determined to rise by arts and learning. He went to study in Oxford, where he allowed himself only four hours' sleep in the twenty-four, and grappled with every species of knowledge, from mathematics to music. Subsequently his mind was deeply impressed by religion, and he found rest at last in Calvinism and Independency. When his party triumphed, he was appointed Vice-Chancellor of Oxford, and then for a season his dream of princely pre-eminence was realised. Oxford never flourished more in learning or piety than when the mighty Nonconformist was at its head, although you may look in vain for his portrait in the Picture Gallery of Christ

Church. After the Restoration had removed him from his office, he became a humble preacher and author in London, employing his time in writing those vast works which rise like a chain of mountains in our libraries, and move our astonishment how one man could have, in less than an antediluvian life-time, written so much. He died in 1683, sixty-seven years of age, and his funeral was attended by such a cortege as had never followed a dissenting divine to the grave before—including the carriages of sixty-seven noblemen and gentlemen, besides a long train of mourning coaches. He was, like his Divine Master, buried in a new tomb; and there, in the neighbourhood of Finsbury, still reposes the dust of this prodigious scholar, able theologian, uncompromising advocate of what he deemed truth; one dear to Independents as a powerful advocate of their polity, and to Calvinists as a noble defender of their version of man and God; dear, too, in no mean measure, to all who respect earnestness, Christian virtue, and gigantic intellectual power.

Let us look next at John Howe, the Platonic thinker and Christian prose poet. John Howe was a comparatively obscure minister—labouring in Great Torringdon, Devonshire—enjoying, indeed, the friendship of the noble house of Russell, and preaching those magnificent sermons which were afterwards published under the title of "Delighting in God," and "The Blessedness of the Righteous," the latter especially containing a singularly rich vein of pious and poetic thought. Still he was in the shadow, till coming one season to London on some errand or other, he, on the last Sabbath of his stay, went to worship at Whitehall Chapel—the chapel attended by the Lord Protector Cromwell, who was a great observer, and looked quite through the deeds and the faces of men. He fixed at once his eagle gaze upon this stranger from the country, and saw at a glance that he was a minister and a great man. He saw it in the gravity and majesty of Howe's countenance, in his lofty and polished brow, and in the serene and piercing intelligence of his eye. After sermon he called him to his presence, inquired his name, and told him he must preach before him next Sabbath. To preach before Cromwell might have tried the nerves of an ordinary man. Ministers have thought much of being asked to preach before the Queen at Crathie, and perhaps felt a little while preaching, although her Majesty was never reputed, with all her merits, to be a great divine. When John Foster attended in Bristol the ministry of Robert Hall, Hall, it is said, could not preach unless Foster was in a place in the chapel where the preacher could not see him, so highly did he estimate and fear his critical judgment. But Howe had to encounter in Cromwell an auditor who was not only a monarch, but a deep theologian, and who, if he had not language for preaching himself, had a thorough knowledge of what a good sermon should be. In John Howe, however, he had met his match, or one at least only a little lower in intellect than himself. It was Schiehallion confronting Ben-Nevis. Howe so preached that Cromwell determined he should be his chaplain;

and as his word was law, the preacher had to remove from Torringdon to London, and every Sabbath to stand up and encounter the gaze and bear the criticism of the two greatest men living—Oliver Cromwell and John Milton. But Howe gave sermons worthy of any audience. Along with Owen's Calvinism, held however in a more moderate form, he had a far loftier imagination, and a style of greater elegance and sustained majesty, along with a vein of contemplation which showed his intimacy with Plato, and which soared as far above the reaches of mere logic as the path of a sunbeam above the motion of a railway train. He gained favour with Cromwell personally, too, by his modest demeanour and disinterestedness. He often petitioned him, but it was always for friends, till Cromwell once exclaimed—"Friend Howe! you have obtained many favours for others; I wonder when the time is to come when you will ask anything for yourself or your family." When the Restoration came, Howe was relieved of his chaplaincy, and soon after of his connection with the Church of England. By the Act of Uniformity, he could only retain his position by submitting to be ordained again. This he would not submit to. "What hurt will it do?" said a Bishop to him. "Hurt!" he replied; "it hurts my understanding; the thought is shocking. It is an absurdity, since nothing can have two beginnings. I am sure I am a minister of Christ, and am ready to debate that matter with your Lordship, if your Lordship pleases; but I cannot begin again to be a minister."

As an ousted minister, Howe had many changes, and

some interesting adventures. He spent some time in Holland, visited Italy even, and greatly admired the pictures and statues there, and was five years in Ireland. Of his journey thither the following curious anecdote is told :—The ship by which he intended to sail was windbound at Holyhead. On the Sunday morning, Mr. Howe and some of the passengers were proceeding along the shore to find a place of worship. They met two men on horseback who proved to be the parson and the clerk. One of the travellers asked the latter if his master was to preach that day. "Oh no!" replied the clerk, "my master never preaches; he only reads prayers." "Would he object that a minister here on his way to Ireland would preach to-day?" "Oh no, he would be very glad." So Howe mounted the pulpit, and preached twice; and in the afternoon his audience was large and deeply affected. All that week the wind continued contrary, and the ship could not sail. Next Sunday, a very large audience assembled to hear the strange preacher. The clergyman of the parish was as confounded as if the late minister of Crathie had found unexpectedly a church full to hear Professor Caird, or Dr. Norman Macleod; and more so, for while the late worthy Mr. Anderson could preach—and, in his own way, preach well—this man could not. He sent his clerk in haste for Mr. Howe, who was in bed sick; but when he heard that the whole country side had turned out to hear him, he rose, and, forgetful of any personal risk, he repaired to the church, and preached with uncommon liberty and power, almost like a dying man to dying men; and when afterwards he related the circumstance, he added,

"If my ministry was ever of any use, it must have been then."

After these troublous times, John Howe settled in a church in Silver Street, London, where he continued an admired preacher till his dying day. His death occurred on Monday, April 2, 1705. A few days previous, Richard Cromwell, son of the great Oliver—now a retired gentleman calling himself Clark, and a most excellent, pious man he was—to whom Howe had acted as chaplain after his father's death, visited his old minister. Their interview was long and affectionate, and they parted amid many tears. Howe, in his dying hours, dwelt with great frequency, and almost superhuman eloquence, upon his favourite theme, the happiness of heaven, and spoke as if he were already within the veil.

Of all the Puritan Divines—next, perhaps, to Bunyan—John Howe has, from boyhood, been our first favourite; nay, if we love him less than the inspired tinker, we admire him quite as much. The late Dr. Hamilton, of London, while praising him highly, and with eminent felicity of phrase, speaks slightingly of his language, as if it were inferior to his power of mind and grandeur of genius. In this we by no means coincide. After deducting a good deal of that scholastic jargon, and involution, and subdivision—which were common to him with many in that age—and which far more characterise the writings of Dr. Owen, there is no Puritan author who, upon occasion, writes with such precision, richness, beauty, and power as Howe. There are passages in his "Blessedness of the Righteous" and his "Living

Temple" which are not easily surpassed; one of them on the Soul in Ruins, we give at the close, though it must be already familiar to most of our readers—and is certainly a curious specimen of that "poverty of style" Hamilton imputes to Howe. John Howe, besides, was not nearly so hampered as some of his contemporaries by system and foregone conclusions. There was often a dignified daring in his mode of thought. He went, in some points, before his age, although it was gracefully, and without spurning the period he had distanced. He either anticipated, or, at least, boldly followed, Fontenelle in his memorable theory about the Plurality of Worlds. That theory has, indeed, been of late vigorously assailed, if not exploded, by Dr. Whewell; but in Howe's time it seemed a necessary deduction from the Copernican system and Newton's discoveries, although not one that would so appear to a common eye. Our theory has long been that, while much of the universe is as yet entirely unpeopled, nevertheless a great colonisation is going on which may yet fill all space with living, intelligent, holy, and happy inhabitants, and that then the dream of the Apocalypse shall be a dream no longer, but literally fulfilled: "Every creature which is in heaven and on the earth, and under the earth, and such as are in the sea, and all that are in them, heard, saying, Blessing, and honour, and glory, and power be unto Him that sitteth upon the throne, and unto the Lamb, for ever and ever!"

———

"'That God hath withdrawn himself and left his temple

desolate, we have many sad and plain proofs before us. The stately ruins are visible to every eye that bear in their front, yet extant, this doleful inscription, 'Here God once dwelt.' Enough appears of the admirable frame and structure of the soul of man to show the Divine Presence did some time reside in it; more than enough of vicious deformity to proclaim that He is now retired and gone. The lamps are extinct, the altar overturned; the light and love are now vanished, which did the one shine with so heavenly brightness, the other burn with so pious a fervour; the golden candlestick is displaced, and thrown away as a useless thing, to make room for the throne of the Prince of Darkness; the sacred incense, which sent rolling up in clouds its rich perfumes, is exchanged for a poisonous, hellish vapour, and here is 'instead of a sweet savour a stench;' the comely order of this house is turned all into confusion; the beauties of holiness into noisome impurities; the house of prayer into a den of thieves, and that of the worst and most horrid kind, for every lust is a thief, and every theft a sacrilege; continual rapine and robbery are committed upon holy things; the noble powers which were designed and dedicated to divine contemplation and delight, are alienated to the service of the most despicable idols, and employed into the vilest intuitions and embraces—to behold and admire lying vanities, to indulge and cherish lust and wickedness.

"What have the enemies not done wickedly in the sanctuary! How have they broken down the carved work thereof, and that, too, with axes and hammers;

the noise whereof was not to be heard in building, much less in demolishing the sacred fane! Look upon the fragments of that curious sculpture which once adorned the palace of that great king; the relics of common notions; the fair ideas of things; the lively prints of some undefaced truth; the yet legible precepts that relate to practice. Behold with what accuracy the broken pieces show these to have been engraven by the finger of God, and how they lie now torn and scattered, one in this dark corner, another in that, buried in heaps of dirt and rubbish. 'There is not now a system, an entire table of coherent truths, to be found, or a frame of holiness, but some shivered parcels.' The very fundamental powers of the soul are shaken and disjointed, and their order to one another confounded and broken; so that what is judged considerable is not considered, what is recommended as eligible and lovely is not loved or chosen. Yea, the truth which is after godliness is not so much disbelieved as hated, held in unrighteousness, and shines as too feeble a light in that malignant darkness which comprehendeth it not. You come, amidst all this confusion, as into the ruined palace of some great prince, in which you see here the fragments of a noble pillar, there the shattered pieces of some curious imagery, and all lying neglected and useless amid heaps of dirt. He that invites you to take a view of the soul of man, gives you but such another prospect, and doth but say to you, 'Behold the desolation.'"

PART II.—BAXTER AND BUNYAN.

WE proceed now to Richard Baxter, the Puritan orator, and John Bunyan, the Puritan dreamer. We remember well when the name Baxter was a kind of reproach, and when Baxterianism was thought a minor variety of the great Pelagian heresy, and deserving of considerable *ex cathedra* condemnation. Pious old Seceders shook their heads when Richard Baxter was named, and said that he was indeed a little better than Arminius or Grotius, but still a dangerous and loose religious thinker. We need hardly say how much this is changed now, and how ready even those who may still differ from the eminent Puritan, in some of their opinions or modes of enunciating them, are to admit the transcendent merits of the writer, the excellencies of the man, and to commend such of his works as his "Call to the Unconverted" and his "Saint's Rest" as two masterpieces of Christian eloquence, as among the best examples of that powerful practical reasoning and strong nervous appeal which may be said, like that Word of the Lord itself, to be "quick and powerful, sharper than any two-edged sword, piercing to the dividing asunder of soul and spirit, of the joints and marrow, and being a discerner of the thoughts and intents of the heart."

Baxter's Life has been written by himself, and by many others since. We all remember how when after his death a Collection of his Sayings was published, as "Last Words of Mr. Baxter," it became so popular that somebody, trading on its success, brought out a supplement, which he called "More Last Words of Mr. Baxter." The incidents of his life need only be rapidly recounted here.

Richard Baxter was born in the village of Eaton, Constantine, Shropshire, in November, 1615. In his youth he had very deep religious impressions. He never went to a university, but gave himself a thorough self-education, delighting chiefly in logic, metaphysics, and practical divinity. A companion was of great service to him in rivetting religious impressions upon his mind, although this companion became afterwards himself a kind of reprobate. Perhaps his example might have shaken somewhat Baxter's belief in the Puritanic doctrine of the Perseverance of the Saints, for he certainly thought this young man a saint, and much better than himself. Richard went to London to push his fortune in the Court, but came back to the country disgusted with Court life, and having his serious feelings confirmed. Returning home, he found his mother dangerously ill, and a heavy snow-storm lying on the ground. He could hardly reach her dying-bed through the storm, and he was shut up by the snow from December to April, watching his parent, who was relieved in May by death. No doubt that long melancholy, snowy winter gave him profound impressions of the vanity and misery of life, and made him at the end a sadder and a wiser man. About the year 1638 he was ordained, having previously pondered many of the popular questions of the time, but not so deeply as he did afterwards, when he saw much to blame in the Church of England, although he was by no means a great innovator. His first employment was as head-master of a school in Dudley, and here he preached his first sermon. Subsequently he removed to Kidderminster, where he laboured for a season with great acceptance. Party spirit, however, between the partizans of the King and the Parliament ran very high, and as he was suspected of siding with the latter, he had to flee for his life—first to Gloucester and then to Alcester, where, while he was preaching, he heard the cannon of the battle of Edgehill firing, and next day, visiting the field of battle, found a thousand bodies lying unburied on the plain, and preaching to him a more awful sermon than he ever preached to others. He settled for a while in Coventry, acting as chaplain to the soldiers in that ancient city, round which were breaking the billows of the Civil War —a terrible time, he confesses, "miserable and bloody days, in which he was the most honourable who could kill most of his enemies." Baxter became during these commotions a decided Puritan and friend of the Parliament, but he never approved of the conduct of the extreme party or Cromwell. Remaining as he did with the army for some time, and removing from place to place in their company, he had the opportunity of seeing and recording his impressions of the anarchy of religious thinking and preaching which obtained among them. It was Revivalism run mad. The wildest fanaticism prevailed. There were sects without number—Baptists, Anabaptists, Seekers, Ranters, Quakers, Familists, Behmenists, Levellers, and others. "Every man his own minister," was their motto; and although these soldiers were not only amenable to discipline during the war hours, and even the bravest of the brave, when these hours were ended they spent their leisure in uttering rhapsodies, compared to which the twaddle of some of our street preachings, and the foam and falsetto of many American camp meetings, are sense, sanity, and wisdom. The picture in Scott's "Woodstock" of an impudent soldier taking the pulpit of a divine, and his place too, and holding forth to the congregation, is by no means a caricature, but a faithful picture. Richard Baxter himself had on one occasion to hold possession of a reading desk in a church, and to carry on a controversy with some inspired troopers belonging to Bethel's corps, "from morn to noon, from noon to dewy eve," being determined, as he said, not to be beaten, as he knew very well they would make a boast of baffling the chaplain; and he succeeded at last in driving them from the field.

From the army where he learned little but skill in controversy and the power of browbeating unreasonable and foolish men, he went again to Kidderminster, was welcomed back with cordial goodwill, and continued there for fourteen years, plying the varied labours of a pastor most diligently and successfully; hearing from afar off the echo of the great events which were transpiring—that strong blow at Whitehall which severed a king's head from his body; the cannonades in Ireland, which crushed cruelty with greater cruelty, as Diogenes trampled on the pride of Alexander with greater pride; the thunders of applause which saluted Cromwell Monarch of Great Britain, and the sound of the acts of marvellous energy by which he sustained his claims to the title. To that great man Baxter was an enemy, perhaps judging of him by his soldiers—his Obadiah Muggletons, Salathiel Bangtexts, Rightabout Thwackaways, and so forth, whom he had met while a chaplain. Cromwell did not mind his hostility; nay, when he heard that Richard Baxter was in London on some other business, he wanted him to preach before him, which he did, not only, like John Howe, without fear, but with faithfulness, telling him some of his mind. And when the Protector sent for him to an interview, he said to him very plainly that the people of England considered monarchy a blessing; and asked how and by whom it had come about that the country had forfeited that blessing; on which Cromwell got angry, and contradicted Baxter, and at it for four hours the two went. We wonder at Richard Baxter's courage. Look at Cromwell's face, in its quiescent state, and you will say that it required firmness of no ordinary kind to have encountered it; but think of those deep-set, hungry, devouring eyes, that great rugged brow, and those large nostrils, inflamed with anger, and then wonder at the man who ventured to beard and to defy it! Baxter gave Cromwell a paper to read. He took it, and returned it; but Baxter doubts if he ever read it, adding very naively, "I saw that what he learned must be from himself." Most true! Richard Baxter derived most of his learning from books; Cromwell derived most of his from his observation of man as a soldier and politician, and from his direct communion with God as a man of piety and of genius—the first of which meets the Supreme

Mind immediately as love, and the other as intellect and inspiration.

Baxter during his residence in Kidderminster was very diligent, we said, and very successful. His church became so full that five galleries were built, one after another, and still it was overflowing. He had only 600 members, but there were not twelve, he said, of whose sincerity he doubted. He got almost all the families in the town to make worship regularly. He was very attentive in visitation and catechizing, and yet he found time for writing a great deal. His plan was first to preach his books, and then to print them. Thus his "Saint's Rest," his "Reformed Pastor," and his "Call to the Unconverted," were originally addressed in the shape of sermons to his people, and then published as books.

When Charles the Second returned, Richard Baxter hailed him with acclamation, being carried away by the hope that Charles, who had been a Presbyterian in Scotland, would befriend that party in England. Some of the Puritanic ministers met the King when he entered London, and presented him with a handsome Bible, which he, the accomplished hypocrite, accepted most graciously, and said it would be the rule of his actions. He soon, however, found out the falsehood of Charles; and when he offered him a bishopric, he declined. Instead of becoming a bishop, he had to leave his charge at Kidderminster and remove to London, where, in conjunction with Dr. Bates, he preached in St. Dunstan's in the West, and became exceedingly popular. On one occasion the crowd was so great that a cry got up that the edifice was in danger. Baxter remained unmoved, and said, with much solemnity, "What is this petty noise to the sound of dissolving Nature!" and instantly the thought of judgment seemed to occupy their minds, to the exclusion of every other, and there was a great calm.

St. Bartholomew's Day, the 24th of August, 1662, came, and ejected 2000 of the best ministers of the English Church. It silenced Baxter among the rest. He withdrew into private life, and then, for the first time, he found leisure or inclination to marry. His wife was young and well-born; he was not old, forty-seven; but his health had never been good; he was thought a little morose in temper, and devoted to study; and, besides, his circumstances were far from prosperous. His marriage, consequently, astonished everybody, and he says himself, "The king's marriage was hardly more talked of." His wife, however, became a blessing to him, cheering him in his trials, and attending him in his imprisonment. She died first, although twenty-five years younger than he, and he wrote a delightful short account of her life. After his marriage he retired to Acton, preaching, like Paul, in his own hired house, and writing some of his practical works. One day, as he was preaching, a bullet fired at him entered the window, passed by him, and narrowly escaped the head of his sister-in-law.

His history after this is nearly all one melancholy picture of misery. He was imprisoned; he was followed by spies and informers; he was chased from place to place; and at last he was put to the bar, and tried by Judge Jeffreys—the most infamous judge that ever polluted a bench. In the year 1685, when Baxter was seventy years of age, he was tried before this cruel man, who exclaimed—" Richard, Richard, dost thou think we'll hear thee poison the court? Richard, thou art an old fellow, an old knave; thou hast written books enough to load a cart—every one as full of sedition, if not treason, as an egg's full of meat.* Come, old knave, speak up: I am not afraid of you for all the snivelling calves thou hast about thee"—alluding to some that stood weeping by Baxter's side. "Your lordship need not," calmly replied the noble old man, "for I'll not hurt you." He was, of course, condemned, fined 500 merks, and sentenced to lie in prison till it was paid. He lay there, accordingly, for two years. He narrowly escaped being whipped, to boot. Such were the tender mercies of Popery, of that bad and unchanged system which is spreading again in our land.

When released, he went to live with a brother minister, in whose house he remained; and, although feeble and old, continued writing and preaching till the end. He died in 1691, seventy-six years of age. His last words were—"I have pain—but I have peace, I have peace."

---

* The famous John Buncle says of Baxter—"He was an author fifty-two years, and in that time wrote 145 distinct treatises, including 4 folios, 73 quartos, 49 octavos, and 19 in twelves and twenty-fours, besides single sheets, separate sermons, and prefaces before other men's writings. His last work was, 'Certainty of the World of Spirits, in 1691.'"

Baxter, as a thinker, was the Duns Scotus—as an orator and writer, the Demosthenes of Puritanism. He was a subtle casuist—too subtle, indeed, to be always direct and honest seeming, although he was at bottom a thoroughly sincere man. He saw things at so many angles and through such a microscopic eye, that he was led occasionally to veer and tack about, and to appear a trimmer. His views were liberal for the time, and his Calvinism very moderate—verging on Arminianism. In the pulpit, he was the most impassioned of orators; his preaching was a whirlwind of earnestness; his great aim was to convince, and for this he employed every weapon, fine or coarse—reasoning, pathos, imagination, and sometimes the most terrific declamation and description, with language always powerful, though sometimes verging on vulgarity. He wrote 168 books and pamphlets. His best are his "Reformed Pastor," "Saint's Rest," and "Call to the Unconverted"—of which last 20,000 copies were sold in a single year. It is an awfully earnest volume, although tinged, of course, with the faults of its age and of its author—harshness of spirit, bitterness of language, and severe and one-sided views. His "Saint's Rest" is, on the whole, a milder and more pleasing book. It abounds in beautiful passages, which, taken in connection with the austerity of the author's spirit, and of some of his opinions, remind you of those golden mosses which grow amidst the bare boulders on the summit of Schiehallion, or those wild and lovely flowers which blossom on the verge of the eternal snows of the Alps.

But now for JOHN BUNYAN! And we cry All Hail to that rarest of rare spirits, that most ingenious and gifted of self-taught men, that Shakespeare of the Barn, that Prince of Dreamers, as poor Dr. MacGinn, the O'Doherty of *Blackwood*, called him once, a little before his own death, after stooping a long time in earnest and pensive thought over his sepulchre at Bunhill Fields. "Sleep on, thou Prince of Dreamers!" he cried. Let us say, "Awake, thou glorious slumberer, and sit up, that thou mayest hear what the world, which used thee so ill when living, thinks of thee in death! Awake, while we recount the outline of thy marvellous story, and sketch the principal features of thy unequalled genius!"

John Bunyan was born in Elstow, near Bedford, in the year 1628. His father was a tinker, but one rather above the common, since he gave his son an education not too frequent yet among the lower ranks—that of reading and writing. He was a wild boy—"roy'd," rather, as we say in Scotland, with hot gipsy blood in him. He was red haired, fiery eyed, big browed, and big boned. He accuses himself of many sins, but in this he was, as in so many other things, looking at himself through the magnifying power of one of the most ardent and excitable imaginations that ever belonged to man. He was neither dishonest nor dissipated nor licentious; but he had contracted the habit of swearing, like too many boys then and now, and was fond of amusing himself by bell-ringing and other diversions on Sundays as well as week days. We find the history of his early days given minutely in his "Grace Abounding to the

Chief of Sinners," the most earnest and entertaining of autobiographies, not excepting Augustine's "Confessions," Rousseau's "Confessions," John Newton's "Narrative," or Carlyle's "Sartor Resartus." What agonies he endured, what hairsbreadth escapes he encountered, what visions he saw, what dreams visited his daily or his nightly spirit —how he at last wrestled out of the Slough of Despond, burst the Iron Cage, escaped the mouths of the Lions, defied the foul fiend, and entered upon a Beulah rest— are set forth in letters of blood in that wonderful history of a human heart, written by itself. He had been first a tinker by trade, then a soldier in the Parliamentary army; had learned, too, the art of tagging laces; but having, after he had obtained peace, felt a strong inclination to proclaim it to others, he was set apart to the ministry in the year 1656, when he was twenty-eight years of age. He became very popular, partly, no doubt, from the fact of his being a tinker turned minister, but principally from the simple, natural, graphic, and vivid style of his genius. Some have argued for the practice of lay preaching from John Bunyan's example, but they forget entirely that John Bunyan had genius, a gift of God to which they cannot pretend. Had Bunyan been alive now, and had he heard some of those miserable imitators of his launching their sham thunderbolts, and kindling their bonfires with the flames of their own presumptuous ignorance and bad passions, a withering frown would have gathered on those big brows of his, and an angry fire would have shot from his eyes as he rebuked, not so much them—the silly victims of flattery and impudence—as the people who were patronising and mingling themselves up with them, and who, sitting and hearing their foolish utterances, although steeped to the lips in disgust, dare not protest against them, but must profess to hope that "good might be done!" Good done by narrow-minded absurdity, by caricatures of God's Word, by false and hateful pictures of God and man alike! Never, never! God does not permit evil that good may come. Truth and love are the only weapons he approves of in the gospel warfare; but where both are absent, there can be no genuine victory, but only, in the long-run, shameful and deserved defeat.

After preaching four years, Bunyan was clapped into prison for doing so. He was at first condemned to perpetual imprisonment, but the sentence was commuted into twelve years; and for that long period he was confined there, he had only two books with him, the Bible and Foxe's Book of Martyrs. There he supported himself, his wife, and family, including one blind child, to whom he was much attached, by tagging laces. It was there that he wrote, among other books, "The Pilgrim's Progress." After the expiry of his term, he was set free through the benevolent exertions of Dr. Barlow, Bishop of Lincoln. He resumed his itinerant preaching till the proclamation of Liberty of Conscience by James II. After that event he was enabled by the contributions of his friends to erect a meeting-house in Bedford, where his preaching attracted large audiences to the close of his life. He frequently visited London, and preached to vast crowds. Twelve hundred would assemble at seven in a dark winter morning to hear the wonderful Tinker, author of the Pilgrim's Progress. One day three thousand assembled to hear him at a Town's-end Meeting-house; one half could not get in, and he himself had to be pulled over the heads of the people ere he could reach the pulpit. His popularity, especially among females, led to scandals against his character, which seem. however, to have been entirely destitute of foundation. His death was brought on by a characteristic cause. He heard of a father in the town of Reading who was on his death-bed, and who was going to disinherit his son. Bunyan determined to act as peacemaker, rode from Bedford to Reading, effected the reconciliation, but, in returning, had got, it is supposed, wet, took ill in London, died after a short illness in the house of a friend, a Mr. Stradwick, a grocer, and was buried in Bunhill Fields. This was in August, 1688, when he had reached his sixty-first year.

Such is a very brief sketch of Bunyan's life. (If our readers wish to know more about him, there are such biographies as Ivimey's, Southey's, Macaulay's, Robert Philip's, and George Offor's.) His genius and principal works we have often characterised, and even yet we can hardly trust ourselves to speak about them. In many points our admiration of Bunyan's theology has yielded to further enquiry; but our admiration of the genius, the eloquence, the infinite skill and ingenuity, the sustained and ever-increasing interest of the story, the wealth and beautiful variety and exquisite discernment of character, the acuteness and good sense, the knowledge of Scripture, the grasp of great Christian principles, and the frank, genial, kindly, child-like spirit of the whole, is as fresh as when we read the enchanting parable, and wept over its pages at our mother's knee. We cannot but quote Cowper's fine lines about Bunyan's masterpiece :—

> "O thou whom, borne on Fancy's eager wing
> Back to the season of life's happy spring,
> I, pleased, remember, and while memory yet
> Holds fast her office here, can ne'er forget.
> Ingenious dreamer! in whose well-told tale
> Sweet fiction and sweet truth alike prevail;
> Whose humorous vein, strong sense, and simple style,
> May teach the gayest, make the gravest smile;
> Witty and well employed, and like thy Lord,
> Speaking in parables his slighted Word!
> I name thee not, lest so despised a name
> Should move a sneer at thy deserved fame;
> Yet, even in transitory life's late day,
> That mingles all my brown with sober gray,
> Revere the man whose Pilgrim marks the road
> And guides the Progress of the soul to God."

CHAPTER V.

THE SCOTTISH COVENANTERS—PART I.

IN several chapters we have gone over the leading men among the Puritans, and we come now to speak of their brethren across the Border—the stalwart children of the Scottish Covenant. And here let us make a preliminary observation. We said that in considering the Puritans we had paid the chief attention to their leading men. In considering the Covenanters we prefer speaking of them as a whole; and we do so because, while the leading men of the Puritans were the master-minds of their time, those of the Covenant were less distinguished, less outstanding, although in some points quite as noble, and were, if not the originators, yet the followers, exponents, and promoters of a great national movement. The Covenant had no Cromwell, no Milton, no Bunyan, Baxter, Howe, or Owen. They had only such men as Argyle, Baillie of Jervistoun, Cameron, Renwick, Peden, Balfour of Burley, and Hackstoun of Rathillet, who nevertheless, as belonging to the popular movement, did good service in their day, and whose names are indelibly impressed upon the memories and hearts of the Scottish people.

The Solemn League and Covenant was first formed at a General Assembly held in Edinburgh, in August,

1643. Previous to this, however, there had existed what was called the National Covenant, a document dating from the days of James I. of England, and which included simply an abjuration of Popery, and an obligation, ratified by an oath, to support the Protestant religion. In the troublous times that followed, and as arbitrary power and superstition were ever renewing their encroachments under Charles I., the National Covenant was again and again renewed. Not long after the famous case of Jenny Geddes, who, when the Dean of Edinburgh proceeded, in the High Church of St. Giles, to read the liturgy, lifted up her stool and launched it at his head, exclaiming, "Villain, wilt thou read the mass at my lug?" the Covenant was renewed with great solemnity in Grey Friars' Church, Edinburgh, on the 1st of March, 1638. First of all, a stirring sermon was preached in the church, then an immense parchment was produced, spread on a gravestone, and subscribed by such numbers that the paper fell short, and many had only room for adding their initials. Some wrote their names in their own blood. The enthusiasm was prodigious. The city became a perfect caldron of boiling emotion. Edinburgh then reminds us of Paris in one of the Federation feasts of the French Revolution, when

> "Men met each other with erected look,
> The steps were higher that they took;
> Friends to congratulate their friends made haste,
> And long inveterate foes saluted as they past."

This enthusiasm, however, speedily died away, although it was only to revive in a sterner and more permanent form.

When the Civil War at length began, Scotland was denied a Parliament; but a Convention of the Estates was summoned, and Commissioners from England having been invited to join the deliberations, it was resolved to form a "Solemn League and Covenant between the three kingdoms, as the only means for the deliverance of England and Ireland out of the depths of affliction, and the preservation of the Church and Kingdom of Scotland from the extremity of misery, and the safety of our native king and kingdom." Shortly after the General Assembly met in the New Church aisle of St. Giles, and there the Solemn League and Covenant, which had been originally a Civil League, became a Religious Covenant. When the famous Henderson of Leuchars read the draft of the amended Covenant in the meeting, many of the aged ministers wept for joy, and there was a general satisfaction felt by the laymen and English Commissioners too. Then followed the Assembly of Divines in Westminster, who, after a long sederunt, sanctioned the Covenant at the same time that they drew up the famous Westminster Confession, the Larger and Shorter Catechisms, and other documents which sought to establish a uniformity of doctrine and worship over the whole three kingdoms. And in this the Presbyterians would undoubtedly have succeeded, had they not been opposed on the one hand by the Erastians, and on the other by the Independents, the one party resisting it on their principle that the Church was the creature of the State, and the Independents on theirs of religious toleration. The latter went a noble length for that time; farther than many people go yet, when they hold that it is "the will of God that since the coming of his Son, a permission of the most Paganish, Jewish, Turkish, or Antichristian consciences and worships be granted to all men in all nations." Yet they did not in this go farther than Jeremy Taylor; nor so far, since he embodied, in his famous parable against persecution, a still broader principle, because extended to pre-Christian times. There, we remember, Abraham is represented as receiving into his tent an old wearied wanderer in the desert, feeding and sheltering him till he discovers he is a Parsee, or worshipper of fire, and then he turns him out to the wilderness. But God comes to the patriarch and says—"Have I borne with this man for a hundred years, and canst thou not bear with him for a single night?" No wonder that the Covenanters hated bishops when their doctrines were so narrow, and those of the biggest bishop in genius and learning in all England were so broad. Men never hate their foes so much as when they feel that they are in some points far ahead of themselves.

Nevertheless, the very narrowness of the Covenant—like the narrowness of an awl or wedge—was the source of its power at first. But although Charles II. became a Covenanter—a thing that seems to us now as wonderful as though Louis Napoleon were becoming a Methodist—yet, as his accession to that side was like everything else about him, false and hollow, it did, in the long-run, no good to the cause of the Covenant. And when Cromwell was dead, and Charles established on the throne, he became the bitter enemy of those who had restrained while they professed to idolise him. As Bucklaw, in the Bride of Lammermoor, vowed that having, when under hiding at Wolfscrag, had to eat pease bannocks and drink sour wine, he would value soft lodging and good feeding all his life afterwards, and never get into the Jacobite scrape any more, so with Charles II. Having been under the curb of the Covenant, and forced to listen to the long sermons and prayers of the Scotch divines for a considerable time, he determined never to be so cabined, cribbed, confined again; nay, he seems to have sworn to hate and persecute his old friends with all the rancour of a renegade—no doubt, stimulated, too, to this by the influence of the bad counsellors who were about him. Victim after victim was now sacrificed to Charles's newborn zeal against the Covenant. Argyle, "Gillespie Grumach"—the favourite of Sir Walter Scott's caricaturing power in his Legend of Montrose, and whom Aytoun calls the "master-fiend," but who died with great courage on the scaffold—were the first to suffer, and were soon followed by Guthrie, minister of Stirling—who long before met the executioner of the city as he entered the West-Port to sign the Covenant, and read in this an omen of his future fate, but who died bravely, exclaiming with his last breath, "The Covenants, the Covenants, shall yet be Scotland's reviving!" Soon after, by an Act of Parliament, Presbytery was abolished, and Episcopacy reinstated. Some of the Presbyterian ministers apostatised—prominent among whom was the unhappy James Sharpe, minister of Crail, afterwards so famous for his bloody and cruel death at

Magus Muir. This man had been sent to London to secure the Presbyterian forms of worship, but was tampered with by the Government, and accepted the Archbishoprick of St. Andrews as the reward of his treachery. In November, 1662, 400 ministers, rather than sacrifice their consciences, went out of the Church, left their quiet manses, their livings—not large, indeed, but comfortable enough—and walked away with their families, either to sleep with the fox and the blackcock on the moors, or to live upon the cold hand of charity. Very different from the Disruption of 1843. There were elements of grandeur in that event too, but there was much that was melodramatic and sensational about it. Lord Jeffrey wept when he saw the Free Church going out from Egypt, as they called it—although it was only from an Egypt of fleshpots to a wilderness of quails and manna. We would rather reserve our tears for the 400 Covenanting ministers who, not in the merry month of May, but in the gloomy month of November, left their manses, pleasantly situated among wooded nooks, amid green pastures, and by the side of still waters, and threw themselves immediately on the care of the God who feeds the young ravens aud lions in the wilderness. "Scotland," says an historian, "was never witness to such a Sabbath as the last on which those ministers preached;" it was a day of tears and bursts of irrepressible sorrow. In place of them a wretched herd of spiritual pretenders, the Curates, were appointed. When Falstaff levied his immortal troops, it seemed, according to himself, that he had pressed the gibbets and jails to furnish such a ragged regiment; and so, when the Curates commenced their ministerial labours, the people in the North, from which region they chiefly came, complained that all the herds had become ministers, and that the cows were no longer properly cared for. And it is satisfactory to know that they were treated, as they were, "the dregs and refuse of the northern parts"—sometimes barred out of the churches, sometimes hissed and hooted at in them, and sometimes their boots were filled with ants, and their feet made to limp as vilely as their sermons.

And, now, the penalty of success must be paid by the Covenanters. Their cause had culminated and declined, and as the "loser always pays," they, having lost, must submit to a terrible penalty. The Persecution began; its blood-red orb arose slowly, first smiting with a red ray or two a victim here and there, and then, as it ascended to the zenith, consuming and withering hundreds and thousands of brave martyrs and confessors. As the churches were filled with the odious Curates, the people in the South and West, who did not like an "ill-mumbled mass," began to frequent field meetings, where the ejected ministers played, of course, the principal part. At first, these meetings were peaceable—as peaceable and as picturesque as our tent preachings used to be—but by and by, when attempts were made to suppress them, and penalties enacted, both against the officiating ministers and the worshipping people, arms began to be seen, and the attitude of the worshippers was that of devotion and of defiance mingled. For ten years, in spite of every attempt to prevent and punish them, the majority of the people in the southern and western shires—in Nithsdale and Galloway, Ayrshire and Fifeshire too—worshipped in the open air. "Their psalms made the wilderness to rejoice; and mingled pleasingly with the bleating of sheep, the distant cry of eagles and blackcocks, and the musical thunder of cataracts and streams; the radiant faces of their young men and maidens made the desert to blossom as the rose; the voice of their preachers became a wild melody, and seemed reverberated from the blue dome of the sky overhead; thousands of visages lightened or darkened, sweetened or stormed, as the preacher kindled with his theme or melted under it; sometimes infants were baptised in the clear water that was rushing by; sometimes marriages were celebrated at these mountain altars—God and Nature giving away their children; and sometimes thousands communicated amid the wilderness, and at the close of the Sacramental work sent up a voice of holy song 'like a steam of rich distilled perfumes' heard afar on earth, heard farther still in heaven, and welcomed there as incense or as the morning and evening sacrifice. Seldom since Jesus trod the Galilean hills has there been such worship in this world. The great sky was transfigured into a temple; every heart said, 'How dreadful is this place!' and as the evening drew on, and still the services unweariedly continued, the stars rising over the mountain tops seemed looking down in love on the scene, and listening with interest to the great tidings which were there

> "'By Cameron thundered, or by Renwick poured,
>   In gentle stream.'

And even when a dark shadow of clouds gathered over the landscape, and when, like a grim spectre, the storm appeared above their heads, and

> "'Lightning, like a wild, bright beast,
>   Leaped from his thunder-lair,'

the softness of the scene was only lost in its sublimity, and every heart in the assembly felt that the God who was speaking was on their side, that that thunder echoed the deep protest of their consciences, and that that lightning was writing, in its own hieroglyphics, the wrongs of their country and their faith." *

Meanwhile, the country had risen under the galling yoke of suffering—a suffering compounded of fines and imprisonments, banishment and scourgings, stripping of clothes and devouring of substance; and there had been the abortive rising and unsuccessful battle of Rullion Green, a quiet spot among the Pentland Hills. There fifty of the Covenanters were killed, and the same number taken prisoners. One of these prisoners, called Hugh Mackail, a young minister, died with a dignity and an enthusiastic confidence which may make his name long memorable. He was young (only twenty-six), had been extremely popular; was a good scholar; and as he appeared on the scaffold, his face was tinged with a

---

* See our Martyrs and Heroes of the Covenant.

hectic beauty, like that of a leaf in autumn shining in the sun. All this so moved the spectators that there was not a dry eye in the multitude. As he mounted the ladder he told his fellow-sufferers that he felt every step of it a degree nearer to heaven. And when he reached the top these were his bold and noble words—" Farewell father and mother, friends and relations! farewell the world and all delights! farewell meat and drink! farewell sun, moon, and stars! Welcome God and Father! welcome lovely Jesus Christ, the Mediator of the New Covenant! welcome blessed Spirit of Grace, the God of all consolation! welcome glory, welcome eternal life, and welcome death!" And with this sublime ejaculation he mounted the chariot and was not, for God took him.

Some of the prisoners were sent to the Bass Rock. We saw that noble old sea hill not long ago as we passed through East Lothian, and thought of what it had once been and of those who once were imprisoned there. A soft, quiet, autumnal light was shining meekly upon its massive form. The ocean was breaking, we knew, in softest music, scarce audible, upon its broad base; and the sea-birds, on half-slumbering wing, were circling its sides. All, from the deep azure over its head to the billows below and the shores of East Lothian around, was, almost ideally, calm. The huge rock seemed a metaphor of peace. But so much the more did it remind us, by the force of contrast, of the days when it stood up, under skies as blue and in the sight of a landscape as fair, a gigantic dungeon, devoted to the purposes of tyranny and to the immurement of the saints of God. There many of the Covenanters were at different times confined. Some of them died through the unhealthiness of the dungeons and the dampness of the rock; others received permission to walk for their health at times upon the summit of the crag. There, if they had been lovers of scenery, they might have admired the magnificent prospect—the Pentlands on the south, the Ochils to the north—the Forth flowing between as if to soothe the ancient wound which made the ridges twain—the Lion of Arthur's Seat and the huge Castle of Edinburgh—the Lomonds of Fife—North-Berwick-Law—the sea outspread eastward and northward in a sheet of silent, trembling, or tossing silver, and in the far distance the Highland mountains, Ben Lomond, Ben Ledi, Schiehallion, and Ben Voirlich, lifting over the rest their free and kingly foreheads. But probably they thought little of all this; their minds were elsewhere. It was of the work of Reformation, of Covenants broken, burned, and buried—of the battles they had fought, of the hopes that glimmered before them still, of success and reprisals, of their own sufferings, or of their families far away: it was such subjects as these that they revolved in their silent promenades on the cliff, or expressed their feelings about in their earnest conversation and psalms of praise. They would thus spend the day, and when the sun had dipped his orb below the Lomond hills, and the ocean was deepening his voice into those cadences which he sings to the stars, they would, without a murmur, retire to their dens, and lie down to dream of heaven and the martyr's crown. "That watch," said good and gifted Jameson of Methven to some persons who were talking of the sufferings of the Covenanters, "gentlemen, was in the Bass Rock," pulling out, as he spoke, an ancient chronometer, which one of his ancestors had had there. And often we can conceive the worthy sufferer, whose name we cannot give, taking out that watch to calculate the slow minutes of his confinement in this accursed though magnificent stronghold of oppression, and sighing, as he bethought him, of how many weeks, or months, or even years must yet lie between him and deliverance.

One man was imprisoned there whose cruel treatment bore terrible fruit. This was one James Mitchell, who had shot at Archbishop Sharpe, but without effect. He was a monomaniac. For some time he contrived to evade pursuit, but was at last recognised at a funeral, and apprehended. He was sent to the Bass Rock, and lay there for some years. He was brought up again for trial, but pleaded a promise of his life which had been made. Sharpe and the Lords of Council denied that any such promise had been given Mitchell, and he was condemned to death. When the Council broke up the records were examined, and there they found the act recorded! Some of the more just and generous sought to get him reprieved, but this was overruled, and the poor creature, haggard, unshaven, withered and wild-seeming, as Habakkuk Mucklewrath himself, was sent, as the persecutors used to phrase it, to "glorify God in the Grassmarket." God no doubt marked this act of glaring injustice, but men marked it too; and there were those among the Covenanters who determined that it should by no means go unpunished.

It led to strong, though suppressed, indignation—to curses not loud but deep—and to purposes of the most determined vengeance. Meanwhile, other oppressive measures were resorted to by the Government. As the greater part of the inhabitants of the western shires would not attend the parish churches, but persisted in worshipping in the open air, and in conventicles, as they were called, the Earl of Lauderdale declared them in a state of revolt, and ordered large forces, including Irish troops and 8000 Highlanders, to take up their free quarters in the country, and to plunder and oppress the inhabitants. This was called the "Highland Host," and seldom has such a horde of savages been let loose upon a land. Think of 8000 kilted demons—half-naked, with shaggy locks and wild eyes, armed with guns, pistols, claymores, dirks and targets, and sometimes with shovels, mattocks, and spades, daggers fastened to the muzzles of guns, iron fetters for binding their prisoners, and thumbscrews for compelling them to answer questions—descending like a herd of wolves upon the West, entering houses, torturing men, women, and children; stopping travellers on the highway and stripping them of their clothes; stealing, or rather robbing, every article of portable furniture, pots, pans, grid-irons, and shoes; seizing upon farm horses, at the plough or in the stable, and compelling them to transport their plunder to the Highlands; terrifying, by their threats, savage gestures, barbarous gibberish of an unknown tongue, blows and rudeness, all sexes and ages, and turning the most populous districts into a howling wilderness. Nothing in modern times can parallel this incursion of the Highland Host, unless it be the employment of the Indians in the first American War against the Colonists—an outrage which is embalmed in the terrible invectives of Lord Chatham and Edmund Burke; or some of the cruelties perpetrated by the brutal Russians under Suwarrof, or the Austrians under the butcher Haynau, who, as the lasher of Hungarian women, gained so bad an eminence some eighteen years ago. The memory of that incursion of savages lives in these regions still, and speaks in the burning hatred with which the tyrannical tools are still regarded. But what said Lauderdale when he heard of these outrages? "Better," said he, "that the West bore nothing but windlestraws and sandylaverocks than that it should bear rebels to the king."

When these men—if we may call them so—had returned to their mountains, laden with pier-glasses, coverlets, eight-day clocks, great-coats, fenders, fire-irons, and all other sorts of "plenishing," as they called it, a body of 5000 regular troops were sent in their room, and distributed in garrisons over the recusant districts. The object of this was, it would seem, to madden the people to resistance, and it was soon gained. But it was in the East that the first muttering of the storm was heard, and that the first blood was drawn in the quarrel—drawn in circumstances of the most extraordinary, and, in some measure, lamentable manner.

It is a May morning in 1679. Transport yourselves to an undulating country,* and there a kind of moorish

---

* Magus Muir is a muir no longer. A large wood covers the spot where it is supposed Sharpe fell. But there is great doubt as to the exact ridge running towards St. Andrews. Observe that party of twelve men on horseback. They are plainly dressed—like what they are, the farmers or little lairds of Fife—and they are all armed with swords and pistols and guns. You see by their looks that they have been disappointed in something or other. Have they been following game, and has the game escaped them? They are gazing at each other with blank visages, and muttering something to themselves. At last towards the west there appears a large old-fashioned carriage in the distance; and look how they prick up their ears, exchange glances, and how a fiery eagerness and joy appear to flash out of their eyes! Yes, they are hunters, and they have been disappointed in their game; but now another and a more valuable quarry is in view. This little band, led by David Hackstoun of Rathillet, and his brother-in-law, John Balfour of Burley, have been waiting for one Carmichael—a contemptible, though mischievous, tool of the prevailing faction—who had given great and just offence to the Covenanters of Fife as a spy, an informer, and cruel torturer of the disaffected; but he has gone some other way, and thus saved his wretched person. But here, here is the Archbishop himself, here is Sharpe—

---

locality. We humbly suggest that the respected proprietor might do something to clear away the dubiety. Among the corn to the west of the wood they show a spot where some of the martyrs (who were executed and hung in chains after Sharpe's death) are buried, and which is said to remain always green, even in the depth of winter. In a wood adjacent is a monument erected to Andrew Guillan, mentioned above, who was executed at the Grassmarket, and his body transferred, hung in chains, and buried there.

the old enemy of the cause, the double-dyed and ten-times perjured villain—here he is, on his way from Edinburgh to St. Andrews, returning home, having probably got in the capital new powers, and devised new schemes, for carrying on the Persecution. Immediately the thought enters their minds—all their minds at once, and it is reflected in fierce glances from eye to eye— "God has delivered him into our hands—the great and capital enemy of the Church is near us—a foeman worthy of our steel—a life the quenching of which is of vastly more importance to our cause than that of the mean and despicable Carmichael; we have been laying a trap for a mere cub and imp of darkness, but here is the old fox and fiend himself." Their minds are made up in a moment. The carriage is travelling fast, but they can travel faster; and, having set their horses to the spur, they overtake the Primate at Magus Muir, about three miles west of St. Andrews. They surround the carriage—cutting the traces, and disarming the attendants, and dismounting them; they then glare in at the Archbishop, and command him to come out of the coach. Look at them as they stand! Hackstoun is a tall, slender man, black-haired and black-visaged, riding a brown horse, wearing a velvet cap, and armed with a broadsword, carbine, and pistols. The two brothers Henryson are mere youths, slender, fair, and tall. Andrew Guillan—a weaver from an adjacent hamlet—is a little, broad, black man, with a curling bushy beard, and is mounted on a white horse. George Balfour of Gilston has black curling hair, is lean-faced, and armed with three pistols and a sword. And the fiercest of them all—John Balfour of Burley, the hero of "Old Mortality"—is a low-statured broad man, with round, ruddy face, a terrible squint, red hair, and the look of one who never gave and never asked for mercy. They seem the twelve apostles of God's vengeance. Sharpe refuses to come out at their bidding, and then they fire into the carriage. On this he and his daughter Isabel—married afterwards to Cunningham of Barns, in Fife—utter the most piteous cries for mercy. Sharpe himself protests, with frantic earnestness, that he would spare their lives, give them money, and even lay down his title of Archbishop if they would spare him. One of the number, named Russell, opened the door of the carriage, and ordered Sharpe to come out, saying the while, "I take God to witness that it is not out of any hatred to your person, nor for any prejudice you have done or could do me, that I intend now to take your life; but because you have been, and still continue to be, an avowed opposer of the gospel and kingdom of Christ, and a murderer of his saints, whose blood you have poured out like water." Saying this, he thrust at the old man with his sword, and wounded him. Sharpe then left the coach, and, creeping on his hands and knees, approached one of the number, Hackstoun probably, whom he recognised, and said—"You are a gentleman, you will protect me;" but Hackstoun replied, turning away, "I will not lay a hand upon you." Another of the assassins, relenting, cried out, "Spare these gray hairs." "Did he spare James Mitchell?" said the fierce Burley, plunging, as he spoke.

his sword into the Archbishop's side. They all then, save Hackstoun, gathered around him, and pierced him with innumerable wounds—showering curses, too, upon his head; and when his daughter threw herself between her father and the murderers, she, too, was severely wounded. Sharpe at last died praying, and the assassins mutilated his body, stamped on it with their feet, kicked his hat before them on the moor, rifled his carriage of arms and papers, and rode off. The body was conveyed in the coach to St. Andrews. And all this was done in broad daylight, within three miles of Sharpe's own house; and the twelve men left the moor unmolested—not so much "as a dog barked at them while their deed was being transacted," and none of them was ever for that action put to death—enough surely, in such an age, to make many exclaim, "It is the judgment of God."

This deed, on the whole, we do not defend. It was a crime, and worse—a blunder. Its circumstances were simply horrible. The man was old, defenceless,—taken at terrible odds,—killed, clinging as it were to the horns of the altar of a daughter's tenderness and misery. Oh, oh! 'twas foul! to see those silver hairs dabbled in blood!—to see his home in the distance sending, you could fancy, its smoke forward to meet him! and to hear the shrieks of parent and daughter, blended in one discordant wail, to which even the wild bay of St. Andrews, one might dream, would have listened in pity! But, in some points, he deserved his fate. He *had* been, as they surmised, in Edinburgh, procuring a proclamation to be passed suppressing field-preachings, under the penalty of high treason; and was even meditating a journey to London, to organise severer measures still. He died thus red-handed—taken in the fact. This dreadful action, however, made the persecution rage hotter than ever. Proclamations were issued, against the deed and its perpetrators, and every attempt was made to discover and seize on them, but in vain. Balfour and Hackstoun made their escape to the West, and found their way to the neighbourhood of Loudon-hill—a blue cone which all Ayrshire sees every day rising to the East, and which is surrounded by bogs and dull moorlands, where the persecuted found a refuge, and where they were predestined to gain one memorable victory.

Robert Hamilton and eighty men had, on the 29th May, entered Rutherglen, put out the bonfires kindled in honour of Charles II.'s accession; burned at the cross all the acts which had been issued against a Covenanted Reformation; published a proclamation condemning the Government, and then retired to the upper wildernesses of Clydesdale. Thither the notorious Claverhouse—it were too closely to imitate himself to imprecate curses on his cruel name, but whose memory is, assuredly, not blessed—was sent with a large party of dragoons to disperse them. He came up with them at Drumclog, on the 1st day of June, 1679, a Sabbath day, four weeks after the death of Archbishop Sharpe. Drumclog lies about a mile east of Loudon-hill. The country around is, as hinted before, an expanse of dreary moorlands, with some sluggish fells or little hills rising lumpishly in the midst, and with morasses interspersed amid the channels of mountain torrents—altogether a place admirably adapted for defensive operations. Claverhouse, leading his troops over a little eminence called Calder-hill, comes in view of a very singular assembly. It is a tent-preaching; but a tent-preaching just ready to tower into an army, and to grasp, instead of the sword of the Spirit, the blade of battle. About two hundred men occupy the centre, flanked on each side by forty horsemen. They stand drawn up on a gently-sloping declivity, and have in their front a morass and a deep ditch. Almost all are armed; although some with rude enough weapons—scythes, pitchforks, and graips. Our old friend, John Balfour, is there—having come from Magus Muir hither—with his face as stern, and his skelly as terrible as ever—a broad blue bonnet on his head, and a trusty shabble in his hand. There, too, are Hackstoun, Hamilton, Captain Cleland, and others. The preaching has begun, and a minister, named Douglas, is waxing eloquent on the arts of tyranny; when, hark! a gun is heard from a neighbouring height, and the watchman who has fired it is seen running rapidly towards the assembly. All cry, "The enemy is upon us." Douglas shuts the Bible, comes down from the little knoll, where he has been standing, grasps a sword, and prepares for battle. The armed men instantly fall into position, and the women and children—for many of both are there—retire to the rear. Claverhouse sends forward an officer, with a flag of truce, and a summons to surrender. It is answered by a shout of defiance; and, after a short silence, the whole army break out in a trumpet-like psalm. How it rings through the desert—awakens the echoes of Loudon-hill—astonishes the foemen, and goes up to heaven, like the sound which made Jericho fall down flat in the grand days of old!

> "In Judah's land God is well known;
>   His name's in Israel great:
> In Salem is his tabernacle:
>   In Zion is his seat.
>
> There arrows of the bow he brake—
>   The shield—the sword—the war!
> More glorious these than hills of prey—
>   More excellent art far!"

Staggered, Claverhouse and his men might be, for a moment, by these solemn sounds; but their courage soon returned, and they raised a loud cheer in reply, and rushed upon the morass. In the attempt, however, to cross and close with the enemy, they were prevented by the well-sustained fire of the Covenanters. They then sent a party to take their foes in flank; but scarcely had they crossed the ditch, when John Balfour and Cleland assailed them, and cut them in pieces. At this critical moment, we see a solitary man running over the moor, and joining the Covenanting army. It is John Nisbet of Hardhill, whose house is near at hand, and who has been sent for, in haste, to the fray. Joining Burley, he cried out, "Jump the ditch, and charge the enemy!" Burley and he proceeded to lead their men across, and attacked Claverhouse's right flank, at the same time that Hamilton and Hackstoun brought the main body into action in front. Claverhouse resisted bravely, but was at last overborne; and, as he and his men rode back over Calder-hill, a countryman, with a pitchfork, made an opening in his famous black horse's belly, so that the bowels hung out a yard—a ghastly spectacle—yet he carried him off a mile! As he rode along, a voice was heard exclaiming to him and his men, "Lads, will ye no' stop for the afternoon preaching!" They at last, after being nearly cut off at the village of Strathaven, reached Glasgow, about midnight, entirely discomfited, and broken up for the time. Such was the immortal skirmish of Drumclog.

The Covenanters lost no time in pursuing Claverhouse to Glasgow, and attacking him there. Owing, however, to the narrowness of the streets, and the height of the houses, they were easily repulsed, and took up their head-quarters in Hamilton. Some dead were left by the insurgents in the streets of Glasgow, and their bodies were shamefully maltreated by the chivalrous Claverhouse and his men. At length, though victorious in driving back the Covenanters, he found he could not maintain his position in Glasgow, and removed to Edinburgh, where he was soon joined by a large army from England, sent down by the Government, under the command of the Duke of Monmouth, Charles's illegitimate son, but a man of mild character—an army of 10,000 strong, and provided with a complete train of field artillery. The Covenanters were now 6000 in number; but they were ill-armed, imperfectly disciplined, and, above all, split up into parties. Some were for, some against, the Indulgence;

and the time that should have been occupied in preparing for battle, was wasted in disputes and mutual recrimination. The army resembled a city in an election time: filled with brawling declaimers, empty pretenders—masses of brute fury or brute favouritism—party spirit and personal abuse raging in every quarter—no order, wisdom, or management; even the cunning and the crafty feeling themselves over-reached—the weak crushed—the honest men and the brave thrust into a corner—the strong and the able themselves rendered useless, and distracted in the general confusion worse confounded of the scene. Meanwhile, while tent was thundering against tent, and preacher abusing preacher, some calling for an election of new officers, and others raving against the "Black Indulgence," the army of Monmouth was slowly drawing nigh. The cry was still—"They come!" and, at last, on the evening of the 21st June, it reached the village of Bothwell, opposite the encampment of the Covenanters.

Sabbath the 22nd dawned, and saw a gallant yet dreadful sight. Bothwell Bridge is in the possession of the insurgents, and forms, along with the houses on their side of it, a very strong post of defence. Advancing to force it, if possible, come on the tall standards, glittering arms, and parti-coloured uniforms of the Royal troops, with the Life-guards in the van, burning to avenge their defeat at Drumclog, and led by Monmouth, seated on a white charger, a beautiful man, with a countenance fair as Absalom's,—by Thomas Dalziel, the grim old soldier, with a large grey beard, which he had never shaven since the death of Charles the First., floating down over his buff coat and steel breastplate,—and by Claverhouse, with his dark locks and crafty eye, looking over the Covenanters' ranks, as if they were his predestined prey, with a savage smile. On the south-west of the bridge were a knot of picked men, under Hackstoun and Hall of Haughhead; guarding the pass, on the river side, were Burley and John Nisbet, with a strong party of horse and foot. In the centre of the bridge was a gateway, which was barred and locked. All this promised well; but, alas! on the moor behind, was a mass of men swayed to and fro by contradictory feelings and currents of controversy—like the trees of the wood by opposing winds—unmanned partly by the phrenzy of faction, and partly by the palsy of fear, who, as a historian remarks, "had neither the grace to submit, the courage to fight, nor the sense to run away." The battle began. Lord Livingston led the attack; but was bravely encountered by Hackstoun—and column after column, trying to cross, were driven back by the close fire of the insurgents; and when a party of the English plunged into the river, to ford it above the bridge, Burley and his troops repulsed them, and not a few were drowned. Thus, for an hour, raged the fight, and the result seemed very doubtful. Monmouth looked anxious; Dalziel got pale with rage; and Claverhouse bit his lip, till the blood spurted out. But now their ammunition began to fail. Message after message was sent to the main body for a new supply;—but in vain. They were too much occupied in abusing each other, and listening to foolish harangues. At last a barrel appears. We see the eyes of Hackstoun sparkle for joy, and a stern smile flicker over Balfour's countenance. They open it in haste;—but, lo! it is filled with raisins, not with gunpowder! Conceive their feelings. If they are too pious to swear, they yet vent their feelings in epithets of burning wrath on the miserable caitiff, or traitor, who has thus deceived them. And to this mistake, whether designed or not, the loss of the battle may be traced. The enemy now makes good his footing near the bridge—the portal gate is burst open—the Covenanters, fighting most gallantly, are slowly pushed back to the open moor—the Royalists follow at their leisure, their cannon in the front, and are permitted to form in battle array upon the plain. The rout now becomes universal. Four hundred have fallen; twelve hundred throw down their arms, and surrender on the spot. The confused and routed mass rolls towards Hamilton. There, Burley tries to rally the fugitives in the streets; and might have succeeded in doing so, had not a shot struck his sword-arm and rendered it useless. "May the hand be withered that fired that shot," said the dauntless man;—"I can fight no longer;" and, turning his horse's head round, he retreated out of the confusion, and we hear of him no more till years afterwards he re-appears in Holland, and is supposed to have died at sea, while returning home to to his own land before the Revolution. This closed the battle of Bothwell Bridge, fought precisely three weeks after that of Drumclog, and the brief gleam of Covenanting success which shone on the moorlands of Loudon-hill, was swallowed up for a season in the blackness of darkness.

It was a heavy blow and great discouragement which the good cause had now sustained, the more as there was not only defeat but disgrace. Many have cried, "All is lost except our honour," and this has been a consolation at the close of many a battle day. But at Bothwell Bridge, everything—men, arms, ammunition, prestige, and honour—was lost, and nothing remained but a scattered remnant, a few sheep in the wilderness, where they had been driven in the cloudy and dark day. Nay, these sheep were not permitted to abide safe in the deserts, but were pursued into them by the triumphant and victorious foe. Claverhouse dashed into Galloway, raging for blood, insatiate of revenge. He had never forgot his defeat at Drumclog, and must wipe out the stain in gore. He made little or no distinction between those who had been at Bothwell and those who had not. He plundered dwellings, seized on horses, killed or imprisoned men, women, and children; and has left in some of the parishes in that region, such as Glencairn, Balmaclellan, and Carsphairn, the memory of a destroying angel, or rather, demon of wrath. The Covenanters, however, though too weak to resist, fell into methods of dodging their foes. The hare cannot face the hounds, but she often escapes by turning and winding. Loth, indeed, was the brave Covenanter, who had not much of the hare about him, to take to his heels; but when he had to run, it was before a superior foe. Often he turned upon his pursuers: he retired as he advanced —like a lion. Skill, sagacity, self-possession, distinguished and secured his retreat; and in the last extremity he was more ready to fight and to die than to yield. The late excellent Dr. Simpson, of Sanquhar, in his book called "Traditions of the Covenanters," has collected a number of striking anecdotes about the wonderful escapes some of the chased ones met with. There was one Thomas Brown, cousin of the famous John Brown, the Ayrshire carrier, who was told that the dragoons were approaching his house. He went out very coolly to meet them, contrived to cross their track, accosted them, and passed off for a stranger. When they approached his own house, the soldiers asked if that "fanatic Brown" was at home. He replied, and truly, that he was not, and so they went on their way, and by and by he parted company from them, and returned home to his own house at leisure.— There was one John MacClement whom the persecutors had in chase. When he succeeded in turning the corner of a hill, he saw a dead sheep lying on the heather; he lifted it up on his back, met his enemies, who mistook him for a shepherd. They inquired if he had seen MacClement: he pointed in a direction where he said he had fled. They set out on the false scent, and thus he escaped out of their very grasp.—One John Dempster was pursued by the dragoons; they were so near him that the horse of one them was pressing on his shoulder. He happened to have with him a pair of large shears, such as are sometimes used in the fields for cutting down weeds; turning round, he plunged them into the forehead of the horse, who reared, cast off his rider, threw the whole party into confusion, and enabled John to make his escape into a wood that was close by, and where they were unable to follow him.—Another Covenanter, called John Fergusson, was working in a hay-field when he saw the enemy approaching. He ran to the brink of a deep dark pool in a river surrounded by thick willows, threw his bonnet and a rake he had been using down the stream, and then plunged under the water, screened by the shade of the willows, and keeping his head above the waves,—his pursuers imagining, from seeing the bonnet and rake floating down the current, that he had drowned himself, and ceasing the pursuit. One is reminded of the famous fictitious scene in "Rob Roy," where that freebooter, having escaped, and swimming down the Forth, pursued by a host of adversaries, loosens his plaid, and allows it to float apart down the river, it is mistaken for himself, and many of the blows and shots aimed at him are diverted by it, and he finally baffles his pursuers; or of the real history of John Colton, who, chased by a whole tribe of naked Indians, reached a raft upon the side of a river, dived below it, and kept his place there unseen—his pursuers coming up, leaping and dancing for a long time on the raft, within a foot's breadth of the head of their enemy, who saw them perfectly well through the openings, and yet had the presence of mind to remain quiet till their departure. But, perhaps, the most striking story connected with Covenanting escapes, is that of Sir Patrick Hume. This brave man had been imprisoned, but contrived to escape. He took refuge in his own family burying-ground, where his wife made him a bed—a bed literally in the grave. Thither his daughter brought him his daily food, at no little risk to herself, what with the gravestones over which she stumbled, and the dogs who barked at her on her way. Then there was the difficulty of secreting the supplies. On one occasion a sheep's head, which was one of the dishes at the family dinner, suddenly disappeared. Great was the astonishment of some of the children at what had become of it, and at the enormous appetite of Grizzy (Grizel was the daughter's name) for sheep's head. She had in reality dropped it very adroitly into her lap, reserving it for her father's use. It was very noble of her certainly, and reminds one of the Roman maiden, who nourished her father in the prison, where he had been condemned to die of hunger, with milk from her own breast. But Grizel Baillie fed her father at the risk of her own blood. In fact, a whole volume, and one as entertaining as "Caleb Williams," "Rookwood," "Jack Sheppard," or Victor Hugo's "Miserables," could be written on the escapes of the Covenanters. Some of them found refuge, like David Haggart, the thief, who, in a haystack, heard two men speaking of him as having broken the jail in Dumfries, and killed the jailer; others, like Charles the Second in the Royal Oak, lurked in the hollows of huge old trees; some got into empty meal chests and barrels; many, besides Sir Patrick Hume, found refuge in church-yards and other haunted spots, where the fear of the dead repelled those who were seeking the blood of the living. But, besides all this, the Covenanters found still securer hiding-places amidst the wastes and wildernesses of the upper regions of the country. Those of our readers who have read "Old Mortality," remember Scott's matchless picture of Burley, lurking in a cave near a cataract, across which there stretched an oak tree, serving him for a bridge; how, when Morton and he quarrelled, Burley spurned the oak away, and, brandishing his sword, cried to Morton, "You are now in my power—fight, yield, or die;" and how Morton replied, "I will not fight with the man who saved my father's life; I do not know how to say yield; and my life I will save as I best can"—springing the while clear over the chasm, and leaving the old homicide astonished and infuriated behind. Some years ago, we visited Creehope Linn, near Thornhill, Dumfriesshire, a romantic spot, where a small, but very spirited, mountain stream descends in a succession of leaps through a beautiful wooded ravine, and were shown a stone niche in a dark nook, called the "Souter's Seat," where it is said a Covenanting shoemaker used, while under hiding, to ply his trade, though how he could retain his composure to work while the wild torrent was wailing around, the gloomy gulph yawning below, and the fear of danger from his foes constantly near him, is more than we are able to understand.

"They now," it has been said, "retreated into remoter wildernesses. Sunless glens; dark morasses, where peat water was the only drink; old forests and the secret tops of lofty hills; dark wooded and rocky dens, by raging cataracts; caves, the mouths of which were concealed by brushwood or by rowan trees, and the sides of which were dripping with a damp, unwholesome dew—such were the retreats into which Scotland's persecuted children were now compelled to carry their Bibles and their swords. The wildernesses of Galloway, Ayrshire, and Dumfriesshire were suddenly peopled with strange, wild-seeming, solitary men, with long, grizzly beards, gaunt visages, and eyes burning with the glow of earnestness—the grey gleam of the partition between enthusiasm and madness—all bearing little clasped Bibles in their bosoms and short but true-tempered shabbles by their sides. Sometimes they met in broad daylight for worship, but in numbers much less, and with spirits not nearly so buoyant, as on that Sabbath morning at Drumclog. The precautions they now took against surprise were much stricter than before, but, at the same time, their spirits were even prouder and more determined. They were like chafed lions or bears robbed of their whelps. The language of their preachers had soared up into a wilder poetry, an austerer symphony, than before. One is reminded of Israel's prophets: of Moses wandering at the foot or on the summit of the fire-girt hill; of Elijah in the cave, listening to the mighty wind, the earthquake, and the still, small voice; of Ezekiel astonished upon the banks of Chebar, or gazing on the valley of dry bones; of John the Baptist feeding on his locusts and wild honey, and clad in his garment of camel's hair, in the midst of that great and terrible wilderness; of Jesus himself treading in majestic solitude the Mountain of the Temptation, or wrestling with the Adversary who encountered him there.

"Their worship was not infrequently performed at night; under the canopy of Scotland's midnight; with Orion in the south shining in meek, yet mighty, rivalship with the Great Bear of the northern sky—with meteors shooting across the deep of the stars—with the wind wailing in its passage over a thousand moors—with streams mingling their many notes with its doleful melody, did these persecuted Christians meet; and their hoarse psalm, and the loud, deep voice of their preacher, did finely harmonise, and make up the full sum of those solemn 'voices of the night.' And as the preacher warmed with his theme, and alluded to that brief gleam of victory which visited their cause at Drumclog, or bewailed the fatal Bridge of Bothwell, fierce eyes became fiercer in the darkness, their Bibles were clasped with greater earnestness to their bosoms, their hands unconsciously grasped their swords, and the whole congregation moved like the waves of a stormy sea, and swore, as it were, one deep, silent oath to avenge their quarrel and the quarrel of their desert-inhabiting God. Few now, comparatively, the voices to sing their war melody, 'In Judah's land;' but rougher and deeper were their accents, and the psalm seemed now the cry of blood going up to heaven from the silent wilderness below, and through that starry desert above, which conducts by its long and burning stages to the Throne of God." *

Another scene, founded on fact, in the Covenant tent-preachings, let us now describe. It is a Sabbath-day among the mountains, and a company of the Persecuted

---

* See our "Martyrs and Heroes of the Scottish Covenant."

have assembled. Around is a mighty chasm of cliffs, called the Cartland Crags, where Wallace used to take refuge, through which a river is flowing, at present so low, owing to the heats of summer, that men could walk all but dry-shod up its channel. A hundred Covenanters —men, women, and children included—are assembled to hear a minister, who stands up in a pulpit of stone, and having a birch tree waving over his head. Between him and the congregation is a clear, deep pool, formed by the diminished stream; and there, after the sermon is over, a row of maidens, all in white, come gliding over the stream, to give away a number of infants who are to be baptised. The baptismal water is lying in the hollow of a large stone, beside the brink of the pool. How beautiful to look down, as you see the boys doing, into the clear water, and see the whole scene, from the maidens, the parents, and the minister, up to the topmost peaks of the sky-striking summits reflected there upon the purest of mirrors. The minister baptises seven infants, in the name of the Father, the Son, and the Holy Ghost, and gives out a psalm, with the words—

> "Lo! children are God's heritage,
> The womb's fruit His reward;
> The sons of youth, like arrows, are
> For strong men's hands prepared."

The psalm is reverberated like musical thunder from the surrounding crags; and all again is silent. Suddenly a large stone falls from the rock above their heads into the pool; a voice is heard from the summit, and when they look up, there is a shepherd's plaid waving in the air in the hand of the watchman stationed above. It is the signal of instant danger, and immediately the whole congregation vanish into caves and hidden recesses, known only to themselves. They vanish almost in a moment; but they have been seen by a party of soldiers who have reached the top of the rock, and who exclaim when they see them, "They are delivered into our hands—they are caught in this nook as in a net; let us down, and they are our own. Halloo, boys! halloo! Remember Drumclog, and let the blasted Whigs perish!" They leave their horses, and rush down a cleft in the crags, and arrive at the spot. But, to their utter astonishment, nothing is to be seen, nothing but a bonnet that had fallen from one of the Covenanters' heads, and the Bible the minister had been using, and which they spurn into the pool. They are utterly unable to discover where their enemies have fled, and awful are the curses and the threats which they utter. But, louder than these curses and threats, hark! a sound like a distant muttering thunder far up the stream. It comes rolling, and roaring, and deepening, as it descends. "What can it be?" The crags shake as if to the sound and stamp of earthquake. "Lord! have mercy on us!" cried the soldiers, falling down on their knees, and looking a hundred ways in their consternation, with pale faces and white lips. Meanwhile, the minister comes out of the cave where Wallace had long ago found refuge, and exclaims, "The Lord God Omnipotent reigneth. It is a powerful voice that comes from the Lord Most High." What is it?—what can it be? It is a waterspout which has burst among the hills, and there the river raging in flood is coming down in its irresistible power. The whole hollow of the cliffs is filled with the waters. An army must have been swept away by that raging torrent. The soldiers perish in a single instant, swept down heaps upon heaps; but far up in the cliffs are the Covenanters, now emerged from their hiding-places, and, with clasped hands and streaming eyes, uttering prayers to the Almighty, and some of them exclaiming, "We will sing unto the Lord, for He hath triumphed gloriously; the horse and his rider He hath cast into the depths of the waters." *

---o---

PART II.—THE SCOTTISH COVENANTERS—*Continued*.

FAR are we from presenting the Covenanters as faultless characters. Had they been so they had ceased to be men, and become very insipid and unconceivable characters. Great virtues almost always imply great faults. The taller and broader a man, the broader and taller is his shadow. The faults of the Covenanters were principally three—bigotry, cruelty, and superstition. They were intensely narrow and bigoted. They saw, or at least, admitted, no virtue, or piety, or merit, in their opponents. The Prelacy was with them "black Prelacy," about as black almost as Popery. The Prayer-

---

* See Wilson's Lights and Shadows.

book, with all its many beauties, was only an ill-mumbled mass. The surplice was a rag of the old whore. Kneeling at the Lord's Supper or at prayer was flat idolatry. The organ was a blast from hell, and there, too, had Arminianism, Episcopacy, and the Black Indulgence been hatched. Again and again they publicly excommunicated the King, and quoted in reference to him the words—"Tophet is prepared of old, yea for the KING it is prepared; he hath made it deep and large. The pile thereof is fire and much wood. The breath of the Lord, like a stream of brimstone, doth kindle it." In all this there was a good deal of truth, and for all this there was a good deal, too, of excuse in the circumstances of the times and in their own persecution; but still, as a whole, it was exaggerated, and among other effects had this, of exasperating and embittering their enemies against them—who had thus some reason for calling them sour, savage, and people who, if they had had the power, would have been as great persecutors as their enemies. Their second great fault was the cruelty which occasionally distinguished their conduct to their adversaries, as in the case of Archbishop Sharpe, and in their treatment of the prisoners they took at the battle of Drumclog, who were put to death in cold blood after the battle was over. But the age was a barbarous one—there was little mercy shown on either side; and when we remember some recent deeds of our own soldiers in the Indian war—the blowing of rebels from the guns, and so forth—we need not boast over the men of the seventeenth century. Claverhouse, after all, was scarcely more savage than Sir John Lawrence, and not so much so, as the Sepoys; and the Covenanters were never guilty of such excesses as the Massacre of Glencoe, in that age, or of the Well of Cawnpore in our own.

The third great fault of the Covenanters was their superstition, which forms, however, a most interesting feature of their character. This superstition was almost a certain result of their solitary and hunted life in the wilderness. Mountaineers are almost all and always superstitious, and the more if they are under any cloud of proscription or of mental darkness. Sir Walter Scott, in the "Lady of the Lake," describes with great power Brian the Hermit, who, as the reputed son of a demon, had to leave the society of his fellows and betake him to the depth of the savage hills.

> "Desperate he sought Benharrow's den,
> And hid him from the haunts of men.
> The desert gave him vision wild,
> Such as might suit the Spectre's child:
> Where, with black cliffs the torrents toil,
> He watched the wheeling eddies boil,
> Till, from their foam, his dazzled eyes
> Beheld the river demon rise;
> The mountain mist took form and limb
> Of noontide hag, or goblin grim;
> The midnight wind came wild and dread,
> Swelled with the voices of the dead;
> There the lone Seer, from mankind hurled,
> Shaped forth a disembodied world."

And before coming out at his chieftain's command—

> "Late had he heard, in prophet's dream,
> The fatal Ben-Shie's boding scream;

> Sounds, too, had come in midnight blast
> Of charging steeds, careering fast,
> Along Benharrow's shingly side,
> Where mortal horseman ne'er could ride;
> The thunderbolt had split the pine,—
> All augured ill to Alpine's line."

It was so in some measure with the persecuted Covenanters. Surrounded by the dreariest, loneliest scenes of nature; sleeping in the neighbourhood of the cataract; wandering whole days along moors and mountains, where not a single living man could be seen; hearing often from afar the whoop of the pursuer and the deep bay of the blood-hound; haunted by memories of past cruelties on the part of their enemies or of themselves; emaciated by hunger, and reading perpetually of the miracles and marvels of a bygone day, their minds sometimes lost their balance, and a gloomy shape of superstition took possession of their souls. If you read Woodrow's history, you will find in almost every page accounts of wonderful and miraculous events, which, however incredible at present, were believed then as if they had been gospel, and which had unquestionably great influence in sustaining their courage, and in intensifying and sublimating their despair. Their superstition, too, was of a very peculiar kind. They did not believe in fairies "dancing their ringlets to the whistling wind," or so much in the ghosts of the departed "revisiting the glimpses of the moon," as in other forms of the worship of awe—sterner, wilder, and less indigenous to Scotland. They transplanted to their own country all the notions prevalent in Judea in Christ's day. They believed in magic and in Satanic agency. Their enemies were all sold to Satan. When they saw Claverhouse or Dalziel riding safe through the battle amid a rain of bullets, they cried out,— "Try him with the cold steel — the Devil has given him proof against lead." Sharpe, they said, deserved to die on Magus Muir, not merely as an apostate, but as a sorcerer. It was, they averred, magical power which arrested their career in Glasgow, and smote them with that ruinous panic at Bothwell Bridge. It was customary, they said, for some of the prelates to meet at midnight and to drink the Devil's health. But they ascribed much to other agents than the old enemy—to God himself. In fact they made God a kind of devil, and attributed to him every sudden or surprising death that befel their persecutors. Sometimes their bowels gushed out like those of Judas. Again, when about to blaspheme or engaged in it, their tongues swelled in their mouths till they could speak no more. Sometimes they were found with mouths gaping wide and tongues hanging out as if bit by a mad dog, but no mad dog had been there. A soldier who had bound good Donald Cargill is afterwards run through the body by a comrade on the very spot he had done so, and expires with an oath so horrible that it cannot be repeated. Sometimes their bodies rotted away piecemeal, and the wine they were about to drink was turned into congealed blood. "Wandering Willy's Tale" in "Redgauntlet" gives an admirable idea of those strange myths which despair and solitude engendered between them in the Covenanting mind. It is a dream of Hell, where the dreamer supposes himself in the company of the doomed persecutors. "There was the fierce Middleton, and the dissolute Rothes, and the crafty Lauderdale, and Dalziel with his bald head and beard down to his girdle, Earlshall with Cameron's blude on his hand, and wild Bonshaw that tied the blessed Mr. Cargill's limbs till the blood sprang, and Dumbarton Douglas, the twice-turned traitor baith to country and king. There was the bluidy Advocate Mackenzie, that, for his worldly wit and wisdom, had been to the rest as a God. And there was Claverhouse, as beautiful as when he lived—with his long, dark, curled locks streaming down over his laced buff coat, and his left hand always on his right spule blade, to hide the wound that the silver bullet had made. He sat apart from them all, and looked at them with a melancholy, haughty countenance, while the rest hallooed, and sung, and laughed, that the room rang again. But their smiles were fearfully contorted from time to time, and their laugh passed into such wild sounds as made my gudesire's very nails grow blue, and chilled the marrow in his bones. They that waited at the table were just the wicked-serving men and troopers that had done their work and cruel bidding on earth. There was the lang lad of the Netherton that helped to take Argyle, and the wicked Guardsmen in their laced coats, and the savage Highland Amorites that shed blood, and many a proud-serving man, haughty of heart and bloody of hand, cringing to the rich and making them wickeder than they would be, grinding the poor to powder when the rich had broken them to fragments. And many, many mair were coming and ganging, all as busy in their vocation as if they had been alive."

Sometimes they thought the Devil came in *propria persona*—in bodily form—to annoy their devotions. One remarkable story occurs to us illustrative of this. A tent-preaching is going on near a river, and the people are listening with profound attention to the minister; when lo! a tall black man is seen crossing the stream to join them. Suddenly his foot slips; he is carried down the current, and uproars for a rescue. All are instantly at work to assist him, but with so little success that ten or twelve stout men who had laid hold of the rope which they had cast to his aid were rather in danger to be themselves dragged into the stream, and to lose their own lives than likely to save that of the supposed perishing man. But the minister, John Semple of Carsphairn, saw the case as it was, and exclaimed, "Quit the rope, it is the Great Enemy! he will burn but not drown; his design is to disturb the good work by raising wonder and confusion in your minds; to put off from your spirits all that ye have heard and felt." So they let go the rope, and, if you believe the narrative, he went down the water screeching and bullering like a Bull of Bashan. We remember the impression made on us when a boy by the story—how when attending tent-preaching near the lovely environs of our own native village, with the sun of summer shining overhead, and the blue stream rounding itself like an arm round the sacred spot, and seeming to linger near and long, and to warble out a low gurgling symphony, with the spiritualities of the solemn scene, and the voice of the preacher rising shrill and clear over a thousand silent auditors, and reverberated from the Grampians behind; often we there glanced an eye of fear, and almost of faith, in case, peradventure, the tall black stranger should be seen again crossing the southern ford of the river. But he came not. And now

"The terrible has vanished and returns not."

Along with the superstitions of dear old Scotland much of its religion, too, has vanished away.

Predictions of future events were said, too, to be very common, and the power of prophecy was largely and lavishly ascribed to such men as Richard Cameron, Donald Cargill, and Alexander Peden. But this leads us to say a few words on these remarkable individuals.

Richard Cameron, famous as the founder of the sect of the Cameronians, was an eloquent, brave, pious, though somewhat fierce-tempered and gloomy man. He was born in Falkland, Fife, and educated in Holland. It had been predicted, it is said of him, by the minister who ordained him—"This head on which I lay my hand shall be lost for Christ's sake, and set up before sun and moon in the sight of the world." This prediction was fulfilled—but previously that brave head had often been laid on the lap of the heather, and often been bared in the breeze, as he uttered his fearless field harangues. He was the most powerful of the Covenanting preachers—his words were fire, his gestures those of the tree in the hurricane, his voice that of the thunder, nor were his actions less bold than his words. Coming down in the company of David Hackstoun, who had found a refuge there ever since Bothwell Bridge, from the wild mountains which lean so grandly northward over the valley of the Nith to Sanquhar, on the 22nd of June, 1686, they affixed to the market-cross of that little town a declaration, disowning Charles Stuart as their king, accusing him of perjury, and every crime, and denying the right of the Duke of York to the accession; and then returned, as the lightning to its black cloud, to their deep wildernesses again. The act, however, was too daring to pass unnoticed. The little band, consisting of about sixty horse and foot, were chased through the wilds of Dumfries and Ayrshire; and at last, on a July morning, were surprised by Bruce of Earlshall at a lonely spot called Airsmoss, where they were so hemmed in by bogs, that their only chance lay in breaking through the ranks of the enemy and dispersing themselves among the desert hills.

Ere the battle began Cameron engaged in prayer. He said three times with great emphasis—"Lord, spare the green and take the ripe." Turning then to his brother Michael, he said—"This is the day I have longed for and prayed for; this is the day I shall get the crown. Come, let us fight on to the last." The skirmish was brief and bloody. Hackstoun had nearly escaped, but his horse stuck in a bog and he was taken alive, although with three horrible wounds in the back of his head. Cameron and his brother died fighting back to back with the most determined courage. His head and hands were cut off and carried to Edinburgh, and presented to his father, an old man, by one in the Tolbooth, for his Covenanting testimony. He was asked whose these were. "Ah!" he cried, kissing them and watering them with his tears, "they are my son's, my own dear son's; good is the will of the Lord." They were afterwards fixed on the Netherbow-Port, with the hands stretched out in the attitude of prayer, and the eyes looking westward to the wild moorlands, where he had so gloriously died. There, said one of the persecutors, there are the head and hands of one who lived praying and preaching, and died praying and fighting. The rest of the Cameronians were all either killed or taken prisoners. Somewhere about the year 1816 or '17, there was a youth under twenty tending sheep in the neighbourhood of Airsmoss. He had often mused over the fate of the brave Covenanters, till one day resting his scrap of paper upon a gravestone erected to their memory, he became inspired, and wrote down, as if the spirit of Richard Cameron held his pen, "The Cameronian's Dream." His name was James Hislop; he perished young and died in a strange land—in the Island of St Jago. The verses are too well-known to require to be repeated.

Happy those who fell at Airsmoss and reached Heaven so triumphantly, if this poet is to be believed; and why should he not? Hackstoun had yet to suffer much and terribly ere his chariot arrived. A gentleman, a scholar, and a Christian, as well as a patriot, he was treated worse than a wild beast. He was brought before General Dalziel, who, on his not answering certain questions, threatened to roast him alive, and would not allow his wounds to be dressed. He was then loaded with irons and conveyed to Edinburgh, making his entry by the foot of the Canongate, riding on a horse with his face backward, accompanied by three of his friends bound to a goad of iron, and with Richard Cameron's head and hands carried on a halbert before him. He behaved then, as always before and afterwards, with the most indomitable courage, and when summoned before the Council, refused to acknowledge their authority by pleading, but told them they were murderers, and that oppression, perjury, and bloodshed, were all found in their skirts. He was found guilty, and executed in the most horrible manner. His right arm and left were first cut off, then he was drawn up to the top of the gallows with a pulley, then suffered to fall down again with his whole weight upon the lower scaffold three times, and then fixed at the top of the gallows. Before he was dead an executioner tore out his heart from his body, stuck it on a large knife, and said aloud—"This is the heart of a traitor," and then threw it into a fire, where it was consumed. The body was next divided into four parts, which were sent to St Andrews, Burntisland, Leith, and Glasgow, and his head fixed to the Netherbow, was near that of his friend Cameron's. "Lovely in their lives, in their deaths they were not far divided."

Let us not omit, in fine, to notice the fate of their kindred spirit, Donald Cargill. This brave minister, nothing daunted by the fate of his two friends, Cameron and Hackstoun, ventured in the end of September of the same year, at a conventicle held in the Torwood, near Stirling, to pronounce a sentence of excommunication against the King, the Duke of York, Lauderdale, and Rothes, Monmouth, Dalziel, Mackenzie, and the Lord-Advocate, giving them all over, whole and several, to the Devil—making no mention, however, of Claverhouse, perhaps upon the principle that it was of no use to bestow on a proprietor what had been so long and manifestly his own already. This daring act troubled the persecutors more than we can at present imagine. We do not think that though some zealous clergyman were now to excommunicate Louis Napoleon, or Disraeli, or Mr. Gladstone, it would cost them a wink of sleep, unless they laughed all night at his absurdity. But it was different then. Mackenzie and the Lord-Advocate trembled at Donald Cargill's terrible Torwood thunder. But they did not cease to persecute the man. It was, we presume, on this occasion that, pursued by his enemies, he leapt the Linn of Ericht, near Blairgowrie. "That was a famous leap you took, Mr. Cargill," said one to him, "when you leapt the Linn of Ericht." "Aye," he replied, "but I took a lang run to it. I ran a' the way from Perth" (fifteen miles). The Linn from that side has never, we believe, been leapt before or since. The intrepid Donald was at last taken in Ayrshire, treated, as we saw, most barbarously, and, in fine, put to death in Edinburgh, 27th July, 1681.

We would say something now of the Women of the Covenant. A noble race of men usually implies a noble race of women too; and this has been found to be the case still more in primitive than in polished nations. At a time when the Roman Empire was declining to its fall, sunk in luxury and vice, and when the Roman women were sadly degenerated from the days when the name Roman Matron or Maiden represented all that was noble in purpose, virtuous in manners, and heroic in character, the Germans, as we are told by Tacitus, preserved their integrity amidst their swamps and dark forests, and their women especially were distinguished by their incorruptible chastity, and their attention to their domestic duties. In the woods of the West, it seems to have been much the same among the Red men; their wives and daughters were, on the whole, true and worthy companions to those magnificent aboriginal races—whom the discovery of America and the emigration of Europeans first corrupted, and have since nearly blotted out from the face of the earth. And so with the high-hearted females of the Covenanting period; they were true, full of a noble simplicity blended with a yet nobler guile, disinterested in their attachments, devoted to their principles, and equally brave and sagacious. Accomplishments they had few or none—it was in that age an unusual thing for a woman to be able to write, still more so to be able to spell. In the days of the Reformation, there were a few prodigies—such as Lady Jane Grey of ill-fated memory—who were possessed of vast and varied scholarship; but this was rare even then, and in later times, was, in Scotland at least, altogether unknown. Neither were they fond of showy dress; their ornaments were not of gold, or pearls, or costly array, but the ornament of a meek and quiet spirit was theirs. The simple snood—the badge of maidenhood—the coif, the tartan plaid were their usual dress, but there was that within that passed show; and the enthusiasm and courage which pervaded Scotland beat nowhere more powerfully than in the hearts of her daughters.

The history of the times is full of illustrations of this noble spirit which characterised the Covenanting women. When the Marquis of Hamilton was sent down by Charles the First with a fleet to Leith to crush the Covenant, the people thronged every avenue to prevent the soldiers from landing, and there was to be seen Hamilton's own mother—a genuine Deborah of the cause —coming out on horseback to meet, and if necessary, to shoot her son, carrying pistols loaded with gold balls for the purpose. During the persecution, too, they took an active part in the good work, and were of material service to their lords. Now they concealed them under beds or in lumber rooms, and then went out and met their pursuers firmly, and answered their questions, perhaps not always, with strict truth. Again, when their husbands were away with their children to be baptised at conventicles, and when the dragoons came in search they filled the empty cradles with rags, and continued to rock them, lest the absence of the infants should excite suspicions as to the cause of the absence of the parents. Sometimes, like the immortal Bessie MacLure in Scott, they sat at the turning of the two ways at the eventide, and told the weary fugitive to take the one and avoid the other, seeing there was danger there—a lion in the path. Sometimes they assisted their husbands in scooping out hollow spots of refuge among the hills. Many a time and oft did they keep the midnight fire burning in their cots, and had a midnight morsel ready that their husbands, cold and wet and hungry, might steal in and spend an hour or two in trembling joy by their own hearthside. And at other times, when this was impossible, whenever the darkness fell—and the darker the better, and better still, if the wind was loud and the rain falling thick,—did these gallant matrons lift up their small bundles of provisions, draw their plaids closely about them, and set out to visit the dark caverns or pits in the sides of the precipice where their husbands were lurking, and feed and comfort them there. When tried by horrid tortures to reveal the spots of their retreat, they refused. When led out, as was often the case, to die with them, they took it right joyfully. When they saw their husbands shot before their eyes, as Isabel Weir did John Brown, they sat down beside their corpses, silent, and with covered heads. And many a drink of whey and piece of oatcake did they, standing at the door of their dwellings, give, at the hazard of their own safety, to haggard wayfaring men, who were pursued by the voice of the blood of Magus Muir, or fleeing from the echo of the rout of Bothwell.

Honour to the memory of such true and noble daughters of Almighty God! No theatrical airs or meretricious graces about them. Never does any one of them, like Charlotte Corday, step out of woman's sphere and become a sublime assassin; nor, like Madam Roland, mingle a certain affectation and grimace with the grandeurs of a heroic death. They were as simple as they were great; their characters seem modelled upon that of Scotland's scenery; their hearts were soft as its vales and yielding as its lochs, while their principles were like its hills—high, firm, and immovable. Let us now paint a well-known scene in which these principles were severely put to the test, and came out from it in the most triumphant manner—triumphant, although it was in the article of death.

There resided in the neighbourhood of Wigtown, in Galloway, three women—two of them daughters of a respectable farmer named Gilbert Wilson, and the other an aged widow, named Margaret MacLachlan, a woman of sense, prudence, and piety. The two younger women were ardent Covenanters, and, although their parents conformed to the Episcopal system, they had obstinately refused to attend the parish church, and had been compelled, on account of their nonconformity, to wander through the hills and wastes of the country. They were all three tried before a Commission Court and condemned to death, because they refused to take the oath of abjuration, and to attend the Curates. The youngest girl, a girl of thirteen years of age, was saved by her father paying a fine of £200 sterling; but the other, Margaret, who was eighteen, was condemned to be drowned along with old Margaret MacLachlan. They were conveyed to a spot near Wigtown, which the Solway Frith covers twice a-day, and there, in the presence of an immense throng of spectators—including Major Winram, Grierson of Lagg, a noted persecutor of the period, whose ruined castle is still visible in the neighbourhood of Dumfries—were bound to stakes in the sand within floodmark, that they might endure all the horrors of a slow and lingering death. The tide is coming in in its blind fury; nearest it is placed the stake to which Margaret MacLachlan, the elder of the two, is bound, in order that the sight of her dying agonies might shake the resolution of the younger martyr. Margaret MacLachan is overtaken by the waves, and without sound or struggle sinks helplessly before their assault. But while she is going down there is heard a sweet, clear voice rising above the surge, and singing those plaintive words of the twenty-fifth Psalm:—

> "Let not the errors of my youth,
> Nor sins, remembered be ;
> In mercy, for thy goodness' sake,
> O Lord, remember me.
>
> "The meek and lowly he will guide
> In judgment just alway :
> To meek and poor afflicted ones
> He'll clearly teach the way."

It is the voice of the young maiden Margaret Wilson ; and when the strain is closed, the voice continues to be heard uplifted in earnest prayer till the waves advance and seem to cover her head and close her mouth for ever. But before her life is quite extinct, the soldiers come up and draw her out of the water, and when she recovers consciousness, their commander, Major Winram, asks her if she is willing to pray for the king. She answers that she wishes for the salvation of all men, and the damnation of none. Amidst the thousands of weeping spectators, one deeply moved, cries out, "Dear Margaret, say God save the King." The poor girl replies with perfect calmness, "God save him if he will, for it is his salvation I desire." Her friends eagerly exclaim, "She has said it, she has said it, set her free." "But will she take the abjuration oath?" rejoins the brutal Winram. I will not," was her firm reply, adding, "I am one of Christ's children, let me go;" and then she was thrown back into the sea, and the ocean waves, less cruel than the savages on the shore, gave her a speedy release, and her young spirit passed away to the God that gave it, and her virgin body was taken into the custody of the great deep, and shall be returned on that glorious day when the commandment shall be given and obeyed,

"Restore the dead, thou Sea."

We may merely mention farther, in reference to this sad and terrible story, that the attempts made lately by Mark Napier to discredit it seem to have entirely broken down, and that new evidence has been produced to prove that it is, in the main, "an owre true tale," and a tale that dashes, as with a thousand foaming waves, a fierce and far-seen light of disgrace and ignominy, contempt and indignation upon the brutal and unmanly character of the Persecutors.

One of the most remarkable characters connected with the Covenanters was Alexander Peden, currently called Peden the Prophet. It must be borne in mind, however, that much has been told about this man that is evidently exaggerated, and without any real foundation in fact, and that the book called Peden's Prophecies is a forgery. Peden was a native of Ayrshire; he led a very wandering and uncertain life. He was for a while imprisoned in the Bass Rock. When forced to leave his pulpit for his Covenanting principles, he is said to have laid an arrest upon it, "that none should enter it except one that like himself, came in by the door;" and accordingly it is said, that neither Curate nor Indulgent entered it till after the Revolution, when one of the Presbyterian persuasion was appointed to be its minister. He prophesied also, we are told, a great many cases of sudden and supernatural death. He joined the Pentland rising, but, foreseeing its destruction, very prudently left it at the Clyde. On Bothwell's fatal day, Peden was forty miles off, and declined to preach, because the Lord's people were at that hour fleeing before their enemies at Hamilton, and their blood running like water. He predicted, however, it is said, a French invasion of Scotland; but that this was not fulfilled is owing, probably, to the success of the rifle guns as much as to the failure of Peden's gift—worthy man! Though often in danger, and after many marvellous escapes, he at last died peacefully in his brother's bed. Two interesting *apparitions* of Peden appear tolerably authentic. One was on the 29th of April, at John Brown of Priesthill's moorland cottage. Peden, who had taken refuge in Ireland, had returned and entered his friend's abode. Worn out with his journey, and now advanced in years, he rested all night under that hospitable and Christian rooftree. When leaving in the morning, he turned from the door and said twice to himself, looking to Isabel Weir, "Poor woman! a fearful morning—a dark, misty morning!" It was that of the 30th April, the last John Brown was ever destined to see. On another occasion, we see the aged wanderer toiling over the moors about Airsmoss. He sat down on the very spot where Cameron, whom he knew and loved, had fallen. He uncovered his head to the sky—

"Its lyart haffets waxing thin and bare;"

he turned up his eyes to heaven and exclaimed, "O to be with Ritchie!" He has now long been with him.

The country was now all but mastered. Most of the clergy were quietly chewing the cud of the Indulgence. The Cameronians had lost their leaders. Hackstoun's head was frowning from the Netherbow; Cameron was sleeping in Airsmoss; Burley was in Holland; Nisbet had been arrested at Fenwick, and was on his sure and rapid way to the Grassmarket; Cargill had been executed in Edinburgh while in the act of prayer; Peden was dying at Sorn, and was soon to "be with Ritchie;" Renwick (of whom more afterwards) still lingered like a ghost among the wilds, pursued by bloodhounds, a high price on his head, and meeting with hairsbreadth escapes every day. The Duke of York had declared that "there would never be peace in Scotland till the whole of the country south of the Forth was turned into a hunting field." A great wild chase all over that region seemed to fulfil his words. Bloodhounds, as we have just seen, were now employed to discover the retreats of the Covenanters, and their deep-mouthed bellow, reverberated by the echoes of the glens and gullies, added a new element of romantic interest to this extraordinary persecution. It was as if a strange storm had enveloped all that chain of mountains whence the Nith, the Dee, the Clyde, and the Annan have their source; while the rest of Scotland was gazing stupefied at the gathered gloom, and hearing the far-off echoes of its thunders. The pretext of trial had long been abandoned—accusation even had now ceased. If a countryman was descried running or walking quickly across the fields, or found reading there, it was enough; he must be a frightened rebel, a Bible-reading fanatic, and was shot. Five wanderers were crouching in a cave in the parish of Glencairn; their retreat was discovered. The soldiers came up, first fired into the cave, then rushing in brought them forth to execution, and, without asking a single question, put them to death. One man, being observed to be still alive, was thrust through the body as he lay. Raising himself up from his couch of blood he cried out with his last breath, "Though every hair of my head were a man, I would die all these deaths for Christ and his cause." This reminds us of Fergus MacIvor's famous exclamation in Waverley —"Were all the blood of my ancestors in my veins, I were free to peril it in this quarrel." But we think the Covenanter's saying the nobler of the two.

One striking and terrible story—less known than that of John Brown of Priesthill (which we need not here narrate), but almost equally thrilling—we may now recount. A widow named Hyslope, residing in Eskdale, had sheltered one of the poor proscribed wanderers, who was ill of consumption, till he died in her house. This act of Christian kindness provoked the anger of Johnstone, the laird of Westhall, who had become a more implacable persecutor than he had once been a zealous Presbyterian. He vented his mean and miserable revenge upon the head of the poor widow, pulled down her house, and, after he had robbed her of her furniture, drove her and her younger children to wander in the fields, and, above all, dragged her son Andrew before Claverhouse, that he might put him to death. Claverhouse, however, strange to tell, had little inclination at the time for more blood. The murder of John Brown was recent, and had rather sickened even him. He, therefore, received Westhall with coldness, regarded the youth with a degree of compassion, and seemed disposed to spare him. But Westhall, eager to signalise his loyalty, insisted on his instant death. Claverhouse consented, saying, "The blood of this poor man be upon you; I am free of it." The captain of a Highland company who was present, was next asked to shoot the lad, but peremptorily refused; and Claverhouse ordered three of his dragoons to do it. When they were ready to fire, the youth was told to pull his bonnet over his face. "No," was his fearless reply; "I can look my death-bringers in the face without fear: I have done nothing of which I need be ashamed;" then, holding up his Bible, he charged them to answer for what they were about to do at the great day, when they should be judged by what was written in that Book. He received their fire without shrinking, was killed, and buried in the moor.

We come now to the premature and ill-starred expedition of the Duke of Argyll. This brave nobleman had been prosecuted by the Duke of York for high treason, because he had taken what was called the Test Oath with a reservation, and was condemned to death. His step-daughter, Lady Sophia Lyndsay, visited him in the Castle of Edinburgh, and he contrived to escape in the disguise of her lackey, carrying her train. In his haste and confusion, he dropt the train when passing the sentinel; but she, with great presence of mind, threw it in his face, with many reproaches for his carelessness, and so besmeared him that he was not recognised, till, reaching the street, he mounted behind her chariot, which was in waiting, as a footman, in passing through the streets threw himself off, dived into a close, and was lost to pursuit. He made his escape to Holland, and returned, in May, 1685, with three ships and a considerable sum of money to try and produce a rising in Scotland. He went first to Orkney, then to the Highlands, and descending from thence into the low country, his army having been routed, tried to make his escape in disguise at Inchinnan, near Paisley, but was arrested and carried to Edinburgh. An order from the king came ordering instant death. He behaved with admirable courage and composure. He said, when brought forth to die, that it was a happier day than that on which he had made his escape from the Castle. He dined, took a short, sweet sleep, or siesta—as was his manner, as was his wont—after it, went up to the scaffold, kissed the instrument of his death, which was called the Maiden, saying it was the sweetest Maiden he ever kissed, and died with his hand uplifted, and the words, "Lord Jesus, receive me into thy glory," trembling on his lips. This was on the 30th of June. On the 6th of July, the Duke of Monmouth's army in England, which had been in communication with Argyll's, was destroyed, and thus the little gleam of apparent morning died simultaneously away from both lands, and a thicker darkness than ever threatened to come down upon Scotland. It was resolved to send a number of the prisoners that had been made out of the wreck of Argyll's army to Dunnottar Castle. Some of our readers must have seen the ruins of that large old fortress, which seem rather like the ruins of some city than a single castle, and against which the waves of the German Ocean spend the force of their huge volumes in vain, and growl, as they recede, like a wilderness of lions, in full discontented retreat. In this place about 1607 prisoners, after they had refused to take the oath of Supremacy, were driven like cattle across Fife, landed at the ferry at Dundee, forced to continue their ignominious march down the sands of the Angus coast, and at last thrust promiscuously, and crowded close on each other into a dark vault, called the Whig's Vault, in Dunnottar Castle. On their way they had been compelled to spend one tempestuous night of wind and rain, without any shelter, upon a bridge over the North Esk in Forfarshire. In the vault there was only one small window, opening on the sea, and they found, when they entered it, that their feet were fast in the mire—mire which was soon, horrible to relate, mingled and almost supplanted by their own excrements. The keepers treated them most barbarously, and would allow them neither bedding nor provisions, except what they could buy out of the miserable pittance they had with them. In a few days, forty of them were removed to a smaller vault still, into which light entered only by a chink, and they had to stretch themselves on a damp floor in order, during the heat and horrid stench, to obtain the benefit of a fresh current of air which blew through a decayed part of the wall. Many of them died of confinement or of disease. Twenty-five made their escape down the steep rock overhanging the sea; but fifteen of these were retaken by the peasantry, and subjected to horrid tortures, bound to the floor of the dungeons, with fiery matches burning between their fingers for hours together, some of them expiring, and others having their fingers burned to ashes. At this stage, the cruelty of their keepers relaxed, and provisions and other necessaries were given them on easier terms. They were asked, too, to take the test and attend their parish churches in future if they were released; but this they indignantly refused to do. About the end of July they were removed to Leith, and those who still stood faithful to their principles were transported to the Plantations, which, we doubt not, with all their miseries, they found more tolerable than the suffocating heat, hunger, and filth of the Whig's Vault. This is altogether a gloomier tale than that of the Bass Rock. Fancy almost loves to see the pious prisoners pacing their ocean pinnacle; but we shiver as we conceive of this mass of bruised mortality, writhing, sweltering, shrieking twisting itself within its narrow and loathsome limits, and the sea without seems uttering a fiercer and hoarser protest around the Northern Dungeon. Let us blush, as we remember that the late king of Naples supplied, in the treatment of his prisoners, a full parallel to the most minute and disgusting particulars of the horrid imprisonment at Dunnottar. We felt our blood boil, while some years ago visiting the Whig's Vault, the more as in the list of sufferers there was included one of our own ancestors, John Gilfillan by name. Nor can we wonder that even still the sailor, storm-driven along the cliffs of the Kincardineshire coast, and the peasant returning late in autumn eve from his labour, and hearing the night-boom of the sea rising like the swell of some great accusing orator's breast and voice when he is growing up to the measure and stature of his theme, regard with awe the shattered but gigantic ruins of this blood-stained castle—see, in imagination, Divine Justice sitting like a sated eagle upon its darkening towers, and mutter a prayer as they are hurrying past the dismantled den of legal murder and oppression.

———o———

PART III.—THE SCOTTISH COVENANTERS—*Continued.*

WE shall now speak of the last of the martyrs, James Renwick, and his singular history. Some preachers indeed continued to haunt and hold forth in the wildernesses after his death, but none of much mark. He was generally regarded as the last, and not least, of the confessors of the Covenant—the Malachi among those modern minor prophets. James Renwick was a native of Glencairn, in Dumfriesshire, and was born in 1662. His father was Andrew Renwick, a weaver, and his mother, Elizabeth Corsar, a woman of distinguished piety. They were poor labouring people, and yet they sent their son James to Edinburgh College. Previous to this he had undergone much spiritual experience of a peculiar kind. When a child of two years old, he of his own accord tried to pray. Some years later the great struggle which comes upon most thinking minds came upon his in the form of doubts as to the existence of a God. Once, looking at the mountains surrounding his native Glencairn, he exclaimed— "If these were all devouring furnaces of burning brimstone, I would be content to go through them all to be assured that there was a God." These doubts faded, and for a year or two he passed his time in devout, solitary meditation on the works and ways of the Most High. A similar case was that recorded of Chalmers by his biographer, who at one time of his life used to wander over the hills and through the woods of Fife, wrapt in a glorious golden dream of God, Nature disappearing from his eyes and its Great Cause seeming to take its place. Such moods of divine contemplation, too, are common with the Theosophists, Mystics, and Brahmans of the East. Sent to the University, he supported himself there by teaching gentlemen's sons. In July, 1681, there is a great bustle in the Grassmarket of Edinburgh. A vast crowd is assembled under the blue sky and burning sun of summer to see a Covenanter die. It is Donald Cargill, the hero of the Torwood excommunication, and the "lang run" and leap of the linn of Ericht. They have come in such multitudes because they have heard of his fame, and know that he will die game, as the saying is. Notice there among the crowd one fair-haired, bright-eyed, beautiful youth, looking with intense interest on the scene. It is James Renwick, only nineteen years of age, who has come forth from his little attic room, where he has been living sparingly and studying hard, to see the venerable Cargill die. Cargill is seventy-one years old, and has long been a noble pillar of the Covenanting cause. Old he seems, but as determined, and firm, and calm, as in the flush of youth or the prime of manhood. The drums are beating to drown his voice or to shake his nerves; but he says, as he mounts the ladder, "The Lord knows I go on this ladder with less fear and perturbation of mind than I ever entered the pulpit to preach. This is the sweetest and most glorious day that ever mine eyes did see." As he lifted up the napkin he said—"Farewell, relations and friends in Christ! farewell, reading and preaching, praying and believing! farewell, wanderings, reproach, and sufferings! Welcome Father, Son, and Holy Ghost! into thy hands I commit my spirit." And still praying, Donald Cargill is turned off. There is a murmur amidst the multitude; but there is one that does not murmur. That bright-eyed youth remains silent, but his eye flashes, his brow flushes, he is stricken to the heart, and returns "a sadder and wiser man," determined to cast in his lot with a people who have produced one that can so nobly live and so bravely die; and the death of Donald Cargill has become the spiritual life of James Renwick.

He lost no time in becoming a member of the Covenanting Church, and the leaders of the body, admiring his talents and his zeal, determined to send him over to Holland for education. He received license to preach there, and returned to Scotland in 1683. His preaching gave a new impulse to the fading energies of his party. His beautiful boyish appearance, the fire which shone in his eye, the bloom which at times blushed upon his cheek, his "pleasant, melting voice," the "seraphic enlargement" of his speech, served to unite in him the charms of an Apollo with the energies and holiness of an apostle. Some, indeed, of the Covenanters, even those that sent him out, looked coldly upon him, thought him wild, visionary, and too enthusiastic. And perhaps he was, but he was still very young; and, besides, energy in that age could not be sustained without enthusiasm. Others received him with the warmest welcome. An interesting account is given of a visit he paid to the house of John Brown, the Ayrshire carrier.

It is a dull, dark night in November. John Brown himself is absent. The family are preparing the wool of their flocks for hodden gray cloth, against an approaching fair in Hamilton. The shepherd is carding the wool. Little Janet, Brown's daughter, and the herd-boy are teasing for the carder. Isabel Weir is nursing her first-born son on one side of the fire, when the dog, which lay basking in the blaze on the other side, suddenly started up, barking and running to the door at the approach of a stranger. Janet and the herd rose too, and are at the door almost as soon as the dog. "Whist, collie," cried the thoughtful girl, "whist, ye maunna speak to the unco man." The herd caught the dog in his arms, and Janet ushered the stranger into the cottage. He is a man young in years, beautiful in countenance, but thin, pale with fatigue and sickness, travel-tired, his shoes worn off his feet, while his plaid hangs wet and drooping about him. Isabel Weir, who had been expecting her husband, looked with some suspicion on the unknown, and left to Janet to discharge the offices of hospitality to the uninvited and unexpected guest. But these the fine-spirited maid discharged admirably, and while the wife was singing to her son, Janet proceeded to take off his plaid, to put him in the warmest corner—to do all, in short, that her mother should have done for him. The herd and the mother smiled at Janet's conduct in mimicking her parent; but the stranger, whose face had brightened up at the sound of the lullaby, was now fairly overpowered, burst into tears and into blessings on the bairn—even "the blessings of one that had been ready to perish." "Surely God," he said "has heard my cry, and provided shelter for my weary head." At this point John Brown himself entered. He recognised Renwick, and a night of plaintive yet joyous talk and reminiscences succeeded. Every one strove to be kind to the preacher. The shepherd brought him clean hose and shoon, the herd his new night-cap, the lasses left their wheels and washed his feet, Isabel Weir made ready for him a warm supper, while little Janet, worn out, lay fast asleep at his side.* Far into the night did Renwick, his fatigue now forgotten, and Priesthill converse, doubtless, about the sufferings of the Church, and their own testimony and prospects. After another day and night of the same happy intercourse, they parted to meet no more on earth; but when, five years afterwards, they met in a better world, they would, doubtless, recall to memory the blessed hours passed in that moorland cottage, and compare what they then *imagined* with what they now *knew*.

Renwick now for years led a wandering life, chiefly among the higher and drearier parts of Galloway, preaching, wherever opportunity served, to the "puir hill folk." Over all that wild but romantic region watered by the river Ken, and overhung by the lofty Cairnsmuir, and the steep mountain of Altrig, he

>"Was known to every star,
>And every wind that blows."

Often, like Elijah, he lodged in a cave; often in the thickest recesses of the wood; often in the deep dank hags of the moss. It was a luxury to find a shepherd's shieling; to enter it and kindle a fire of sticks or heath— sometimes to feed on oatcakes and braxy which the shepherd left, and sometimes, when evening had fallen, there might be seen little children hastening from their parents' dwellings with small bundles of provisions for the lonely minister. These were the ravens who fed the modern

---

* We wish some true-hearted Scottish painter would give us this scene in colours.

prophet! He was often employed in baptising children; and, as if there were a special blessing connected with that ordinance when administered by him, when he fixed a day for the purpose, he sometimes had to baptise thirty children at once; and how beautiful the sight of these thirty innocents receiving the pure waters of the Ken—themselves as pure—while the "Summer heaven's delicious blue" seems from afar to smile down well-pleased! After the Sanquhar Declaration, which was written by Renwick against the authority of James, a reward of £100 was offered for his apprehension, and fifteen distinct searches were made after him. Once he escaped by throwing himself into a hole on the side of a hill which protected him from view by a heap of stones. His energy at this time was amazing. With almost supernatural activity did he pass from parish to parish, baptising, catechising, preaching, protesting against King James and the ensnaring Indulgence which he had offered. At length, young as he was, his health began to fail him. He could no longer mount or ride on horseback; he had sometimes to be carried to the place where he was to preach. Yet, once there, recognising an audience of true-bred Covenanters, and feeling the fresh breeze of the mountain on his fevered forehead—he revived, he strengthened, he was enlarged, he poured out the emotions of his heart and the wrongs of his country in a very sea of eloquence, and the dying "boy" Renwick, was felt to be inspired. In him soul triumphed over body, and seemed, when it reached its climax, to lift up the frail form in scorn, and to say, "What proportion between this poor weak instrument and that effect—strong men trembling and weeping under the Word?" "Not by might, nor by power, but by my Spirit, saith the Lord." We always think that Scott must have had Renwick in view in his beautiful picture of Ephriam MacBriar in Old Mortality. "Ephraim MacBriar was hardly twenty years old, yet his thin features already indicated that a constitution naturally hectic was worn out by vigils, by fasts, by the rigour of imprisonment, and the fatigues incident to a fugitive life. Young as he was, he had been twice imprisoned for several months, and suffered many severities. He threw his faded eyes over the multitude and over the scene of battle, and a light of triumph arose in his glance; his pale and striking features were coloured with a transient and hectic flush of joy. When he spoke, his faint and broken voice seemed at first inadequate to express his conceptions; but the deep silence of the assembly, the eagerness with which the ear gathered every sound as the famished Israelites collected the heavenly manna, had a corresponding effect on the preacher himself. His words became more distinct—his manner more earnest and energetic; it seemed as if religious zeal were triumphing over the bodily weakness and infirmity." And after the sermon—a very wonderful one—is preached, the great novelist says—"Many crowded round the preacher as he descended from the eminence on which he stood, and, clasping him with hands on which the gore was not yet hardened, pledged their sacred vow that they would play the part of heaven's true soldiers." Exhausted by his own enthusiasm, and by the animated fervour which he had exerted in his discourse, the preacher could only reply in broken accents, "God bless you, my brethren. It is His cause; stand strongly up and play the man. The worst that can befall us is a brief and bloody passage to heaven."

We possess a volume of Renwick's sermons, which are, in their boldness, sweetness, and unction, very characteristic of the man. Finer than even these are his letters, which evince learning, ardent piety, and have touches of true genius, as where he speaks of Scotland's moors and mosses being *flowered* with martyrs. He speaks often of Luther in the loftiest terms, and seems quite familiar with his writings. His last letter closes thus: "I go to my God, and your God; death to me is as a bed to the weary."

In February, 1688, this devoted and high-minded man came to Edinburgh, and, while lurking in the Castle-Hill, was discovered by a tide-waiter, who was searching for smuggled goods. He tried to escape at a back-door, and fired a pistol, which drove back his enemies; but, in running down a street, he lost his hat, was recognised, and secured. He was treated, on the whole, with great lenity. Either they were beginning to tire of their bloody work, or there was something in his lovely countenance, and mild and gracious bearing, which melted them. They would have spared him had he made the slightest concession; but he did not seem to wish to live. Death, too, was in his vitals already, and he was weary of life, saying that he was a "broken-hearted man." Nevertheless, his conduct in the cell was calm and dignified, and, before the Justiciary, determined and courageous. He was, of course, condemned as he would not retract; and, as he would not deign to petition for his life, there was nothing for it but death. An impudent Popish priest intruded on him in the Tolbooth, but was repulsed by the one stern word, "Begone!" which became afterwards a proverb in the jail. With his mother and sisters he held some most affecting interviews. The morning of his execution at last dawned, and Renwick bravely prepared to meet it. When the drums beat to guard, he fell into an ecstasy, and said—"'Tis the welcome warning to my marriage; the Bridegroom is coming, I am ready, I am ready." Never was there such a crowd assembled in the Grassmarket as on that day. There seemed a presentiment that here was the last of the Martyrs. The feelings of the multitude, however, whatever they were, were reduced to silence by the stormy music of the drums. Unappalled, the martyr mounts the scaffold. Perhaps the spectacle of Donald Cargill's death is before him, and he seems to see himself standing in the corner of the street, where a flake from that great man's fervour had fallen upon him and is burning about him yet. He sang Psalm 103rd—it may be those verses:—

> "But unto them that do him fear
> God's mercy never ends;
> And to their children's children still
> His righteousness extends;

> "To such as keep his COVENANT,
> And mindful are alway
> Of his most just commandments,
> That they may them obey."

He then read Revelations 19th chapter, describing the coming of the Avenger of Christian blood, whose name is Faithful and True, and whose eyes are as a flame of fire. He then prayed, and thousands who could not hear his words, owing to the drums or to distance, must have been moved at the sight of his upturned countenance, which had become "like the face of an angel." It was the 18th of February, and clouds were darkening the sun as he said, "I shall soon be above these clouds; then shall I enjoy thee and glorify thee, without interruption or intermission, for ever." He next addressed the people, renewing his testimony against the corruptions of the times. At the top of the ladder he prayed again, and at length expired with the words in his mouth, "Lord, into thy hands I commend my spirit; for thou hast redeemed me, Lord God of truth."

When Renwick died, Martyrdom might be said to have borne its last pale flower, and the deep sigh of the multitude said, "It is done." An era had passed away with it, and a new time, less glorious indeed, but less troubled and conflicting, was about to succeed.

The Persecution was now ended, after a period of twenty-eight years had elapsed. It is impossible to calculate how many had perished during the course of it. The historian, Woodrow, who has left such a lengthy and minute account of it, professes himself unable to tell the number. Daniel Defoe, in his little but very interesting work on the subject, refers us, in a stroke of genius worthy and characteristic of himself, to the roll of their number kept under the altar and before the Throne.

Nearly 20,000, at a rough guess, seem to have perished by fire or sword, or water, or the scaffold, or to have been banished abroad, or to the northern islands. Besides these, numbers without number expired of cold or hunger among the morasses of the country. It seemed as if some pestilence, some Black Death had crossed the land, so great was the sacrifice of life, so intense had been the excitement and the terror, and so deep the desolation which was left behind. Since the persecution of the Waldenses, there had been no such persecution in Europe; and Milton's famous Sonnet on the treatment of the Protestants among the Alps of Savoy might almost be applied to the Covenanters on the mountains of Scotland.

The time had now fully come for the deliverance of the country. The Prince of Orange landed in Great Britain. The tyrant James fled to France. But even before this final flight, Edinburgh had risen against its oppressors. There was only one small force in the Castle, under the Duke of Gordon—the rest having been withdrawn from the country to support the king against the Dutch. Great disturbances took place in the city. The crowds who used to assemble at night assembled now in broad day—burned the Pope in effigy—clamoured for a Free Parliament—issued placards setting a price on the heads of the leading members of State—and they so terrified poor Lord Perth, that he had to be protected by a strong bodyguard to his own abode, Drummond Castle, in Strathearn; and no sooner had he reached this safeguard than Edinburgh rose *en masse*. The Palace of Holyrood was first assaulted. It had been turned into a Roman Catholic school and printing-house; it was now stormed, sacked, and well-nigh burned. Scott represents Burley as saying to Morton in the Cave:—Morton had said, "The land has peace, liberty, and freedom of conscience, and what would you more?" "More!" exclaimed Burley, unsheathing his sword with a vivacity which made Morton also start, "Look at the notches upon that weapon; they are three in number, are they not?" "It seems so," but what of that?" "The fragment of steel that parted from this first gap rested on the skull of the perjured traitor who first introduced Episcopacy into Scotland (Sharpe); this second notch was made on the rib-bone of an impious villain (Bothwell), the boldest and best soldier that upheld the Prelatic cause at Drumclog; this third was broken on the steel headpiece of the captain who defended the Chapel of Holyrood when the people rose at the Revolution. I cleft him to the teeth through steel and bone. It has done great deeds this little weapon, and each of these blows was a deliverance to the Church. It has yet more to do to restore the Covenant in its glory, and then let it moulder and rust beside the bones of its master." This spirit-stirring speech is quite imaginary. Burley was, in fact, dead some time before this event. The work was well done without him. The Palace was disembowelled of its Papal contents; Popish books, pictures, and crucifixes were dragged out from the Chapel and burned in the High Street. While this was going on, the news arrived that King James had fled. A proclamation was instantly issued for the disarmament of Papists, and inviting Protestants to rally in support of their religion. Even before this was issued, Scotland from north to south, was up in support of the Prince of Orange. Large bodies of armed Presbyterians were poured into Nithsdale and Clydesdale, where some disturbances and reaction took place, chiefly among Papists and a few discontented Cameronians. Lord Perth had to flee from his frowning castle, and find his way through the snow-covered Ochils to Burntisland, where he entered a ship, but was pursued and seized. Meanwhile, in London, William had a meeting with the Scottish Lords, who, after a consultation of several days, requested him to call a Convention of the Estates of Scotland. On the 2nd of March, the Convention met, and, after some slight opposition, decided that King James by his abuse of power, had forfeited the Crown, and declared the Prince and Princess of Orange to be King and Queen of Scotland. Presbytery was restored, Episcopacy was abolished, and, in the emphatic language of Scripture, the "land rested from war."

To this there was but one exception in Claverhouse, whose history and fate we shall now briefly go over, and then conclude the subject of the Covenanters.

Graham of Claverhouse, we have already often had occasion to mention in these sketches. He was the elder son of Sir William Graham of Claverhouse, an estate near Dundee with an old castle now in ruins. His mother was Lady Jane Carnegie, daughter of the first Earl of Northesk. Young Graham was educated at St. Andrews University, where he was distinguished, it is said, by a knowledge of mathematics, an enthusiastic passion for Highland poetry, and great zeal for the established order of things in Church and State. His abilities recommended him to the notice of Archbishop Sharpe, whose death he afterwards so sternly and fearfully avenged. He joined the army and commenced his military career in the French service. From thence he passed to that of the Prince of Orange, whose life he saved at the battle of Seneff, for which service he was made captain; and the Scottish regiment in the service of the States of Holland shortly after becoming vacant, Graham applied for its colonelcy, but was disappointed, and thereafter left the Dutch service in disgust and came over to Scotland, where he was, owing to the recommendation of the Prince of Orange, appointed to a troop of horse. His deeds in persecuting the Covenanters need not be recounted. His dragoons were laughingly called the *Ruling Elders of the Church*, and their rule was certainly an iron one. Abhorred as Satan himself by the Covenanters, Claverhouse was a great favourite with King James, so much so, that he was made captain of the Royal regiment of horse, sworn in Privy Councillor, and had a gift from the king of the estate of Dudhope, and along with it, of the Constabulary of Dundee. On the 12th of November, 1688, being then with James in London, Claverhouse was created a peer by the title of Viscount Dundee and Lord Graham of Claverhouse. This was a week after his old master, the Prince of Orange, had come over to England; and when James fled to Rochester, Dundee strongly dissuaded him from leaving the country, and offered to collect 10,000 of his disbanded soldiers, and marching through England to drive the Prince of Orange before him—a ludicrous boast, still more ludicrously rendered into verse by one of his own laureates:—

> " O never yet was captain so dauntless as Dundee,
> He has sworn to chase the Hollander back to the Zuyder Zee."

His advice, however, was not taken, and Dundee was compelled to retreat northward, bringing with him a troop of sixty horse, who had deserted from his regiment in England. He reached Edinburgh, where the Convention of the Estates was sitting and settling the affairs of the country. He did not, however, feel himself there at ease, the more as he knew the Westland men had him at feud for his cruel and barbarous conduct in their country, and were watching his motions. He retired, therefore, from the city, and was pursued by General Mackay through the shires of Perth, Angus, Aberdeen, Banff, Moray, and Nairn. At length he gained the Highlands, and on the 1st of May, 1689, at the head of 150 men, joined MacDonald of Keppoch, who was investing Inverness. He remained with Keppoch for six weeks, when suddenly he rushed southwards and came unexpectedly upon the town of Perth, where he made some prisoners, and seized on horses and about 9000 merks belonging to the Royal revenue. From Perth he marched to Dundee, but the town shut its gates against him, being even then rather a radical place; and he had to retire to his own house at Dudhope, where he spent two nights, the last he was ever to spend at home. Thence he returned to Keppoch, and after residing there for six weeks, he marched into

Badenoch to meet Mackay and the Laird of Grant, who had entered the Highlands with an army of 2000 foot and 200 horse. Mackay, though superior in numbers, retired before the dreaded Claverhouse till they passed Strathbogie. Dundee pursued him with great ardour as far as Edinglassy, where he heard that Mackay had received some reinforcements, and after resting a few days he returned to Keppoch. Here he was joined by the flower of the Highland clans, under MacDonald of the Isles, MacDonald of Glengarry, the Captain of Clanronald, Sir John MacLean, and Cameron of Lochiel (Evan Dhu, as he was called, the famous chieftain who, when his clan were once bivouacking in the snow, when he found one of them that had rolled a large snowball to use as a pillow, kicked it away as a luxury, and gave the man a sound rating as a degenerate Highlandman), besides some Irishmen. Many of these recruits were wholly unable to distinguish between King James and King William; but they hated the Sassenach, and they had great faith in "Dark John of the Battles," as they called Claverhouse. He now found himself at the head of 2500 men, and with these he advanced to Blair-in-Athole. Meanwhile, General Mackay, who was at Perth, came northwards to encounter him, at the head of 3000 foot and two troops of horse. He marched immediately through the Pass of Killiecrankie. Many of us are familiar with that magnificent pass, where a haughty mountain-land seems to have thrown up entrenchments to secure itself against all invasion, and where the spirit of beauty, following fearlessly after, has wreathed those rugged bastions with green loveliness, peopled them with the music of streams, and surprised them into involuntary smiles. Now, a broad road pierces the Pass, and the traveller looks with ease and enchantment up to the rugged cliffs above, and down through fragrant birches and thick copsewood to the bottom of the glen, where

> "Deeply, darkly, far below
> Goes sounding on a lonely river."

But then the road was so narrow that two men could hardly walk abreast; it was lower down, too, than the present, and ran along by the base of the rocks, having on the one hand a succession of steep precipices, and on the other the Garry, leaping from one dark pool to another, and almost invisible from the thick wood surrounding its waters. So dismal, indeed, was then the aspect of that romantic glen—which now coaches and a railway pass every day—that, when the soldiers of Mackay arrived, they refused at first to go any farther, declaring that it was the mouth of Hell. We cannot but think that Dundee committed a great error in strategy in not seizing on this pass before Mackay—although it is an error that has led to beneficial consequences to the country. When Mackay's soldiers defiled from the Pass, he saw the Highlanders posted on an eminence to the north, and proceeded to draw up his men in line three deep, having a narrow plain before them, and the tremendous gorge they had just passed and the roaring river Garry behind. About half-an-hour before sunset—on the 27th of July, 1689, the broad sun of summer, hanging low above the mountains and coal-black pines of Blair-Athole to the west—the battle of Killiecrankie began. Dundee resolved to charge in person, although he had the precaution to exchange the scarlet cassock and gleaming cuirass which he had worn through the day for a dull buff-suit to disguise him. When the signal was given, the Highlanders raised a great shout, which was reverberated from the rocks and woods around; while the Royal forces, discouraged by the position in which they were placed, replied to it with a low and spiritless cheer. The brave Lochiel noticed the difference, accepted the omen, and cried out, "They are beginning to faint already." Instantly the Highlanders proceeded to strip themselves to their shirts and doublets, and rushed down the hill, firing their pieces. The right wing of the Royalists returned the fire briskly, and did considerable execution, especially on the MacDonalds of Glengarry. But the clansmen continued to advance, till, when close upon the hostile ranks, they threw down their guns, cried out, "Claymore!" and, drawing their broadswords, dashed with a dreadful yell upon the enemy, before they had time to screw their bayonets to the end of their muskets. The same result followed as afterwards at Prestonpans. The dark torrent of the clans, crested by their flashing swords like the foam upon the billow, broke the line of the regulars to pieces. A general panic seized upon the troops of Mackay, and they fled down the hill in irretrievable disorder, behaving, for the most part, according to Mackay himself, "like the veriest cowards." Dundee rode at first at the head of his forces, but, as he noticed one detachment of the MacDonalds not advancing, he rose up in his stirrups, waved his hat, and shouted on them to follow him. While raising his arm, a musket ball struck him under the right armpit, and inflicted a mortal wound. A soldier, named Johnston, caught him as he dropped from his horse. "How goes the day?" said the dying man. "Well for the King," replied Johnston; "but I am sorry for your lordship." "Since the day goes well for my master," replied Dundee, "it is less matter for me." With these words he breathed his last. His body was stripped by some of his own followers. It was afterwards carried to a cottage, and, in fine, wrapped up in two plaids and buried in the Old Church at Blair-Athole—a church which has long ago itself perished. No monument was ever erected to his memory. The hand that shot him is, to this hour, unknown, and various fabulous rumours have floated about. Some say that he was shot by his own servant with a silver button—Claverhouse having got from the Devil proof against lead! Others, that one of his old Covenanting friends, who had wrongs to avenge, had followed him to the braes of Killiecrankie, and gained his object there. But we find similar rumours whenever one man is identified with a cause and falls suddenly. It was so with Gustavus Adolphus and Charles the Twelfth —both fell on the battle-field, and both were said to have been assassinated. We do not judge quite so harshly of Claverhouse as when we wrote a little book on the Covenanters a good many years ago. We cannot, indeed, praise or justify him; but we should, as Christians, forgive him. The tendency even of our day with many professing Christians, is to extreme and unjust severity to those who differ from them either in principle or practice. Let us, while emphatically condemning Claverhouse's conduct to the Covenanters, and while granting that Sir Walter Scott has painted him in colours too tender and glowing, grant, too, his invincible courage, his unswerving fidelity to his master, and, as we stand in the lovely valley which connects Killiecrankie with Blair-Athole, and remember that he was buried there, if not a soldier without stain or reproach, yet certainly one of the bravest of the brave, be ready to accommodate to him the lines written by the Mighty Minstrel over the grave of Wogan :—

> "No! for 'mid storms of fate opposing,
> Still higher swelled thy dauntless heart;
> And while despair the scene was closing,
> And shut thy brief but brilliant part:
> Thy death's hour heard no kindred wail;
> No holy knell thy requiem rung;
> Thy mourners were the plaided Gael;
> Thy dirge the clamorous pibroch sung."

The victory of the Highlanders was most complete. Mackay's baggage, cannon, stores, everything, fell into the hands of the insurgents; 2000 of the Royal troops were cut to pieces or taken prisoners. The claymores had inflicted the most terrible wounds upon the dead and wounded; heads were cleft down to the throat; skulls were cut off above the ears; both the bodies and cross-belts of some of the slain were found to have been cut through at one blow, and pikes and small swords were severed like willows.

Had Dundee lived, the panic of Killiecrankie would have extended through the length and breadth of Scotland; and the reaction against the infant Government of William would have been very powerful, and, to say the least of it, very troublesome. But he had fallen in the arms of victory. No head in the battle had been more completely severed from its body than he had been from the body of the Jacobite enterprize; and, after a little more struggle, dissensions began among the Highlanders themselves, and there was no one with commanding enough genius to reconcile them. One is reminded of that impressive passage in the "Lady of the Lake" which describes the battle between the Sassenach and the Gael in the gorge of the Trossachs, carried on in the absence of Roderick Dhu who had been, unknown to his followers, beaten in fight, and sent as a captive to Stirling:—

> "The horsemen dashed among the rout
>   As deer break through the broom;
> Their steeds are stout, their swords are out,
>   They soon make lightsome room.
> Clan Alpine's best are backward borne,
>   Where, where was Roderick then?
> One blast upon his bugle horn
>   Were worth a thousand men!"

In the absence of their Roderick, the Highlanders were again defeated, and Mackay was at last able to pass through the Highlands without meeting the slightest resistance, and to carry into execution his favourite plan of subduing the Highlands by building a line of forts to overlook them—the first being erected at Inverlochy, near Fort-William, which commanded at once the passage along the line of lakes which now form the Caledonian Canal, and the communication by sea with the Western Islands and Ireland.

While the Highlands were thus subjected to a slow but sure process of pacification, in the Lowlands the religious commotions were to a great extent appeased. There was now in many parts of Scotland, a Sabbath feeling prevailing. The storms of a long night had passed, and

> "The morn was up again; the dewy morn,
>   With breath all incense, and with cheek all bloom,
> Chasing the clouds away with playful scorn,
> And living as if earth contained no tomb."

Scotland's Reign of Terror was over. People resumed their ordinary habits of industry. The moors became once more deserted and silent, save for a few hero worshippers, who, like Old Mortality, long afterwards, visited them, for the purpose of erecting monuments to the dead who slumbered there. The churches were again crowded with congregations. The hateful curates had fled, and many of the ejected pastors, who had once expected, when a better day should come, to be able simply to say with old Simeon, "Lord, now let thy servants depart in peace," and so to die, were reinstated in their parishes, and permitted to spend their closing years quietly among their original flocks. No summary revenge had been taken by them upon their persecutors. This, if the passions of some of the fiercer of the Presbyterians demanded, the policy of William's wise and lenient Government resolutely refused, so that, on the whole, there was general peace and contentment.

In the ecclesiastical state of the country, a decided improvement had taken place. The majority of the Scottish Protestants had now got their will, their Church was settled on the basis of Presbyterian parity; their worship was restored to that elemental simplicity which yet exists; but there remained, we must not omit to notice, many of the real roots of the evils which had been luxuriating for more than half a century in Scotland. We mention only two—the perplexed state of the law of patronage, which led to that secession of which we mean to speak afterwards; and, secondly, the grand fundamental error which underlies all the thought and all the efforts of all parties at that period—namely this, the thought that there is any possible plan of reconciling the claims of Church and State, except by identification, a thing at present and that may for ever be impossible; or by subjection, which is resisted by both; or by compromise and bargain, a game at which both have played for centuries without coming to any satisfactory conclusion. In closing this rapid view of the Covenanting sufferings, we may say, that seldom do we find in history a nobler specimen of the resistance of principle to power than here. There was a great disproportion between the efforts made to suppress the Covenanting principle and that principle itself. It was not, in our judgment, sufficiently large; but from the tenacity with which it was held, from the severity with which it was persecuted, and from the resolution with which the sufferings were borne, it gathers around it both the air and reality of grandeur. It sufficed to arouse the depths of the Scottish spirit. In no part of the history of that country do we find a more marked, strenuous, and long-continued expression of the *perfervidum ingenium* of Scotland. Scottish Covenanters were not great in prosperity—few parties are; but the alchemy of suffering brought out the rich qualities of self-denial, stubborn endurance, unlimited trust in divine aid, a strange wild eloquence and insight, a courage which never quailed, and an integrity which was never shaken. In the recollection of these distinguishing excellencies, posterity may well forget the faults which unquestionably they committed. But let us blend with admiration for their energy and zeal, sorrow that they effected not still more.

CHAPTER VI.

THE SECESSION AND RELIEF CHURCHES IN THEIR CRADLE.—PART I.

IN our former chapter, we left Scotland in a state of spiritual quiet as well as of political peace. Within the Highland line, indeed, there might be heard now and then mutterings as of far-off thunders; but these began to die away, and in the south all was comparatively still. But although there was stillness, it was, to some extent, especially in ecclesiastical matters, a deceitful stillness. William of Orange was a sincere lover of religious liberty in general, but his views of its details were either too latitudinarian, or, at all events, too liberal and advanced for that age, and in his attempts to conciliate all parties, he ended, as usually happens, by giving general offence, and nearly rekindling those flames of religious dissension which the Revolution had quenched. He strongly urged the General Assembly to admit, upon terms of free and easy communion, the curates as Episcopalian incumbents into the communion and ministry of the Presbyterian Establishment. This the more determined and zealous of the Presbyterians resisted; and, to overcome their resistance, Parliament was persuaded to pass an Act declaring that such of the curates as offered to subscribe the Confession of Faith, to submit to the Presbyterian form of government, and against whom no scandal could be proved for thirty days, should remain as parish ministers in the maintenance of their position and the receipt of their salary. Much indeed might have been said in favour of this. It seemed a healing measure. It augured a certain statesmanlike largeness on the part of the King, and it even showed a forgiving spirit; for these curates had been bitter enemies of the Orange dynasty. Still, the wounds of the country from Prelatic oppression were too recent and raw—the aversion to the curates themselves too widespread and too deep—to justify such a measure. Accordingly, Assembly after Assembly threw out the proposition, which at last, however, was carried, and, by the year 1712, hundreds of Episcopalian ministers were admitted into the Church of Scotland; and the Assembly which met that year in an address to Queen Anne congratulated her and her Government upon the fact. During the same period, the character of the eldership was changed by a similar admixture; and the country generally was scandalised by the sight of some of the old persecutors—whose hands had reeked with carnage in the killing times—walking to and fro in the churches, and distributing the elements of Christ's passion among the assembled communicants.

About this time there began to appear in Scotland those two famous parties which, under the name of the Moderates and Evangelicals, were destined to play so important a part in the Ecclesiastical History of Scotland. Probably neither party has been fairly represented by its opponents. On the one hand, the Evangelicals denounced the

Moderates as the mere tools of power and time-servers, without any religion, unless it were a species of Naturalism wearing the cloak of Christianity, and having even less morality—as cold, dead, and selfish. On the other hand, the Moderates accused the Evangelicals of being harsh, stern, bigoted, intolerant, enemies to the arts and the amenities of life, to science and literature, to progress and enlightenment. Both were partly right, and both were partly wrong. Both served, in fact, as all opposing parties do, to correct each other's errors, and to modify each other's excesses. The Evangelicals kept the Moderates back from the extreme of Erastianism, and from losing Christianity altogether in the sands of mere Pagan ethics. The Moderates kept the Evangelicals from wild fanaticism and fierce persecution. The Evangelicals produced great men in their own style—such as Erskine, Moncrieff, and many others. The Moderates produced men of high accomplishments and literary powers—such as Robertson the historian, Blair the preacher, and Jupiter Carlyle, as he was called, the devotee of the fine arts. The real evil lay not so much in the struggle between those parties as in the triumph of either of them. Thus, when Moderatism came to its meridian it was felt to be a yoke that our fathers were not able to bear, and hence came the Secession. And when Evangelicalism culminated, it sought to concuss Government into measures which Government scouted, and thence came the Disruption of 1843. There should always, perhaps, be two parties in a church; when there is only one, it ceases to be a party, and becomes a despotic power.

When Queen Anne ascended the throne and the Union between the two kingdoms was concluded, several measures were passed which tended greatly to grieve the stricter Presbyterians. First of all, when the General Assembly was deliberating on an Act declaring Christ to be the sole Head of the Church, the Queen abruptly dissolved the sitting. Again, an oath of abjuration, so constructed, as to compel the swearer to the approbation of an English Act of Parliament, which provided that the successor to the throne must be of the Episcopal communion, gave great offence to many, and some of the ministers, including the famous Boston, refused to swear it. But, especially, the Law of Patronage was, in 1712, restored in all its grinding force, and the people were deprived of their highly cherished power of choosing their own spiritual teachers. Hence came forced settlements, pushing ministers into churches at the point of the bayonet, conducting ordinations under the protection of the military, and so forth. Some of the Moderate ministers, such as Professor Simpson, in Glasgow, went considerable lengths in new views of doctrine; although, it is amusing now to those who have watched the recent progress of speculative thought, to find historians of the Secession bewailing so lugubriously doctrines which are now held by some in many Evangelical Churches—such as, "that the heathen have some obscure connection with the redemption of Christ, and that the souls of infants are, when born, pure and holy." The Assembly did not condemn these views very severely, but prohibited him (Simpson) from preaching them; and, of course, they could not foresee that his errors were, as was afterwards the case, to multiply and assume a deeper dye. As it was, the stricter of the clergy were much incensed at the leniency of the Assembly. This feeling was strengthened by what was called the Marrow controversy. A treatise, called the "Marrow of Modern Divinity," written by an Englishman of the name of Fisher, had found its way into Scotland. It became a great favourite with some of the more orthodox divines—such as Boston of Ettrick, Drummond of Crieff, and Hogg of Carnock. It taught some doctrines which were thought by the dominant party to verge on Antinomianism, although, to those who read it now, it seems to be for the times, in some points, a wonderfully sensible treatise—holding the doctrine of the freedom of the Gospel, approaching that of universal atonement, and slighting the fear of hell and hope of heaven as motives for the believer's obedience—at least, reducing them to their proper place. But the Assembly took those ministers to task who were circulating that work, and condemned it as contrary to the Word of God and to the Confession of Faith. The "Marrowmen," as they were called, twelve in number, and including Ebenezer Erskine, and Ralph his brother, resisted this, but in vain; it led to keen controversy and ecclesiastical action, and would have issued in the retreat of these twelve men from the Church, or rather their expulsion, and the formation of the Seceding body ten or twelve years earlier than was actually the case, had not a Royal Letter arrived recommending peace and deprecating divisions.

Afterwards, causes of offence continued to multiply.

Professor Simpson became an Arian, and was only suspended, not deposed as Boston wished. Professor Campbell, of St. Andrews, published certain tracts and lectures containing what were counted formidable heresies, and yet was employed by the Assembly on business of high trust and importance; and when he was brought at length to the bar, he was dismissed from it uncensured and uncondemned. It would seem that the leaders of the Church of Scotland aimed at an eclecticism of opinion for which the country was not, and perhaps may be long ere it is, fully ripe. The Scotch hold their religious tenets so strongly—with a grasp as firm as that with which they hold their guineas —that they have no patience with those who entertain different views, or who even would seek to make modifications upon theirs. They are far sounder than the Apostles themselves, and would have thought Paul, in some points, a Latitudinarian, James an Arminian, and Peter a Papist. They make little allowance for diversity of training,—for the progress of ideas—for the new methods of Scripture criticism—for the effects of time in modifying belief. They, as Edward Irving says of them, handle an idea and a creed as a butcher an ox, feeling all along its sides and buttocks, shoulders and limbs, and looking upon everything less substantial as a mere ghost. It is partly a matter of prejudice with them—their fathers thought so and so, and they love, and justly, the memory of their progenitors; partly a matter of national pride— their religion has been praised so much that they think it must be perfect, and that a portion of their national credit is gone if they let it slip; partly owing to a certain national stiffness and obstinacy of character; and is partly, shall we say, a matter of economy characteristic of them as a people. Have they paid so much blood, and tears and latterly money, for their faith; and shall they give up any part of that which cost them so dear? At all events, the last relics of the beggarly elements of the past will be found, and not for a long while to come, dead "by a Scottish dyke side," and improvements in worship, and innovations the most unavoidable in modes of thought, will have got old in most other countries before they are fully recognised, except by a minority, in our dear, old, decent, delightful, dour, and dogged Caledonia—which, though heterodox in the sight of the rest of the world, hugs its heterodoxies to its bosom as the only truths, and believes all others wrong and mad, somewhat on the principle of poor Nat. Lee, the tragic poet, who, shut up in a lunatic asylum, insisted upon it that all men, except himself, were mad, but that numbers had prevailed over right.

Still, our fathers had a good deal to complain of, not merely about the strange doctrine which was creeping in, but about the death-like coldness of the Moderate preachers and their people. In our day, the Broad Church thinkers in both England and Scotland, such as Kingsley, Jowett, Wallace, &c., are among the most zealous and active divines of the day; but in Scotland the brood that followed the Campbells and the Simpsons were usually lazy drones, and the sleep in their pulpits had extended to the pews. A spiritual lethargy was creeping over the land. And then there was the standing grievance of Lay Patronage, which began, too, to get worse and worse. First, the patrons sometimes handed over the right of choosing a minister to the Presbytery, and they often resigned it to the people. But at last, an overture was brought forward to the effect, that where patrons neglected or declined to exercise their right of presentation, the minister should be chosen by a majority of the heritors and elders, if Protestant. This was sent down to the Presbyteries, the majority of which declared unequivocally against it; but the General Assembly being determined on gaining their point, overruled, in the most tyrannical manner, the decision of the inferior courts. They counted eighteen Presbyteries who had not reported at all as on their side, and by this unblushing unfairness of calculation, made out a majority for their measure.

A crisis had now come in the history of the Church when a master-spirit was required. An hour had arrived, and a man must be ready to meet it. And that man was found in the famous Ebenezer Erskine.

This remarkable man was the son of a minister called Henry Erskine, of Cornhill, who had been ejected from his charge during the Persecution, and narrowly escaped imprisonment in the Bass Rock. It was fitting that the first Seceder should spring from a Covenanter. He was born in 1680, and, in 1703, was settled at Portmoak, a parish beautifully situated on the banks of Lochleven, and under the shadow of the Lomond Hills. He was, from the moment of his entrance on the ministry, a most exemplary clergyman; but became more earnest and more evangelical, it is said, after overhearing his wife and his brother Ralph conversing upon religious subjects in a bower in the garden one evening.—" These," he said to himself, "have ideas and feelings to which I am a stranger —they possess a valuable *something* which I have not." After this he became more emotional in his religion, although he never approached the verge of the fanatical as his brother Ralph sometimes did. He had less fancy than Ralph, but he seems to have had a stronger judgment. He possessed great natural eloquence—a delivery grave, plain, and impressive—and a voice of vast power and compass. He was tall, of a piercing eye, commanding presence, lofty brow, and a majestic mien. "I never saw," said a minister of the time, "so much of the majesty of God in any mortal man as in Ebenezer Erskine." Adam Gibb, of Edinburgh, having asked a person if he had ever heard Mr. Erskine preach, was answered in the negative. "Well then, Sir," replied Mr. Gibb, "you never heard the Gospel in its majesty."

Ebenezer Erskine had stood forth already on what he deemed the side of truth and righteousness. He had, in 1712, resisted the abjuration oath. In 1717, his name had been numbered among the twelve Marrowmen. And he was constantly at his post resisting every effort to wreathe the yoke of patronage round the necks of the people. And at last, an opportunity was furnished him for making a bold and conclusive stand for Church liberty; which, as connected with the history of the Secession body, and with that of the Ecclesiastical history of Scotland in general, has become forever memorable.

In 1731, he had been translated from Portmoak to

Stirling as a scene more worthy of his masterly powers, and had soon after been appointed Moderator of the Synod of Stirling and Perth.

It was the duty of the retiring Moderator to preach a sermon suitable to the occasion; and this he did, accordingly, at the opening of the Synod on the 18th of October, 1732. He chose for his text the words in the Psalm, "The stone which the builders rejected, is become the head stone of the corner."

Curious enough, that the movement which produced the Secession Church, and that which led to the Voluntary controversy with all its marvellous results, were both inaugurated by single sermons, preached by divines, till then, little known. In the year 1830 the Rev. Andrew Marshall, of Kirkintilloch, preached in a Secession Church in Glasgow, a sermon on the words, "The dark places of the earth are full of the habitations of cruelty," which acted like a trumpet call in rousing first Scotland, and then England, and other lands, to the evils connected with Church Establishments—a trumpet call which was echoed on Monday, the 1st of March, 1869, in the clear and piercing tones of W. E. Gladstone, when he proposed the disestablishment and disendowment of the Irish Church. But that noble blast had been preceded and anticipated by the majestic and lion-like voice of the Secession Luther, when he thundered in the kirk of Perth, and the thunder said,—"Seeing the reverend Synod has put me into this place where I am in Christ's stead, I must be allowed to say of this Act, what I apprehend Christ himself would say of it, were he personally present where I am, and that is, that by this Act the corner stone is receded from, Christ is rejected in his poor members, and the rich in this world put in their room. If Christ were personally present where I am, by the Synod's appointment, in his stead, he would say in reference to that Act, 'Inasmuch as ye have done it to one of the least of these little ones, ye did it to me.' By this Act Christ is rejected in his authority, because I can find no warrant from the Word of God to confer the spiritual privileges of his house upon the rich beyond the poor; whereas, by this Act the man with the gold ring and the gay clothing is preferred to the man with the vile raiment and the poor attire." He added, "Whenever we discern the danger coming either from open enemies, or pretended friends, or our fellow-builders going wrong, let us give the cry like faithful watchmen, and though they be offended, there is *no help for that*. It is a heavy charge that is laid by God against some, as above, that they were dumb dogs that could not bark, but preferred their own carnal ease unto the safety of the Church."

"No help for that," indeed! offences will come—offences cannot but come. The bleak wind of March blowing against the ears of nobility as bitterly as against the rags of the mendicant, gives a little offence it may be; and it may be, too, that the man who, spitting against a North-easter, spits in his own face, is offended when the effluvium returns. The bats in a barn and the owls in a deep grove are mightily offended when the light of morning breaks in upon their cherished gloom. The Augean Stable, with all its oxen, was, we doubt not, greatly offended when

Hercules turned the river Alpheus into it to remove its accumulated filth. The buyers and sellers in the temple were offended to the quick when Christ smote them with his whip of small cords. And so the patrons and patron-patronisers, and expectants and dependents on patronage were desperately offended when denounced by the manly voice of the First Seceder. Action was instantly taken against him. The Synod, by a majority of six, declared him deserving of censure—Mr. Moncrieff, of Abernethy, Mr. Merk, Moderator, Mr. Wilson, of Perth, and ten other ministers, with two ruling elders, protesting; and Mr. Erskine and his son-in-law, and Mr. Fisher, of Kinclaven, appealing to the General Assembly. In May, 1733, the General Assembly met to decide Mr. Erskine's case, and a most interesting meeting it was expected to be. Exactly one hundred years after (1833), the General Assembly met to pass the Veto Act, and thereby sought, although vainly, to undo the effect of what the General Assembly had done so long before. We sat a young student in the gallery of the High Church, Edinburgh, on a May forenoon in 1833, and heard Chalmers, who was the retiring Moderator, deliver one of the most eloquent discourses that even he ever preached; on the text, "He that is unjust let him be unjust still; he that is righteous let him be righteous still," closing with a very solemn appeal to the meeting on their awful responsibilties in what they were about to do. At the bar of the Assembly of 1733 stood forth Ebenezer Erskine, along with William Wilson, minister of Perth, Alexander Moncrieff, minister of Abernethy, and James Fisher, minister of Kinclaven. Mr.

Erskine alone was allowed to be heard, and he proceeded to read a remarkably clear, cogent, and eloquent defence of his conduct. By a majority of votes, however, he was condemned to be rebuked and admonished. This was done; but Mr. Erskine produced a paper he had written in expectation of what was to follow, which he requested to read to the Assembly. The request was refused, the paper was left lying on the table, and the brethren retired. The matter might have dropped here had not Mr. Naismith, minister of Dalmeny, noticed the paper, which had fallen over the table, lifted it, read it, and, his face glowing with indignation, risen up and fiercely and with a stentorian voice called on the Assembly to stop and consider the insufferable insult they had received through that paper. The four brethren were recalled, appeared before a Committee of the Assembly on the morrow, and, refusing to retract, the Assembly ruled they should appear before its Commission in August, and if they persisted in their refusal they were to be suspended, and, if they acted contrary to suspension, might be deposed. On the sentence being intimated to the four brethren, they proceeded to read a short paper of complaint against the summary treatment they were undergoing, but were not permitted, and the officer was ordered to thrust them out of the court! August came, and Erskine and his followers appeared. "I saw," says Adam Gibb, who was there a young witness, "Mr. Ebenezer Erskine standing at the bar in a most easy and undaunted but majestic appearance, amidst warm and brow-beating reasonings against him, particularly by the Earl of Isla." He read a powerful defence of himself, but, in spite of it, the Commission proceeded to suspend him and the other brethren. They protested against this, and were summoned to appear at the next meeting of the Commission in November. By this time the country was moved in their favour, and petitions from Presbyteries in all parts of Scotland poured in requesting them to be treated with leniency; but, as the four brethren would make no concession, the Commission did not depose but loosed them from their respective charges, and declared them no longer ministers of the Church of Scotland—they having told the Commission that though suspended in August they had not ceased to set the Act at defiance, and to exercise their spiritual gifts. They instantly drew up a Protest containing the remarkable words—"We for these and other weighty reasons, to be laid open in due time, protest that we are obliged to MAKE A SECESSION from them, and that we can have no ministerial communion with them till they amend." And on the fifth day of December, 1733, they, along with Ralph Erskine and Thomas Mair—who did not, however, take part in the proceedings—met at Gairney Bridge, a small village about three miles south of Kinross, and there did form themselves into a Presbytery, were constituted by prayer, appointed Ebenezer Erskine Moderator, and empowered two of their number, Wilson and Moncrieff, to draw up a testimony setting forth the reasons of their Secession. Honour to those four brave brethren! One of themselves, Mr. Wilson of Perth, very pleasantly and ingeniously compared them to the four living creatures in Ezekiel's vision —"Our brother Mr. Erskine has the face of a man; our friend Mr. Moncrieff has the face of a lion; our neighbour Mr. Fisher has the face of an eagle; and, as to myself, I think you will allow that I may claim to be an *ox*, for, as you know, all the laborious part of the work falls to my share." And thus the Secession Church began.

———o———

PROGRESS OF THE SECESSION—RISE OF THE RELIEF CHURCH.—PART II.

THERE does not seem, at first sight, very much in the four names appended to the first seceding protest, "Ebenezer Erskine, William Wilson, Alexander Moncrieff, and James Fisher." And yet, taken in connection with what has happened, and with the known ability, worth, and courage of the four men, we cannot but look upon that quaternion of Christ's and Scotland's soldiers with very considerable reverence and respect. Not to be named with Scotland's great thinkers—her Humes, Napiers, Browns, and Leslies —nor with her men of genius, her Burnses, Scotts, and Wilsons—nor with the first three of her pulpit orators and divines, Knox, Chalmers, and Edward Irving, they were, nevertheless, men of mark and mould, men that discerned their time, did their work, proved equal to the crisis that created them, and founded one of the most useful, popular, and powerful of our Scottish Churches. Of the first of these four we spoke fully enough before. The second of them, William Wilson, was sprung from the West country, and both his parents had been disinherited on account of their religious opinions. His mother was the daughter of a landed proprietor in Forfarshire, and was disowned by her proud parent because she was attached to the principles of the Covenant. Young Wilson became a good scholar—a master of theology and of Latin, a fluent, if not eloquent, writer and speaker. He refused a tempting offer to make him heir of the large possessions his mother had lost in Forfarshire on the condition of his abandoning the prospect of the Presbyterian ministry and becoming an Episcopalian. This offer did not after all tempt him, for he spurned it instantly. When licensed he was settled as the third minister of Perth, and in the Fair City he exercised a ministry of great power and success till the era of the Secession. Colonel Gardiner, whose name is so famous in Scottish history for his remarkable conversion, his piety, and the courage with which he fought and fell at the battle of Prestonpans, was a frequent visitor of Mr Wilson's, and almost domesticated in his family. Wilson became, as he said, the ox in the fourfold Living Creature of the New Church; was plodding, painstaking, and clear-headed, capable of any amount of work, although destitute of the popular gifts of some of his brethren. Alexander Moncreiff was the son of a proprietor in Perthshire. The estate was Culfargie; it lies on the banks of the beautiful river Earn, not far from the spot where it meets the Tay, and a little beneath the little town of Abernethy, with its ancient Pictish tower lying so sweetly in the shadow of the Fife hills. This estate had been in the Moncreiff family for centuries. Young Alexander studied at St. Andrews and then at

Leyden. When he returned he was invited to the pastoral charge of Abernethy, at his own doors, and he soon, with characteristic fearlessness, joined the ranks of the Evangelical party; wrote a book against Simpson and in favour of the Divinity of Christ; and, in fine, cast in his lot with the Secession Testimony. Moncreiff was of a peculiarly bold and ardent temperament, and who, having the face of a lion, feared not the face of man. Yet though he blenched not before man he bowed most reverently before God. He was a man of great, almost constant, prayer. He was perpetually uttering, both in private and in the pulpit, brief ejaculatory petitions, and has been compared to one of those inhabitants of the sea which cannot remain long beneath the surface of the water at a time, but must come up frequently to breathe. So *he* must, at times, look up and imbibe a little of the air of heaven! When preaching he sometimes paused, shut his eyes, and engaged in prayer. "See," said an old woman, "Culfargie is away to heaven, and has left us all sitting here!" The son of Culfargie, Matthew Moncreiff, was also a remarkable man. He preached very short, never longer than half an hour, but it was like one of the bursts of Vesuvius—all force, passion, and fire. When he ceased (people said) you thought he expected the judgment day to be to-morrow morning. He never used notes, nor even wrote his sermons. Coming down from Abernethy to preach in Dundee on one occasion, he wrote a sermon and committed it, but could hardly get on at all. A person who had often heard him was present, and stepping up, said—"Mr. Moncrieff, you don't seem in your usual to-day." "No," he replied, "I had written what I thought a good sermon, but the devil stole it from me. However I'll defy him in the afternoon, for I myself don't know the text yet." He went at it again, and preached with all his wonted force and fervour. James Fisher, the younger of the four fathers of the Secession, was an Ayrshire man, was born in Barr parish, of which his father was minister, in January, 1697, and was ordained at Kinclaven in 1726. He early took the side of the Protesting party in the Church, and attached himself strongly to the side of Ebenezer Erskine, whose daughter, too, he married. He was a man of penetrating judgment and great theological knowledge. He was transferred from Kinclaven to Glasgow, where he continued to minister till 1775. He died at the age of 78, having long survived his three coadjutors. He wrote a book called Fisher's Catechism, containing a commentary upon the Shorter Catechism. It is a book of much merit in its way, very clear, minute, and comprehensive, and was at one time to be found in almost every Seceder's house in Scotland. We remember once inquiring, when commencing our theological studies, at a very able minister, as to what books we should read, and he said—"Read Fisher's Catechism; it contains, in a small compass, as much as twenty systems of divinity."

One of the first things done by the four brethren after their meeting at Gairney Bridge was to draw up a testimony, called the First or Extra-Judicial Testimony, prepared by Messrs Wilson and Moncreiff, setting forth with great ability the principal reasons why they had seceded from the judicatories of the Established Church. The grounds they stated were as follows :—1st, The long series of inroads which had been made upon the constitutional rights and liberties of the Church, inroads which had come to a climax in the Act of 1732, respecting the settlement of vacant parishes, an Act not only tyrannical in itself, but which had been passed in the most unconstitutional and illegal manner, against, indeed, the expressed will of the great majority of the subordinate courts. 2nd, That the ruling party were pursuing such measures as did corrupt the doctrines of the Confession of Faith. 3rd, That the prevailing party were also chargeable with imposing new and sinful terms of communion, inasmuch as ministers were now restrained from testifying against the present course of defection and backsliding, on pain of ecclesiastical censures. And 4thly, That the ruling party had persisted in their corrupt courses, notwithstanding all attempts to reclaim them. These different reasons were stated at length, defended with ability and candour, and the testimony was closed by such solemn and weighty words as the following: —" Therefore it is not only warrantable for us, but we are laid under a necessity to lift up a testimony in a Way of Secession from them against the present current of defection, whereby our constitution is subverted, our doctrine is corrupted, and the heritage and flock of Christ are wounded, scattered, and broken; that we may not partake with them in their sins, and may do what in us lies to transmit unto succeeding generations those valuable truths that have been handed down to us by the contendings and wrestlings of a great cloud of witnesses in Scotland, since the dawning of the Reformation light amongst us."

In the Assembly of 1734 milder measures prevailed, and the four brethren had the sentence against them recalled, and were restored to their ministerial status. To this, probably, the Assembly were moved by the popular disturbances which took place in the parishes from which they had been expelled. When, for instance, Fergusson, minister of Killin, went to intimate the sentence against Mr. Wilson from his pulpit in Perth, he was met at some distance from the city by a vast multitude and prevented entering. Principal Campbell of St. Andrews was treated in the same way when he went to Abernethy to intimate the sentence against Mr. Moncreiff. The preachings of the Seceding ministers, meanwhile, were attended by vast crowds, and at the dispensation of the Lord's Supper at Abernethy, in the spring of 1734, there was such a concourse of people from every part of Scotland as had never been witnessed since the Covenanting days, and which struck the dominant party in the Church with terror.

The four brethren were not seduced by the milder spirit of the General Assembly, but continued to hang aloof, meeting for prayer and conference, but exercising no judicative authority. The Reforming party in the Church, headed by the famous Willison of Dundee, were very anxious that the first Seceders should "let bygones be bygones," and should return unto the bosom of the Church. The four brethren, however, wished more evidence on the part of the rulers of repentance for the past and of security for the future, and they soon gave the world the reasons for their refusal in the shape of another brief testimony. Meanwhile the Assemblies of 1735 and 1736 supplied new grounds for continued secession by arbitrary acts, encouraging forced settlements, and going against the wishes of the people in the choice of ministers, so that at last the four brethren determined to act in a judicative manner, as well as to continue in a state of secession; to take young men on trials for license; to send supply to parishes where forced settlements had been made; to answer demands for preaching which came pouring in upon them from many parts [of Scotland, and even from Ireland, where a pious sailor had carried the tidings of what was going on here, and whence there came a petition, signed by 3000 people, and, in short, as they said, to "follow the Lord's leadings," who was evidently bent on bringing a new church out of the bowels of the old.

In 1737, they were joined by Mr. Thomas Mair and Ralph Erskine, who had previously only sympathised with, without adding themselves to the movement. Ralph Erskine was a great accession to the body. He was a man of natural eloquence, of fine powers of fancy, was a poet as well as a prose writer, though often odd and quaint, the author of a book of great and peculiar merit, called the "Gospel Sonnets"—without a quotation from which in our boyish days, a sermon was hardly thought quite sound, and which even, if we mistake not, such distinguished men in the Established Church as Dr. Kidd, of Aberdeen, and Dr. Chalmers, did not disdain sometimes to quote; who wrote also a treatise of considerable merit, entitled, "Faith no Fancy," and some remarkable sermons, such as one entitled, "The Contest of the Divine Attributes." Ralph was minister of Dunfermline, where, a few years ago, a fine monument to his memory was erected. Soon after, Thomas Nairn, of Abbotshall, and James Thomson, of Burntisland, joined their ranks and swelled their numbers to eight.

The Church became alarmed at their progress, and summoned the eight brethren to appear before their bar and answer for what were called "high crimes." They obeyed the summons, and read a deed they had drawn up declining the authority of the Assembly. The Assembly were inclined to depose them, but through the influence of good Mr. Willison of Dundee, delayed it for another year. On the 15th of May, 1740, they passed an Act of Deposition against them, and, though unable to deprive them of their flocks, they did all they could, and but too successfully, to deprive them of their manses and churches. Ralph Erskine and James Thomson were allowed to retain their churches till new places of worship were ready. At Stirling, the church bells were forbidden to be rung, and the people found the church doors locked. They would have proceeded to burst them open had not the noble Ebenezer Erskine himself come forward, with the pulpit Bible in his hands, and saying to the vast multitude that not he, but his opposers, were answerable to Almighty God for the proceedings of that day, led the way to the valley on the north of the town, and began to preach to them there. Nobler scene there is not in all Scotland. To the north-west, are the gigantic masses of the Highland mountains—Ben Lomond, Ben Ledi, Ben Voirlich, and Ben Venue, watching the early wanderings of the Forth; north is the green chain of the Ochil hills; while on the east you see the river turning and winding through the beautiful plain or Carse of Stirling, as if in agony of reluctance to leave a scene so fair. Between these two different, yet united, and unequalled prospects, on that Sabbath morning, stood up Ebenezer Erskine, still as strong and powerful as ever, although sixty summers have passed over him, and gave out for the opening psalm the words—

> "O Lord, thou hast rejected us,
> And scattered us abroad;
> Thou justly hast displeased been,
> Return to us, O God!
> The earth to tremble thou hast made,
> Therein didst breaches make;
> Do thou, therefore, the breaches heal,
> Because the land doth shake."

How that psalm, issuing from three or four thousand lips, must have sounded, awakening the echoes of the Castle Rock, and seeming to bind the blue heavens to the green earth in a chain of harmony! An impressive prayer followed, and the preacher took for his text the words, "The men marvelled, saying, What manner of man is this, that even the winds and the sea obey him?" The sermon must have been equal to the occasion. Such a man in such a scene could not have failed. Tears were seen streaming down some cheeks; on others there kindled up a glow of enthusiasm as perhaps they turned from the glorious landscape to the great sermon, or remembered the Covenanting gatherings of their early days, and thought within themselves,

> "Surely the ancient spirit is not dead;
> Old times, methinks, are breathing here."

Turn we now and see what is doing, in similar circumstances, in the Fair City of Perth. Mr. Wilson and another gentleman—Andrew Ferrier by name—repair to the church. They find it locked and barricaded against them—nay, the magistrates themselves drawn up with their myrmidons to obstruct the entrance, and an immense multitude assembled in front. Approaching the door, Mr. Wilson, with ineffable dignity, exclaimed, "In the name of my Divine Master, I demand admission into His Temple." Thrice he made the demand, and thrice it was refused by the authorities. The multitude behind began to stir. Mr. Wilson felt its motion like that of some mighty monster heaving at his back; some were getting indignant, and there was a cry to stone the magistrates and force an entrance into the church for themselves and their minister. But Wilson turned round, and with a calm commanding air sternly forbade the execution of their purpose. "No violence," said he, "my friends; the Master whom I serve is the Prince of Peace."

Mr. Ferrier proceeded to seek admission for his minister, and, failing in this, solemnly protested against the conduct of the magistrates, as conduct for which they must answer before God and men. They replied that they would take men in their own hands, and would answer to God when they were called to do so.

At this juncture, the Deacon of the Glovers' Corporation stepped forward, and said to Mr. Wilson, that if he would accept the Glovers' Yard for the services of the day he was most welcome to it. He at once accepted the kind offer, and immediately repaired thither, followed by an immense concourse. And as he was moving, with the multitude like a vast train behind him, a poor, sneaking probationer, called John Halley, was thrust into his old pulpit, and began the public services there to a beggarly account of empty benches.

Arrived at the Glovers' Yard, the intrepid Wilson commenced the labours of the day. He had not, like Erskine, the Grampians and the Forth in view; but the Tay was not far off, with its melodious murmur. Moncrieff Hill stood up to the South, and the peak of Schiehallion terminated the northern vista. Above all, there was before him a great assemblage of eager auditors hanging upon his lips. He lifted up the Psalm-book, and in tones half of reproach and half of forgiveness, read out the words—

> " He was no foe that me reproached,
>   Then that endure I could;
> Nor hater that did 'gainst me boast,
>   From him me hide I would.
> But these men, who mine equals guide,
>   And mine aquaintance hast,
> We joined sweet counsels; to God's house
>   In company we pass'd."

After a fervid and affectionate prayer, he opened the Bible amidst dead silence, and read out for his text, "*Let us go forth, therefore, unto them without the camp*, bearing his reproach," and proceeded to preach a powerful sermon. In the close of the day—which had been to him one of great anxiety and feeling—he retired, worn and weary, to his dwelling. His daughter Isabella, then twelve years of age, had witnessed the whole scene, but did not very well understand what it meant. She felt confounded and perplexed, wished to ask her father, but was afraid—yet continued to hover about his apartment. He saw her at last, and, guessing her thoughts, he called her to him, and said—"My dear Isabella, this has been a day of trial; but we have reason to be thankful that it has not been a day of shame. If any one ask you, my dear Bell, why your father lost his kirk, you may just say as good Mr. Guthrie before his death directed my mother to say of him if she were asked why he lost his head, 'That it was in a good cause.'" She long survived her father, and the whole of that day, and these words of his, remained indelibly and vividly impressed to the last in her mind.

The Secession body had thus received a fair start, and its history from this date does not require particular elucidation here. It grew not rapidly, not like Jonah's gourd, in a night, though not slowly either, but regularly and irrresistibly. In its progress, it was split up into two bodies—we allude to the Burghers and Anti-burghers, who divided from each other about a burgess oath, which one party found themselves at liberty to take, while the other deemed it opposed to Seceder principles. This division, however, like that between Paul and Barnabas, only served to lengthen the cords as well as to strengthen the stakes of the new body. The gulph between them was never very deep, and, after a separation of 73 years, they were happily re-united in 1820. In the course of this book, when we come to speak of Methodism, we shall have occasion to allude more particularly to the quarrel between the first Seceders and George Whitfield, which led him to entertain such a strong prejudice against the Secession, and hence the well-known story of his looking up to heaven and asking—"Father Abraham, are there any Episcopalians in heaven?—'No.' Any Independents?—'No.' Any Presbyterians?—'No, no.' Any Seceders?—'Oh no, no, no!'" In their opposition to Whitfield, however, and to the Revival at Cumbuslang, our fathers developed a portion of what has been the true mission of the Secession—that of diffusing a zealous, earnest, yet common-sense Christianity; not of a retrograde if not of an eminently progressive kind; fond of fixing the one foot firmly before shooting forward the other; averse to extremes of thought and to excesses of feeling; employing its energies principally in practical work, to which all its efforts and all its culture have ever been rendered subordinate. Of late years it has greatly distinguished itself, first, as a missionary Church, supporting a great number of successful missionary stations, and cherishing a warm missionary spirit; and secondly, as a keen supporter of the Voluntary Cause, that Voluntary Cause which, when the Dissenting Churches of Scotland took it up, was a poor, feeble, beggarly bantling, but which has now become a Queen, and is soon about to take to her her great power and reign. While the moral and spiritual influence of the Secession Church has been healthy and useful, its intellectual influence has been very considerable. It has such names on its roll of eminent worthies as the Erskines, the Moncreiffs, the Browns, grandfather, father, and son; Dick of Glasgow, Ferrier of Paisley, Ballantyne of Stonehaven, Dr. Jameson of Edinburgh, author of that stupendous work, the "Scottish Dictionary," Jamieson of Methven, Drs. Heugh, and King, and Mitchell; Michael Bruce and Robert Pollok, among its minstrels; Dr. John Brown, author of "Rab and his Friends," and Coventry Dick, among its literateurs; Dr. M'Crie (who, however, left its communion latterly) among its historians; Henry Calderwood, Professor of Moral Philosophy, Edinburgh, and Dr. Cairns of Berwick, among its philosophers; Dr. Eadie of Glasgow, and Davidson of Edinburgh, among its scholars; and among its popular and able preachers, such men as John Kerr of Glasgow, Drs. Edmond and Macfarlane of London, W. B. Robertson of Irvine; Hamilton MacGill, Dr. M'Kerrow of Manchester, Drs. Jeffrey of Glasgow, and a whole host of others. We may here, too, as well take in the names of Relief celebrities, such as Gillespie; the famous orator Struthers, who was reputed during his day the most eloquent preacher in Great Britain; his namesake, Gavin Struthers of Glasgow; such vigorous writers as Professor MacMichael; solid scholars as the late Dr. Lindsay of Glasgow; and such men of original genius and powerful popular influence as Dr. William Anderson. But now a word or two on the rise of the Relief body.

The father of the movement, which originated in that body, was the Rev. Thomas Gillespie, minister of Carnock.

He was born near Duddingston, in 1708, was introduced to Boston, and through him underwent serious impressions, and resolved to be a minister. He joined the Secession Hall, which was taught under Mr. Wilson, the brave minister of Perth, but remained only ten days there, feeling, after a conversation with the Professor, dissatisfied with their views. He went to Northampton, where he studied under the famous Dr. Doddridge, and was licensed and ordained among the English Dissenters. Returning to Scotland, he joined the Established Church, and was presented to Carnock, and settled there, signing the Confession of Faith, with a reservation as to the power of the civil magistrate. His views of the connection between the Church and the State, which he had probably imbibed in England, were far before his age, being those of an out-and-out voluntary. He was himself a man of good talents, deep piety, and great fidelity in the discharge of his duties—although of a timid and melancholy temperament, struggling all his life, as Luther did, with sore fleshly and spiritual temptations. Such a man could not be at home in the bosom of such a Church of Scotland as was then, and where Principal Robertson—the historian of Scotland and America—was exercising a despotism over reclaiming congregations somewhat, though afar off, resembling the high-handed conduct of his own historic heroes, Cortes and Pizarro, to the American Indians. The Assembly, which did Robertson's will implicitly, had forced one Richardson into the parish of Inverkeithing. The Dunfermline Presbytery had resisted this strenuously, and it was determined that one of them should be deposed; and as Gillespie had been the leader in the opposition, he was fixed upon as the victim. Deposed in Edinburgh, he walked home to Carnock (four miles west of Dunfermline). When entering the garden before the house, his wife met him. "I am no longer minister of Carnock," he exclaimed. "Well," cried the noble woman, "if we must beg, I will carry the meal-poke." He determined to continue to preach, and did so—first, in the church-yard, then, driven out of this, on a little hill near the mill, and then on the highway and a piece of waste ground beside it. Great crowds attended his ministry. He got a chapel built for him in Dunfermline, and there he set up a church of liberal Presbyterian principles—standing for awhile alone, and celebrating the Sacrament without any assistance. Afterwards he was joined by Boston of Jedburgh—a son of the famous Thomas, who, like him, had been thrust out from the communion of the Church; and when Gillespie went to assist at his first sacrament, one Mr. Collier, who had come from England, and was settled in Colinsburgh, Fife, joined the pair of Protesters, and there, on the 22nd October, 1761, the first Relief Presbytery was formed, consisting of three ministers and five elders.

Ever since, the Relief Church continued to maintain a respectable and growing place in the Ecclesiastical history of Scotland. It held some peculiar views, such as Free Communion, and for a long time its students continued to attend the Established Hall. It was supposed to be less rigid, both in doctrine and in discipline, than the Secession Church, and its power in Scotland was not so great. Nevertheless, it produced many able men and eloquent preachers, and its liberality of feeling recommended it to the growing liberality of the time, so that when it wedded the Secession in the year 1847, it reminded men of a strong tributary like the river Earn uniting itself to the larger and more majestic Tay; and they have since flowed on in perfect harmony.

CHAPTER VII.

RISE OF METHODISM.—PART I.—WESLEY.

WITHIN three centuries there have been four great spiritual developments or crises in Great Britain—that of the Reformation, that of the Puritanic and Covenanting times, that of Methodism in England, and that which has occurred in the days of Chalmers, Irving, and other distinguished Christian men in our own era. In the Reformation there were harsh and fiery elements blended with the movement: the destruction of monasteries, the seizing of ecclesiastical property, the persecution and martyrdom of the Reformers, Smithfield fires, civil wars, and political convulsions. But through all this dire thunder and tempest, the clear voice of the gospel was heard, as the "lute mingles with the cymbal's clash," as a strain of sweet and soul-ravishing music has sometimes been heard amidst the tumults and uproar of the midnight tempest. The religion reared by the Reformation was, on the whole, of a manly, though somewhat pugnacious kind, which, when it waked, waked to fight, and when it slept, slept in its armour. The Reformers' views of religion were rather negative than positive; they were fonder of attacking and defending than of calmly constructing or profoundly inquiring. Their virtues were martial virtues, their spirit that of men from whose eyes many of the scales of Popery had not yet fallen. In the Puritanic Revolt some of their fierce elements continued, and were blended with a sterner self-denial and a more ascetic spirit; a greater separation between the Church and the world, and a far higher, a more daring, and more thorough-going theology. In both there was a great deal of the emotional, but the emotion was rather stern than soft; more the enthusiasm of passion than the effervescence of sentiment. Even their snivel when they did snivel, their cant when they did cant, and their turning up of the eyes and elongation of the visage, when they did make long-faces and throw up their looks to heaven, as if they were weary of earth, were connected with attributes of mind and character which rendered them, if not respectable, terrible, and if men did not believe in, they trembled at them. The men and divines of that period were too much occupied in laying deep and broad the foundations of religion, and in stripping it from the gewgaws of superstition, always to submit to the restraints of common sense, or to preserve the equilibrium of good taste. But whatever the errors and excesses of the Puritans and Covenanters were, they were venial or positively virtuous compared to the vicious practice and latitudinarian laxity of opinion which the Restoration of Charles II. rendered fashionable. Then the elements of religion, and morality too, were all in confusion; for although there were noble divines at that time in the English Church, while men listened to them with admiration for their eloquence and believed in their words as constituting the creed of a loyal gentleman, they never dreamed of putting them in practice. The Revolution of 1688 came, and brought to both England and Scotland inestimable blessings, including the privileges of civil and religious freedom, and very considerable intellectual stimulus too. It reared such mild, able, and thoughtful defenders and expounders of Christianity as Addison, John Locke, Atterbury, Tillotson, Sherlock, and Richard Bentley. But there was about the religion as well as the style of such men a certain coldness and hesitancy: they wanted warmth and life and fervour. Compared to the men of the Reformation and of the Puritanic age, these defenders of the faith and preachers of the Word had little firmness of personal conviction or strength of devotional feeling. They were sincere, but hardly in earnest. They had sufficient orthodoxy, but no propagandist zeal. They were content with holding their own faith and defending it against all comers, but had no desire to circulate it to others, particularly to the lower ranks. While the upper seats of the synagogue and the Bench of Bishops in that age were well filled with able and learned men, the lower clergy, as we may see from Fielding's novels, were extremely coarse and inferior persons, being reduced by their limited means to eke out their incomes by dealing in pigs, horses, and cattle. Meanwhile, the working classes were sunk in the grossest sensuality and the most brutal ignorance. Apart from those vices which are too common still, their greatest delight was in grinning through collars, bull-baiting, attending cock fights, pugilistic matches, and fairs, which were usually scenes of riot and debauchery.

Religion and morality were both at a discount, and it has been said truly by a poet,

> "Imagination in that age was dead,
> And cold beside it lay the corpse of Faith."

Many efforts indeed were made by the good and godly to stem the current. Richardson wrote his famous novels, "Pamela," "Clarissa," and the rest, in which his object was to excite horror at vice by painting its fearful consequences, and to show that virtue was its own reward. Young poured out his magnificent "Night Thoughts," in which he denounced earthliness and revealed the doctrine of immortality written around the stars. And Dr. Johnson, in his "Rambler" and other writings, exposed the vanity of this world, and unbared the stings which, while they punish the votaries of pleasure, point upwards to a future and fairer state of existence. But whatever influence these writers exerted, it was only over a class. They did not touch the general mass of the community, or produce any profound or permanent impression. That was reserved for a humbler order of men, who at this time arose and obtained the name of Methodists, and who, humble as were their powers and pretensions, reared at least two men of a very high and peculiar order—namely, John Wesley and George Whitfield.

John Wesley is a name with which all are familiar as representing a large and active and very useful denomination of Christians. Yet against him, or at least against his system, there were long in Scotland strong prejudices, which, like all strong prejudices, rested in a root of truth, but grew up amidst surroundings of falsehood. If Wesleyanism laid perhaps too much stress upon works, this was necessary in an age wholly given to practical Antinomianism. If it cherished emotion and excitement above measure, this, too, might be requisite in a period when there prevailed so much of

"The waveless calm, the slumber of the dead."

Nor are we to judge of Methodism by the rant, cant, and absurdities of its caricaturists—modern revivalists, and others, who have run off with all that is extravagant in the Methodistic system, and have left all that is valuable behind. We are to judge of it chiefly as it was adapted to the age when it appeared, not so much by what it is now as by the power it occupied, the place it filled, the work it did in its day and generation. The Methodism of our age has many deficiencies, and is not, we think, in some things quite up to the mark in reference to modern theological progress; but it is in others more liberal than the majority of sects, and it did at the beginning great, much needed, and undeniable good.

The principal agent in rearing Methodism into a system, and giving it wide acceptance and lasting power, was undoubtedly John Wesley. We speak afterwards of the great eloquence and burning energy of George Whitfield; but he was not the founder of Methodism, and the power he exerted was more of a temporary kind. Whitfield preached with the tongue of angels; Wesley organised the church with the prudence, and more than the prudence, of men. Whitfield converted souls individually; Wesley, in collective masses. Whitfield caught men singly, as by a fishing rod; Wesley took them in nets. Whitfield, like Saul, slew his thousands; Wesley, like David, his tens of thousands. "Whitfield was all soul; Wesley all system. After a preaching paroxysm, Whitfield lay panting on his couch, spent, breathless, and death-like. After his morning sermon, Wesley would mount his pony, and trot, and chat, and gather simples till he reached some country hamlet, where he would halt his charger, and talk through a little sermon with the villagers, and remount his pony and trot away again." Whitfield's sermons were distinguished by overwhelming but convulsive power; Wesley's by quiet conversational interest. Whitfield cared nothing for pastoral work, and had no head for ecclesiastical polity; Wesley was a man for governing, and ruling, and constructing. Whitfield was never at home except when preaching under the cannopy of heaven, in those "airy pluralities" of which he himself beautifully speaks; Wesley, to the work of an evangelist, added the care and anxious oversight of a bishop. Whitfield's power died with him—he founded and wished to found no church, and even imprecated on his head the curse of God if he should ever make the attempt to connect his name with a sect; Wesley devoted his life-long existence, all his skill and learning, and knowledge of human nature, to building what has ever continued to be a powerful and prosperous body. Whitfield was a mountain torrent, collecting suddenly and bursting out impetuously, sweeping irresistibly on, and uttering a voice of far-heard thunder more than proportionate to its volume of waters, doing much but speedily drying up, disappearing and leaving its channel empty; Wesley was a calm deep river, flowing on majestically, enriching the soil through which it flowed, and gathering around it gradually cottages, castles, villages, and large and populous cities, rising like the creations of its quiet yet powerful waters.

John Wesley was a native of Epworth, was the second son of Samuel Wesley, rector of that parish, and was born on the 17th June, 1703. When he was six years of age he was awakened by a great light in his chamber, and looking up saw the roof streaked and spotted like the skin of the panther with flames of intense brilliancy. He rose, went to the window, and mounted on a chest. One man of the company assembled without stood up on another man's shoulders and lifted out the boy. The house almost immediately afterwards fell in. When John was taken into a cottage where his father and the rest of the family had found refuge, the old man cried out—"Come, neighbours, let us kneel down! let us give thanks unto God! He has given me all my eight children; let the house go, I am rich enough." John was educated at the Charter House, whence he was removed to Christ Church College, Oxford. He was elected Fellow of Lincoln College, and ordained in 1725. At this time of his life he was distinguished by his classical attainments, skill in debating, and talent for poetry. He had been all along a virtuous and grave young man; but the perusal of Law's "Serious Call," a book which also greatly impressed Dr. Johnson, turned his thoughts into a deeper channel and made him more decidedly pious.

We saw that the Secession Church began with four

brethren. And so the Methodist body, which now numbers thousands of clergymen and millions of members, began with four young men, who met together some evenings in the week to read the Greek New Testament. These were John Wesley, his younger brother, Charles (a very remarkable man, whose hymns are full of genuine poetic as well as spiritual fire), Mr. Morgan of Christ Church, and Mr. Kirkman of Merton College. To these were gradually added others, including James Hervey (afterwards the well-known popular author of the "Meditations," and "Theron and Aspasio") and George Whitfield. By and by, the club, if it could be called so, amounted to fifteen. Not contented with religious conference, prayer, and reading, they began to such practical works as visiting the sick and prisoners in jail. This roused enmity against them, which manifested itself in a shower of nicknames. They were first called Sacramentarians, then the Holy Club, and in fine, Methodists—a term which, derived from an ancient sect of physicians who practised a new method of curing, fastened on the young men, and has since stuck to the society they founded. Wesley's father wished him to succeed him in Epworth, but he declined the offer. He was, during his residence at Oxford, marked by various interesting peculiarities. He was exceedingly liberal in his gifts, giving away much of his small income, and even grudged the expense of getting his hair cut, as leaving him less for the poor, and hence he wore it long, and flowing over his shoulders. He was a great walker, and speaks of having in one year accomplished 10,050 miles. Continuing to reside in Lincoln's College, and keeping pupils there, he was constantly employed, when leisure served, in going out to the highways and hedges as an itinerant preacher. In the year 1733, he commenced a practice of reading while travelling on horseback, a practice he pursued for forty years. His frequent journeys, hard study, and constant abstinence began to tell upon his health. Spitting of blood began, and one night he thought himself dying, and cried out through the clotted blood he found in his mouth—"O prepare me for Thy coming, and come when Thou wilt!" He took the advice of a physician, who put him upon a regimen through which he recovered his strength, and lived nearly sixty years afterwards. At this time the trustees of the new colony of Georgia were in need of persons to preach to the Indians, and John Wesley along with his brother Charles and some other missionaries, including a few German Moravians, were chosen. He set sail from the Downs in October, 1735, and during the voyage out he arranged every hour of his time with that marvellous regularity which he had begun to practise in Oxford. He might well be called a Methodist, for he was the most methodical man that ever lived. He landed at Savannah, where he immediately set himself to do all the good in his power, in preaching, in founding libraries, and so forth. He was prevented, however, by the disturbed state of the colony from preaching the gospel to the Indians. He gave by and by a good deal of offence by his High Churchism, refusing the Sacrament to Dissenters, and by his ascetical practices. And he raised quite a storm against himself by his conduct to a lady, a Miss Canston, who refused to marry him, and whom, after she had married another, *he* refused to admit to communion, without assigning a reason. Legal proceedings were instituted against him; he was treated very unfairly; the case was put off again and again; and at last, hopeless of fair play, and afraid of the effect the report would have on his character when conveyed home, he determined to set off for England, and reached it after an absence of a year and nine months. In America he had voluntarily undergone great hardships; often slept on the ground amid heavy dews of the summer night, and awoke in winter sometimes with his hair and clothes frozen to the earth in the morning; would wade through swamps and swim over rivers in his clothes, and then travel on till they were dry.

Wesley had met some Moravians in America, and, when he returned, kept up communication with that body. He even went abroad and visited Hernhuth, the head-quarters of what he called this "lovely people." The Moravians were eminently pious, a little mystical, too, in their religion, and had done good service by their missions in Greenland. There was something in their simple manners, warm-hearted piety, and their dash of superstition withal, that pleased certain imaginative Christians. We find Cowper the poet speaking of them as having planted

"Sweet Sharon's rose
'Mid barren wastes and everlasting snows."

Dr. Chalmers, in his last Astronomical Discourse, has panegyrised them in his most glowing style; Schleiermacher sprung from them, and owed much of his peculiar idiosyncrasy to them; and John Wesley, who was a great believer in ghosts, dreams, and visions, found congenial society and kindred beliefs in the brethren of Hernhuth.

In September, 1738, Wesley began, systematically, that long course of evangelistic labours which were to render his name famous and his influence so enduring. He commenced to exhort and preach, often three or four times a day, at the prison and other places of the metropolis, and made frequent excursions to the country, where his followers became rapidly more numerous. Hearing that Whitfield, who had also been in Georgia, was returned to England, Wesley went to London to meet him, and they renewed their sweet counsel. Some extravagant scenes, aping the Pentecostal phenomenon, took place about this time, at which their sensible admirers will now blush. In spring Whitfield went down to Bristol, and commenced preaching in the open air to immense throngs, and with prodigious vehemence and effect. Wesley continued his labours in London and Oxford alternately; but yielding to Mr. Whitfield's urgent request, Wesley went down to Bristol, and commenced preaching in company with his great coadjutor, and remained after he had left, his ministry producing marvellous bodily effects, with some of which Samuel Wesley, his elder brother, was by no means satisfied. In Bristol, in May, 1739, the first stone of a Methodist meeting-house was laid.

It may be as well to notice here that John Wesley was rather ill to please about the time and mode of his conversion. Most people, when he was labouring at Oxford and Savannah, full of zeal, of methodical duty, of reading and prayer, thought him a very good man. And so we doubt not he was. "By their fruits ye shall know them;" and his fruits were fresh, and fair, and abundant. But he appears to have been haunted with a desire for some sensible evidence—wished to pass through some quick and decisive operation—as if conversion were something like amputation, to be performed within a given time. In this craving he was strengthened by one of those good enthusiastic Moravians, and at last his ardent wish was gratified, as most such wishes are, by fulfilling themselves. While a person in Aldersgate Street was reading Luther's preface to the Epistle on the Romans, on the 24th May, 1738, at a quarter before nine in the evening, Wesley's sudden conversion, as he thought, took place. He certainly after that time gave one additional evidence of goodness. He ceased, he tells us, to be a servant, and became a son. His fear of God, which had been slavish, became more filial. He left Sinai behind him, thundering in its wilderness, and he found himself standing free and fearless upon the sides of Zion. And though it were for nothing else, we are disposed to say—Honour to John Wesley for introducing into our theology a milder and more merciful regimé, and teaching thousands and millions who have embraced his views to be less terrified at God and to love him inconceivably better!

Such liberal theological views on his part led gradually to an estrangement between him and Whitfield, who was all his life a flaming Calvinist. Methodism was now a fact in the country, and Wesley proceeded to consolidate it by the most admirable generalship and methodical management. His great object was to secure its unity, to form innumerable parts into one compact whole; and this he managed, by the formation of various classes and class teachers, and by getting all the ministers of the denomination subject to a Conference—a kind of Parliament, with almost all a Parliament's powers and prerogatives. He introduced, too, the element of lay preaching, and of continual shiftings of ground on the part of ministers. His own power over this body during his life-time was all but despotic. All the chapels built were vested either in him or in trustees, bound to give admission to the pulpit as he should direct. He himself, too, appointed all the lay preachers, and employed them as itinerants among the different societies of the persuasion. Nothing more tended to the success of Methodism than the strict and orderly discipline established by its founder; and although this led, in some cases, to harshness and tyranny, and even on several occasions to resistance and to the formation of large bodies dissenting from the original stem, the original church still continues strong, compact, and flourishing in every quarter of the globe, and remains an everlasting monument to the organising genius of John Wesley.

The rest of this extraordinary man's career was little else than a long series of labours. He was benevolent as an angel and restless as a demon. Although he had now a chapel built for him in London, he was almost perpetually travelling, preaching, or writing. He moved through England, Wales, Ireland, and Scotland, confirming and watering the churches he had founded. He usually preached two sermons a day, sometimes four or five. He was a very early riser, and famous for gathering up the fragments of time. He needed little sleep, although latterly, when he used a carriage, he sometimes napped in it. He was unhappy in his domestic circumstances, and was eventually separated from his wife. He was on intimate terms with some celebrated men. Dr. Johnson liked to converse with him, only he complained that he was always too much in a hurry for one who, like himself, loved to fold his legs and have his talk out. He knew and admired that marvellous man Swedenborg. He once saw Robert Southey, the poet, when Southey was a boy, patted him on the head, and blessed him; and Southey said to James Everett, long after, with tears in his eyes, that he felt John Wesley's hand and his blessing on his head still. He died on 20th March, 1791, eighty-eight years of age. He was abundant in labours to the last. His final sermon was on the characteristic text, "Seek ye the Lord while he may be found; call ye upon him while he is near." While on his deathbed he said one forenoon—"I will get up;" and while they were preparing his clothes, he broke out with astonishing spirit—

> "I'll praise my Maker while I've breath,
> And when my voice is lost in death
> Praise shall employ my nobler powers.
> My days of praise shall ne'er be past
> While life and thought and being last,
> Or immortality endures."

His last words were—"I'll praise! I'll praise!" He was buried on the 9th of March, and, to prevent a crowd, between five and six in the morning; and in the forenoon, Dr. Whitehead, who afterwards wrote his life, delivered his funeral service to an immense concourse of people, including divines of all denominations. An inscription was placed on his tomb, the conclusion of which is striking—"After having languished for a few days, he at length finished his course and his life together, gloriously triumphing over death, on the 2nd March, 1791, in the 88th year of his age."

John Wesley was unquestionably a great man. He did not want his faults, and he had bitter revilers and scandalmongers that made the most of them. But he had, nevertheless, most of the elements which constitute a good and noble man. He was a philanthropist and a Christian; a gentleman, a scholar, and a saint; was liberal, generous, courteous, a powerful controversialist, an attractive preacher, the most indefatigable and persevering of men; and in all that constitutes a leader and builder of a church unrivalled. In personal appearance, though not tall or bulky, he was in youth attractive, in middle age commanding, and in age most venerable.

―――*o*―――

RISE OF METHODISM.—PART II.—WHITFIELD.

IN the firmament of the church as well as of the world, there are great varieties of luminaries. There are large, single, and steady stars; there are vast constellations, there are careering comets, there are dull orbs, the very light in which is darkness, and there are whizzing and short-lived meteors. The dull orbs include, unfortunately, a vast number of ministers and of men. These are your commonplace men, folks with a creed and a confession of faith, dexterous policy and courting of the people or of the upper classes for practice; who find their strength in their weakness and their success in their suppleness; who are perpetually running about and cajoling their flocks, as a fearless youth in the north of Scotland was saying the other day, "buzzing about them like a honey bee." Then there are the stationary, steady, and large luminaries, leaders of churches, fathers of presbyteries; or, in the world, municipal rulers, and members of Parliament. Then there are the meteor-like men, who make a great noise for a season, but soon crackle out their little hour and disappear in darkness—Orator Henleys, Bellews, *et hoc omne genus*. Then there are the men who form constellations in themselves, so varied are their powers and so vast their breadth of influence—the Jeremy Taylors, Chalmerses, Halls, Wardlaws, Wesleys, and so forth, in the church; and in the world, the Walter Scotts, Wordsworths, and Shakespeares. And last, there are the comets in the sky, not perhaps so weighty or vast in bulk, but brilliant in colour, swift in motion, eccentric in orbit, and lurid in aspect—such as in the world the Shelleys and Coleridges, and in the church the George Whitfields and Edward Irvings.

It may appear a singular conjunction of names, but we cannot help sometimes connecting into one group the three men—George Whitfield, Edward Irving, and

Percy Byssche Shelley. The three men at first sight seem excessively different—a Methodist orator, a modern Scotch puritan, and a pantheistic poet; the son of an innkeeper, the son of a tanner, and the son of an English baronet; a Calvinist, a Millenarian, and a Pantheist. And yet they had all certain generic resemblances amidst their specific differences. All three were enthusiasts—thoroughly, burningly sincere, earnest as flames of fire; all were men of genius; all were rather one-sided, and slightly *cracked;* all three were good men, with all their faults and mistakes; and all three were warm and self-sacrificing lovers of their kind, although the first showed his love by wielding hell-flames and uttering infernal thunder, the other by holding the belief that Christ was coming soon to burn up the globe and consume the majority of men, and the third by denying the personality of God, and substituting some dream of intellectual Beauty or form of airy Love as Deity instead.

The secret of the power of such men lies in this—that they are like, yet very unlike, that very race they love and labour for, and that they therefore in the first instance repel and ultimately attract them. All these men were at first received with obloquy and opposition, which broke the heart of two of their number, shortened the career of Irving, and would have driven Shelley to suicide had he not been snatched from it by the storm which drowned him. To this obloquy, however, there surely, though somewhat slowly, succeeded a "late remorse of love." Their virtues were appreciated, their talents recognised, their efforts to do good separated from the mistakes they committed and errors they taught and fully acknowledged, and their names added to the roll of earth's worthies, with the greater eagerness that the act of doing so had been unworthily delayed. When men have great faults and great merits, the faults during their lifetime act as clouds to the sun; but when they die, just as clouds kindle up around the sinking or sunk luminary, and add to the relict-splendour of his beams, so faults go to swell the glory and become fuel to the fire of the fame of the noble men who have left the scene. The "Great Soul of the world is just," and it decides on this wise :—"These men had personal errors, against which they strove, and strove to some purpose. They had extravagant and extreme views, and advocated them in an imprudent way; but they had all some truth to tell, they had all a certain mission to discharge, they were all men of supreme sincerity, as well as of great gifts; and, therefore, though they may not be classed with the more perfect specimens of humanity, yet they have deserved well of their race, and must be ranked very high in the temple of the immortals."

George Whitfield was born in the Bell Inn, Gloucester, and if this be a reproach it is one that applies to his Master, who, as Jeremy Taylor quaintly says, was

> "Born in an inn,
> A star the sign."

His father, Thomas Whitfield, died when George was two years of age. His mother continued to keep the inn, and seems to have been a thrifty, managing, and exemplary woman, as well as a very kind mother to George. He seems to have been a careless boy, neither better nor worse than many of his standing; although he afterwards accuses himself very bitterly of such sins as lying, stealing, and foolish jesting. He was greatly given, too, to reading romances, and it should be remembered that romances then were of a very loose and immoral kind. All such statements, however, we are always disposed to take with much allowance. And even then Whitfield tells us that he could recollect early motions in his heart, which satisfied him afterwards that "God loved him with an everlasting love, and had separated him from his mother's womb for the work to which he ultimately called him." His mother married again, and the marriage proving unhappy, it brought on him much affliction, during which he sometimes read and profited by religious books. He early discovered those talents for elocution which contributed to make him afterwards so famous, and was very nearly led to give them a theatrical direction. A play written by the master himself was enacted by the boys, and Whitfield took a woman's part, and appeared in girl's clothes, of which event in his history he was heartily ashamed. He was even for a while a drawer in the Bell Inn, clad in a blue apron, and crying like Master Francis—"Anon, anon, sir." Yet while thus occupied he composed two or three sermons, and instead of romances began to read Thomas à Kempis.

At the age of eighteen he went to Oxford. To this ne was moved by his worthy mother, who heard that one might live there cheaply as a servitor, and who saw her son's tendencies to a public life to be irrepressible. He had first studied very hard at the grammar school to prepare himself for the university. When he entered Oxford he heard much of the Methodists, the men living "by method," including Wesley and his friends, and was ultimately attracted to them and became one of their number.

The life of Whitfield has been often told, and to do it justice in a short paper is quite impossible. Robert Philip's life of him is, with a good deal of rubbish, the best, and is easily accessible, and on the whole accurate and candid. At Oxford he exhibited some extraordinary extravagances, lying whole days and even weeks on the ground in prayer, choosing the worst kind of food, and dressed in a patched gown and dirty shoes. He began to preach at twenty-one, being then ordained deacon, and is said by his first sermon to have driven fifteen people in Gloucester mad, which, when told the Bishop, he said he hoped the madness would last till next Sunday. He graduated B.A. at Oxford, became the chaplain of the Tower, preached also in other places, both town and country, with unprecedented popularity; crossed the seas, and joined the Wesleys in Savannah, Georgia; projected an orphan house for the destitute children there; came home to advocate their claims, and raised vast sums of money for it; was ordained priest by Bishop Benson; preached in London to enormous crowds, was compelled at last to begin open air preaching, which practice he continued to the close of his career; returned to America, where he was attended by immense throngs, and made the acquaintance and awakened the astonishment of Benjamin Franklin; arrived at Savannah and laid the foundation of the new orphan-house; coming home, engaged in controversies with Wesley about Election and Reprobation, he being a strong Calvinist; revived his cause, which was sinking, and succceded in rearing two tabernacles, one in Moorfields and the other in Tottenham Court Road; visited many parts in England, Scotland and Wales; married a Welsh lady in 1741, at whose death he chose the strange text, "For the creature was made subject unto vanity, not willingly, but by reason of him who hath subjected the same in hope;" returned again to America, where he remained four years, came home again, and was introduced to the Countess of Huntingdon, who appointed him one of her chaplains; visited Ireland, made two more voyages to America, and at last, on his seventh visit to that country, was cut off very suddenly at Newburyport, in New England, when he had only reached the 56th year of his age, and seemed not past the prime of his most active and energetic existence. He had indeed somewhat in previous years exhausted himself with labours, and had been afflicted with severe colds; but during the summer of 1770 he had revived wonderfully, and had preached every day. On Saturday the 29th September he had addressed great multitudes for two hours, and retired to rest bent on preaching the next day. But during the night his rest was much broken by oppression in the lungs, and an attack of asthma carried him away at six in the morning. He might thus be said to have died in harness, and almost literally in the pulpit. John Wesley, in accordance with Whitfield's expressed desire, preached in England his funeral sermon.

Such is a cursory sketch of Whitfield's life. But there are two or three points about him on which we would desire more particularly to dwell. First, the character of his preaching, along with some illustrative anecdotes; secondly, his connection with the Seceders in Scotland; and thirdly, the general question as to the result and value of that style of preaching of which his was perhaps the best example. First, let us look to the general character and give some illustrative anecdotes of his matchless eloquence.

Whitfield possessed all the natural qualifications of a great orator. He was tall and well-proportioned, slender in youth, enormously stout as he advanced in life. His complexion was very fair, his features regular, his eyes blue—one of them squinted a little (hence his name "Dr. Squintum"), a peculiarity which Edward Irving also had in his vision, and which rather added to than dertacted from the effect. His voice was very strong, so strong that he could be heard a mile off in the open air: it was also exquisitely melodious and well managed. His action was at once powerful and full of grace. A plain man describing his eloquence once said that he preached like a lion, denoting no doubt his impression of the force, vehemence, and withal majesty and naturalness of his manner. Had his intellect and knowledge been equal to his eloquence, George Whitfield would have been the Shakespeare of divines, nay, almost a supernatural being. But his learning was limited, his knowledge of theology narrow, and his views were neither comprehensive nor profound. Yet he cannot be denied the possession, apart from his oratory, of high genius. His letters and journals, amidst a great deal of pietistic twaddle, contain some glowing pictures of nature and some gleams of true imagination. His leading moral qualities were heart and sincerity. "That man," said Mirabeau of a very different character (Robespierre), "will go far, for he believes every word he says." George Whitfield believed every word he said, and some of his words were tremendous words to be believed or uttered. Yet terrible as were many of his denunciations, all who heard him thought him to be a man of warm heart and boundless benevolence. His whole conduct in reference to the Orphan House in Georgia proved this. How he laboured for those friendless ones including several negroes! How he "remembered the forgotten!" If when thundering hell flames he resembled Moses in the midst of Sinai's uproar and darkness, when weeping over his poor orphans he was the image of Jesus Christ himself.

His great faults, besides a little vanity, and latterly a desire to propitiate the great when they came around him, were his impetuosity of temper, his yielding to the power of impulses, and his somewhat censorious habits of public speech. All that were not on his side he denounced as infidels, or at least unconverted men. Jonathan Edwards, when he visited him, warned him of these faults. By the way, what a meeting that must have been between the most intellectual of Calvinistic thinkers and the most eloquent of Calvinistic preachers! The one all ice, the other all fire; the one all logic, the other all passion; both holding the same doctrines, but in the one Calvinism being frozen into snow, like the water on the Andes, in the other coming down in the shape of furious torrents. Edwards, the author of the "Freedom of Will," might be compared to Chimborazo in his altitude and corpse like cold; Whitfield to Cotopaxi, flaming out billows of fire through a covering of everlasting snow.

His elocution was inimitable. He never hesitated, except when he paused to utter a flood of tears. Sometimes he wept excessively and stamped loudly and passionately. The effect of his vehemence after his preaching on himself was dreadful. He often vomited blood for hours, and in his exhaustion men trembled for his life. News of his sudden death were circulated constantly, and were rendered credible by his enormous exertions. He delighted in sensational and highly wrought points and paroxysms of eloquence. Sometimes he would set before his congregation the agony of Christ as though the scene were actually before them. "Look yonder," he would say, stretching out his hand and pointing while he spake, "what is that I see? Not my agonising Lord! Hark, hark! do you not hear? 'O my Father, if it be possible let this cup pass from me: nevertheless not my will but thine be done.'" This he introduced often in his sermons, and with an effect that never diminished. "Sometimes at the close of a sermon," says Southey, "he would personate a judge about to perform the last awful part of his office. With his eyes full of tears, and an emotion that made his voice falter, after a pause which kept the whole audience in breathless expectation of what was to come, he would say —'I am now come to put on my condemning, my black cap. Sinner, I must do it. I must pronounce sentence against you.'" And then in a tremendous strain of eloquence, describing the eternal punishment of the wicked, he recited the words of Christ—"Depart from me, ye cursed, into everlasting fire, prepared for the devil and his angels." The effects he produced were wonderful. Often he had twenty thousand people weeping, or awe-struck into a silence profound as the grave. Often

"Those who came to laugh remained to pray."

A man in Exeter went to hear him with stones in his pocket to stone him, but dropped them before the sermon was far advanced, and came up to him at the close and said—"I came to break your head, but you have broken my heart." A shipbuilder was once asked how he liked him. "Like him, Sir! I tell you that every Sunday I go to the Parish Church I can build a ship from stem to stern under the sermon; but were it to save my soul, under Mr. Whitfield I could not lay a single plank." David Hume heard him in Scotland, and tells an anecdote of his preaching. "After a solemn pause he thus addressed the audience—'The attendant angel is just about to leave this and ascend to heaven; and shall he ascend and not bear with him the news of one sinner out of all this multitude reclaimed from the error of his ways?' And then he stamped with his foot, lifted up his hands and eyes to heaven, and cried aloud— 'Stop, Gabriel! stop ere you enter the sacred portals, and yet carry with you the news of one sinner converted to God!'" Franklin describes himself going to hear him once, determined to give nothing to him, as he disapproved of the object for which he pled. "I silently resolved he should get nothing from me, although he was to finish with a collection. I had in my pocket a handful of copper money, three or four silver dollars, and five pistoles in gold. As he proceeded, I began to soften, and concluded to give the copper. Another stroke of his oratory made me ashamed of that, and determined to give the silver; and he finished so admirably that I emptied my pocket wholly into the collector's dish, gold and all." "At the same sermon there was one who, being of Franklin's mind about the object, took the precaution to empty his pockets ere he went; but as the preacher went on he felt a strong inclination to give something to the cause, it was so eloquently enforced; and he applied accordingly to a neighbour who stood near him to lend him some money for the purpose. The man, probably the only one in the church who had remained quite cool, and who was, by the way, a Quaker, said in reply—'At any other time, friend Hopkinson, I would lend to thee freely; but not now, for thee seems to me to be out of thy right senses.'" A hundred similar stories might be given. The biggest and most complex audience was to this mighty preacher simply an instrument of less or larger compass, on which he could play whatever tunes he pleased, and which was quite passive in his hands, both when he roused it into a tumult of terror or melted it into a passion of tears.

We promised to say something about Whitfield's connection with the first Seceders. Before he came to Scotland his fame had got before him, and both Ebenezer and Ralph Erskine wrote him, urging him to come over and help them. They knew he was the most powerful preacher living, and they knew that he was an avowed Calvinist, and had quarrelled on that account with John Wesley. They thought therefore, very justly, that he would be a most valuable ally to them; but they showed too great a disposition to keep him to themselves, and tie him down to a belief in the divine right of presbytery, and in the heaven-born origin of the Secession Church. But Whitfield was far too broad in spirit and unfettered in his motives for this. He wished to be and was in ecclesiastical matters a "chartered libertine," as independent as Paul himself of presbyteries, synods, and churches generally, ready, as he said, to preach the gospel in the "Pope's pulpit" if he found no other, and who had preached it on the stages of wrestling matches and strolling players. He went indeed to Dunfermline, preached in Ralph Erskine's large chapel there, and was delighted to hear the sound of the host of rustling Bibles, to which he had never heard anything equal anywhere else. But in farther conference they came to a complete rupture. Whitfield's account of it is amusing. They were angry at him for not making the Solemn League and Covenant his study. "Ralph Erskine said they were the Lord's people. I then asked whether there were no other Lord's people but themselves; and supposing all others were the Devil's people, they certainly had more need to be preached to; and therefore I was more and more determined to go out to the highways and hedges." One of them preached in Whitfield's hearing on the words, "Watchman, what of the night?" but "so spent himself in talking against Prelacy, the Common Prayer Book, the surplice, the rose in the hat, and so on, that when he came at the close to invite sinners to Christ, his breath was so gone that he could hardly be heard. What a pity that the last was not first and the first last!" An open breach was the consequence. "I retired, I wept, I prayed, and after preaching in the fields sat down, dined with them, and then took a final leave." Yet the first Seceders were able and excellent men, and let it never be forgotten that they lifted up their voices most emphatically against those Cambuslang and Kilsyth revivals of the last century, which Whitfield countenanced by his preaching and presence, but which seems now, to us at least, like all such works, to be on the whole rather outbreaks of fanaticism, deliration, and spiritual delusion, than to proceed from that God who is the God not of confusion but of order and peace, of intelligence and love.

We promised, in conclusion to say something about sensational and terroristic preaching. There can be no doubt that George Whitfield was the prince of sensational preachers, and that he wielded, although not exclusively yet to a very awful extent, the language and the power of terror, even in its physical forms. Sensationalism, no doubt, and terror both existed before him. We find them in the Reformers to some extent, in the English divines—such as Jeremy Taylor, Bunyan, and Richard Baxter—and very notably in some of the French preachers, such as Massillon and Saurin. But Whitfield not only surpassed all these in popular power, but he used the elements of sensationalism and of terror more largely and habitually, and he may be said to have founded a school in the Christian Church which has by no means even yet died away. To him we owe mainly, in this country at least, florid and theatrical pictures of the death of Christ, appeals to the emotional nature, extravagant and overdone statements as to the nature of conversion, a frequent craving after physical effects, such as tears and bodily transports, or bodily convulsions under the Word, and the painfully frequent and unmitigated proclamation of the terrors of an eternal, and probably a literal, hell. Now, in Whitfield's own case we can, to some extent, excuse this. He was not a man of very high culture or of very refined taste—he was a man of prodigious passions, passions which if they had not found a vent in oratory and his form of religion, would have made him a very sensual man. He had besides, owing to his imperfect knowledge of divinity and literature, but a moderate stock-in-trade, so to speak, and had to recur often to his tropes of terror and bursts of excited eloquence, and he addressed very often the coarsest audiences the age could afford—colliers, the riotous rabble of Moorfields, or the loose debris of country markets. It may be doubted if similar preaching is as much in place in the present day, and this the caricaturists of Whitfield do not perceive, especially when they come to Scotland, where if the hearts are colder the heads are clearer and harder than in our sister land, and where silly anecdotes and bold misstatements of facts, and pictures of terror, conceived in the spirit of Dante but destitute altogether of his genius, fall utterly powerless. Sensationalism and terrorism do not suit our present habits of thought. Men are now beginning to investigate religious subjects, and they do not want to be disturbed either by outcries of "Fire! fire!" or by spiritual cajolery and delectable pictures, which seem to have little foundation in reality. Sensationalism and terror are not in keeping with the spirit whether of the universe or the Bible. The universe is on the whole a very calm and orderly system. Its volcanoes and floods, tempests and eclipses, are regulated by laws as unfailing and irresistible as its tidal movements or its planetary revolutions, all moving on a plane and to a purpose far above the reaches of fanaticism, and not to be bended to its weak and insane pleasure. The Bible is a remarkably sensible book, with no fanaticism in it, and with the element of love far overpowering the element of terror. With the exception of a very few figures, it says nothing about the nature of the future state at all; and its descriptions of Christ's sufferings are exceedingly short, subdued, and unostentatious. Sensationalism and terrorism do ill, by turning men's minds away from the evil of sin to its physical consequences, consequences which we see in this life extended to the innocent as well as to the guilty. If we are to read sin only in its results, why is it that some of the best of men are as miserable as the worst? They do not really convert. Conversion means a divine spiritual education, and the betterment produced thereby; not a sudden spasm or a few tears, or an exaggerated or entirely false theory about God and man, enthusiastically preached, unthinkingly accepted, and often

afterwards readily relinquished. They turn the sensuous element into a new channel, and provoke a reaction in its favour, and they produce many undeniable cases of madness. We find a powerful and painful testimony to this in Dr. Maudesley's recent and most admirable book on the "Pathology of the Mind." We quote a passage or two quite startling in their truth:—" The practical religion of the day, the real guiding gospel of life, is money-getting; the professed religion is Christianity. Now without asserting that riches are not to be gotten by honest industry, it may be maintained that the eager passion to get rich—honestly it may be, but if not, still to get rich—is often inconsistent with the spirit of the gospel professed. The too frequent consequence is, that life becomes a systematic inconsistency or an organised hypocrisy. With a profession of faith that angels might adopt, there is too often a rule of practice which devils need not disdain."
" I do not hesitate to express a conviction that the excitement of religious feelings, and the moroseness of the religious life, favoured by some religionists, are habitually injurious to the character, and a direct cause of insanity. Young women who betake themselves too fervently to religious exercises, and thus find an outlet for repressed feeling in an extreme devotional life, fly to a system which expressly sanctions and encourages a habit of attention to the feelings and thoughts." Still more strongly does this accomplished philosopher and physician say—" The fanatic religious sects which every now and then appear in a community, and disgust it by the offensive way in

which they commingle religion and love, are really inspired by an uncontrolled and disordered sexual instinct." "Exaggerated self feeling, rooted often in sexual passion, is fostered under a spiritual cloak, and drives its victim either to madness or to sin." He strongly denounces, too, those who use the weaknesses of women to minister to their own base ends under a religious guise.

Sensationalism and terrorism, in fine, by misrepresenting Christianity, are driving many to utter infidelity. Intelligent men are saying—" If Christianity be a theatrical excitement, founded on the agonies and blood of God's Son himself—a tragedy, with Christ for the chief performer; if it be a flight of fireworks to which the vast majority of the human race are to form the fuel; if it be a great coming scheme of conflagration to the world and glorification to such a small church as can be gathered out of it by the advent year 1871 or 1873; then we for our part are done with Christianity, we cannot swallow these versions of it, and we would prefer to stand back from it altogether." Oh! if our well-meaning obscurantists were but knowing what mischief they are doing by their narrowness of spirit, their conventionalism of creed, their pumping up of false and faded excitements, their belated terrorisms, and their weak, withered cant, to the very cause they seek, and perhaps seek sincerely, to support, they would change their tactics, they would alter their scheme of thought and their mode of talk; they would become humbler, sadder, and wiser men, and would at length learn that the clock of the world does not stand still at the hour in 1770, when the brave George Whitfield left it, or at the hour in 1834, when Edward Irving died; but is moving onwards and onwards, at an always accelerating rate, and for evermore.

CHAPTER VIII.

NATURE AND EXTENT OF LIBERTY OF CONSCIENCE.

WE propose annexing to this little volume the following thoughts on the Nature and Extent of Liberty of Conscience, especially as that liberty should be exercised in the light of the present day. The subject is delicate and difficult, and we cannot commence without praying Him who is the Infinite Light, and who above all beings enjoys perfect liberty, to aid us in its consideration.

Liberty of thought and liberty of conscience differ chiefly in this, that while the one refers to thought employed upon all subjects, including scientific, political, philosophical, and secular, the other refers to the exercise of the mind upon moral and religious topics exclusively. Conscience, when stripped of mystical jargon, is just a name for the intellectual power of man employed upon a particular set of subjects, and the moral sense is simply the feeling springing out of that exercise. All agree that liberty of thought and liberty of conscience are, within certain limits, native and inalienable rights of man; and the only question on which there is difference of opinion is in reference to the nature and extent of these limitations.

Now, in reference to thought on common subjects, it is obvious that one has a right to entertain any proposition that is not contradictory, and that is supported by a proper amount of evidence. I may be wrong in judging or weighing the evidence that convinces me, but no one can quarrel with me for entertaining, after inquiry, my opinion, whatever he may think of its validity. Even proverbially " every one may have his own think," and you can only alter or seek to alter that *think* by producing fresh evidence or exposing the fallacy of what has been the medium of your conviction. Here comes in the question about *authority*—Should not authority have weight in determining my thought? Certainly; but that authority is not and ought not to be absolute. Suppose it to be the authority of parents : parents are not infallible. Should it be that of great thinkers and philosophers: they are not infallible either. Seniors have and should have influence from their longer standing; but seniors too are men, and though they have the start of their juniors, that start is not infinite. Authority, in short, is only a weaker kind of evidence, weaker than that of the senses, weaker than that of the reasoning and investigating understanding, and is, like other evidence, to be carefully examined and scrupulously weighed before it is accepted as conclusive.

In reference to Conscience, it is somewhat different. Conscience, or the Reason of man working upon moral and religious subjects, is naturally free to believe whatever it sees upon evidence to be right. It is not mere feeling that stirs within a man when he abhors what is evil and cleaves to what is good. It is feeling, indeed, but feeling which may be called the *solution* of a principle which has been founded upon evidence, evidence either gathered by the individual or handed down from generation to generation. Why do I shudder when I see a deed of violence or hear of an act of base treachery? Because my reason has evidence, collected either by itself or founded on past experience that such a thing is wrong, criminal, offensive, and creates the feeling that it is so in me of indignation and a desire for punishment. Now here, too, comes in the principle of authority. And so far as the authority which seeks to dominate over my conscience is that of man, however superior in age, or knowledge, or intellect, or station, or time, it is simply evidence which I must weigh as I do other evidence in forming my conclusion. It has and can have no *absolute* power over me, for the same reason as in the former case—my seniors, or parents, or superiors, or the wise men of a past generation, are not more infallible than myself.

But now comes the difference between the limitations of Reason and those of Conscience. In Reason and its exercise we know of no infallible authority. In the domains of Conscience we do; and that is the direct Word of God. That there is any such authority is not indeed universally conceded. All Rationalists deny it; Papists shift it from God's Word to the Church—it and it only on earth do they believe infallible, at least as an interpreter of the Divine Will; but all Protestant Christians admit that the Will of God is revealed in the Scriptures, and where accurately ascertained to exist, must be implicitly obeyed.

It is then, solely with believers in the Book of God, as containing a revelation from God to men, that we have at present to do. All such agree that where God's Will can be gathered out of that Word, they are bound to accept it as their belief. But a number of considerations here present themselves. First of all, it is no easy matter to ascertain from the Scriptures what the Will of God is. The Scriptures are a collection of treatises, tracts, and histories, written in dead languages, written a long time ago, written at various times, and by persons of various degrees of mind, information, and probably of inspiration, and written often in obscure and figurative language. Hence, to gather the truth out of these multifarious writings, to reconcile apparent contradictions, to follow the gradual process of thought and religious opinion which is manifest in them, is confessedly one of the most difficult of tasks, has exercised the minds of the greatest scholars and thinkers, and has developed great diversity of view amongst men of equal calibre. Calvinists and Arminians, Pelagians and Unitarians, Protestants and Papists, have all defended their theories, though wide as the poles asunder, by plausible interpretations of the Scriptures. This I mention not as an excuse for scepticism, but as as an argument for modesty and caution, and to show that Reason has a great deal to do with the Word of God. It must not only bow before its authority, but it must first ascertain its meaning.

Secondly. Without denying at all the inspiration of the Scriptures, it has now become quite obvious to thinking men that that inspiration varies in various portions of the Book. It is not the same in the lists of proper names in Chronicles and Nehemiah as in the divine songs of Isaiah or the profound deliverances of Paul of Tarsus

It is not the same in the description of the Temple in Ezekiel or in the mystical mazes of the Apocalypse—parts of Scripture about which there have been ten thousand conjectures but no clear explanation—as in the Parables or Sermons of Christ. Here, then, is another call for the exercise of Reason to settle the different modes and degrees of inspiration. Bowing before the Book, it cannot bow so profoundly at some words as at others, and it reserves prostration only for what is oracular and manifestly meant to command belief and obedience.

Thirdly. It is impossible to ignore or wink at the facts which have become so palpable of late, that there is a process of critical inquiry going on which threatens considerably to modify men's judgments about particular portions of the Canon, about the authorship and age of the Pentateuch, about the authority of the Book of Daniel, about the two-fold origin of Isaiah, about the inspiration of the Apocalypse, and the authenticity of the Gospel of John. It is not my part at present to say what I think of these researches and conclusions. In some points they may be near the truth, in others they seem rash and premature. Enough for my present purpose that such researches are proceeding in all Churches of the Reformation—that it is wholly impossible to put them down by force; and that here again Reason must play her part—must decide by her own standard how far they are right and how far they are wrong—must, in other words, find out and determine what *is* the Word of God in the Scriptures before it bends before its authority as infallible and supreme.

After all this, however, it is still possible for Christians to find an oracle in the Bible—a "Thus saith the Lord," which for all practical purposes, and some theoretical, is sufficient; and in this we should cordially rejoice. Not only have we not followed any cunningly devised fable, but we need neither the infallible stamp of the Church of Rome nor the trumpery hope of a New Revelation from Heaven, in which some well meaning men believe; we need nothing more than a continued exercise of our own instructed Reason to find enough in the Scriptures for our spiritual guidance; aye, and we may make new discoveries in them too by the improved methods of modern interpretation.

But although we thus cordially admit an ultimate authority in Scripture, as properly limited and understood, yet where, we ask, is the evidence for the ultimate and oracular authority of human documents, such as Creeds and Confessions? We deny not that such documents had, and worthily served, their day. They were landmarks of progress and beacons of light in the age when they were first produced. But now they are anachronisms and ruins. They are full of crannies and crevices, through which you hear the winds whistling with a sound half melancholy and half scornful. Much truth they still contain, because a great part was collected faithfully from the study of the Scriptures; but they never contained the whole truth, being only extracts from its volume—a volume that has, besides, been enlarging and widening since with the progress of the human mind, till these old extracts, compared to its present size, look miserably petty and fragmentary. And they are seen now, besides, to contain many blunders—

blunders of scriptural interpretation, blunders of natural and mental philosophy, and blunders of theological doctrine. They hold, or at least you can directly infer from them, such dogmas as Eternal Reprobation and the Damnation of Non-Elect Infants. They hold that the world was made in six literal days. My friend, Dr. Anderson of Glasgow, went down to the Presbytery of Glasgow three years ago with a copy of the Confession of Faith marked in nine places as opposed to the Word of God and to common sense; and I, though a younger and inferior man, claim for myself and others a similar liberty. The mere size of these documents is a powerful objection. The Confession of Faith is not indeed a very large book to be read; but it is a very large book to be believed—a very large book of human composition, verily, to be put on a level with the Book of God! It should never be forgotten, too, that since these Standards have been written, not only have Science, Philosophy, and Scripture Criticism been advancing at a great rate, but there has more fully developed itself in the human mind the element of *Individualism*. Men in ancient times thought in masses, or rather followed implicitly the thinkings of other and greater men. People are now beginning more (remembering that it is as individuals they must be justified or condemned) to think on religious topics, and indeed on all subjects, for themselves; and that any independent thinker can, in this age of restless research and all-sided inquiry, consent, *ex animo*, to all the propositions in a thickish octavo volume, or even in the Shorter Catechism, is simply impossible. And hence many who have no sympathy with progressive views are compelled, by a felt necessity in the case, to entertain the idea of abridging these documents greatly, and reducing the immense heap of credibilia which exists at present in them to a few leading and vital principles.

It is true that efforts are being made at present,* with the particulars of which the newspapers have informed everybody, to make more stringent a yoke which neither we nor our fathers were able to bear, and to extend the weight of that yoke to a portion of the community who have yet been comparatively free from it—I mean the laity. Hitherto it has generally been understood that the laity were exempted from those vows and obligations, at least in their extent and minutiæ, by which the clergy are fettered. But now matters are changed, and attempts are being made to stop the utterance of individualistic thought among laymen by severe pains and penalties, including inquisitorial investigation, public citation, and probably ultimate expulsion. Such cases in themselves do not perhaps fall properly into the sphere of pulpit criticism; but when viewed as indications of tendency, as straws showing the direction of the wind, as bearing on the general question of Christian liberty, they assume paramount importance, and call for special notice.

There are various reasons why the laity should be exempted from such severe treatment as has befallen some of them recently. It is not to be supposed that as a rule they have enjoyed leisure or received education

---

* The Author alludes to the well known Coupar-Angus Heresy Case, proceedings in which, he is glad to say, are now dropped.

fitting them to form personal convictions on many of the immense number of topics contained in the Standards of their Church. In ninety-nine cases out of a hundred, they have not read these documents at all, and in connecting themselves with a religious body they have never dreamed that they were pledging themselves to aught but a general concurrence with the main doctrines and facts of Christianity, and a special preference for the peculiar ecclesiastical position of the particular Church. Beyond this they do not consider themselves bound, and can only be driven by an act of ecclesiastical despotism. When a minister looks abroad over his people on a sacramental occasion, he never supposes that he is looking at a collection of thoroughly equipped and profoundly orthodox lay divines. He sees only a number of persons, male and female, moderately well informed on religious topics, and willing to be better instructed; who have a general belief in Christianity, and a love for the Saviour, at whose table they are seated. A few of them, he is aware, go much farther, and are highly intelligent and far advanced believers. But he is aware, too, that especially in this age there are probably some who hold heterodox opinions, or whose minds are disturbed by sceptical doubts, and yet who in the main are worthy, sincere, and well-conducted men. All this, if he knows his congregation at all, he may know perfectly; and with this state of matters, if he knows human nature, he will rest satisfied, or at least feel that to make rude and violent efforts to improve it would be very useless. Suppose he should hear that one or other of his members were vending his doubts or propagating his heterodox opinions, he would, before taking action, inquire (first) privately if these reports were true; (secondly) of what nature the doubts were; and (thirdly) in what spirit they were propounded. And if he found that they were not of a very vital kind, and that they were brought forward in an humble and Christian spirit, he would, as on the whole his wisest course, refrain from interfering, and feel assured that the matter would soon drop. Even if he discovered or heard that the doubts or questions were of a graver kind, he might, before proceeding to extremities, inquire whether there were not others in the Church, perhaps in its high places, who were currently understood to hold similar opinions; whether it were not likely the accused would avail themselves in self-defence of the knowledge of this; and whether he would not by this inquiry be the means of disturbing the peace of his Church, of troubling waters he could not calm, of raising a devil he could not lay. If he dared these consequences, it might then become a question, if not for him for others, whether he were strong enough to master the situation and to cast out the heresy which was so widely spread, and whether altogether it were not better for him to let the matter alone, and the heresy and the heretics to run their course and to find their level. This, it appears to me, would have been the conduct of sense and wisdom; but this has *not* been the conduct of the clerical parties to whom I refer.

In the present excited, uncertain, and transitional state of thought both in England and Scotland, it were the easiest thing in the world to create a heresy-hunt which would end in the confusion, irritation, and perhaps disruption of any Church whatever. Suppose I know a man in my Congregation who believed in Millenarianism, were I (who once held that view myself, although I now look on it as a mere crotchet and Jewish dream, remembering with shame and indignation that I had once been its public advocate) to proceed to prosecute the person, and to prove to him that it was entirely opposed to the Confession of Faith and the Catechisms Larger and Shorter, not to speak of the Secession Testimony, how easy it were for that person to protest that the doctrine was held by some excellent and able ministers in the U.P. Church, and then carry the case to the Synod, and create quite an ecclesiastical row. What a fool I would be to start such a hunt! And what less can I call those who seek to pull up a man for denying Verbal Inspiration, while it is notorious that there are dozens in his Church who either deny it altogether or hold it in twenty contradictory ways? Where would such a system end? And if private members are to be prosecuted, why not leading ministers? Why should there be different weights and different measures? But men, it is said, that propagate heresy should have no mercy. For my part I honour the man that speaks out his thoughts, whatever they be. But why, it is said again, should they not leave the Church if they differ from its doctrines? Certainly, considering the usage they have met with, and the illiberal, stupid, and detestably narrow views advocated by the ministers with whom they have come in contact, I wonder that they have not left, shaking the dust of their feet behind them.

But the question arises—If they leave why do not the entire liberal party in that Church leave too? And, query, What are the doctrines of that Church? Whether are we to gather them from the small men in the provinces or from the large men in the capital? Whether is Dr. Julius Wood or Dr. Candlish in the right about the Atonement? Whether are we to take the Shorter Catechism or the *North British Review* as the true exponent of Free Church views about the Creation of the World, the Antiquity of Man, and other knotty questions? And whether is the divine in the North, who has become notorious, or Walter Smith of Glasgow the proper representative-man in point of orthodoxy of that Church, of which the one is about the obscurest and the other one of the most distinguished members—both members, mark you, yet differing as widely in many religious views as the centre from the pole, as Saturn from the Sun? I denounce as a piece of unjust and contemptible oppression seeking to crush private individuals for holding opinions which are known to be entertained more or less fully, and defended more or less openly, by distinguished divines and professors in the same communion.

I close with two or three remarks founded on what has been said. First. Let us try to forgive and pity the most narrow and bigoted of our fellowmen. It is very difficult to do so. I fear after all it is seldom done; though it is something even to try and to wish to do it. One's blood is but too apt to rise when we hear of men, and ministers too, professing, and we should hope entertaining, warm appreciation and love for the Lord Jesus Christ, and yet seeking, with cat-like stealthiness of motion, to entrap the unwary, with vindictive determination to pursue them, with foul-mouthed fury to defame them, and, what is infinitely worse, compromising the glorious liberty and catholic character of Christianity itself by the most narrow-minded views and the most unguarded statements. Christ says—"He that is not against us is on our part." But these ministers tell you there can be no virtue, and imply there can be no salvation, except by believing their creed and breathing their spirit, which is, I fear, little less exclusive and less persecuting than that of Papists themselves. It is sad to think of such things being said, and seemingly believed, in the nineteenth century. It is sadder to remember that some who utter them are really good, though extremely mistaken men; not better, however, and certainly not one whit less mistaken or less illiberal, than many sincere Papists, who hold that there is no salvation out of the Romish pale, and that there is no faith to be kept with those heretics for whom nothing but perdition is reserved. It is sad to think that if the union goes on a number of the U.P. Church ministers (although certainly not the writer of this) must call such men brethren, and try to love them as such, instead of blaming them as bigots, and pitying them as fanatics. And it is saddest of all to remember what a handle all this will give and is giving to those who are enemies to religion, and have no other wish for the whole Church than is implied in the words—"Cut it down; why cumbereth it the ground?"

Secondly. Mark the bearing of this upon the Christian

laity and their prospects. There is with many of the more intelligent of that class a considerable aversion to join Churches in the present day, owing to the unsettled state of religious opinions. And when they do join, they like a large margin. They love Christianity, they love Christ, they value the privileges of the Church, but they would like to retain in many points the liberty of thinking for themselves. They like edification and the culture of the spiritual nature; not overbearing dogmatism and eternal controversy in the pulpit. Now before these men, such proceedings as those I am commenting on throw formidable obstacles, and they will be ready to say—"If our opinions and our tongues are to be subjected to such espionage—if we are liable to be subjected to discipline for every speculation we may indulge and every doubt that we may utter, utter perhaps simply to relieve its pressure on our own minds—then we must withdraw from these Churches, or we must avoid connecting ourselves with them." And I can assure the clergy that the loss of such thoughtful and conscientious men will not be made up by the largest rabble of tame slaves and subservient noodles that can be forced into the fold by the whip of terror, the fear of popular clamour, the energy of revivalistic convulsion and claptrap, or by any other cause whatever. If the Church cannot retain her intelligent and influential laity, she must perish, and deserves her doom.

Once more, let us ever act as disinterested and decided lovers of truth. Few, alas! in any age, have been ready to exclaim—"Above all things truth! Above names, prejudices, prepossessions, systems, creeds, even crotchets, the greatest obstacles of all!" The true lover of truth will be as humble as sincere in his researches, and will walk all his life bending before her footprints, while he essays to follow her whithersoever she goeth. And this being his feeling, he will not shrink from her society, and desert her when she seems to tread new, or steep, or dangerous ground, persuaded that Truth is never more herself than when she leaves the trodden vale and aspires either to the rugged and storm-swept summit, or descends into the deep and dragon-swarming abyss. He knows that the scale and tale of truth are infinite; that the universe is the result of causes immovably, infinitely complex in kind, and which can be proved to have been operating for millions of millions of years. He feels therefore that to dogmatise on subjects so vast—many of the roots and ramifications of which are as deep as the oldest handiworks of God, and as distant as the remotest stars of heaven—is pitiful presumption, and is equally so whether on the heterodox or orthodox side. Would that men, instead of fighting so fiercely about their "little systems," were more generally convinced of the largeness of their ignorance, of what a vast sphere of darkness surrounds them, and were more thankful for every gleam of new light, come from whence and from what or whom it may. Surely by this time of day we should have learned to despise the cry of "Danger from too much light." Such a cry should never have been heard to chirp after the poet of Childe Harold had thus sung—

> "Yet let us ponder boldly; 'tis a base
> Abandonment of reason to resign

> The right of thought, our last and only place
> Of refuge : this at least shall still be mine.
> Though from our birth the faculty divine
> Is chained and tortured, cabined, cribbed, confined,
> And bred in darkness lest the truth should shine
> Too brightly on the unprepared mind,
> The beam pours in ; for Time and Skill will couch the blind."

Of this we may be certain, that Truth, in her rapid and resistless march—however much of the rubbish of the Past she may leave behind her or trample on as she travels—can *never* destroy the deep foundations of Moral Obligation, or the genuine principles and the blessed spirit of the Christian Religion.

NOTE.—The Author intends a second volume, including the Fathers of the Voluntary Cause, the Heroes of English Dissent (Hall, Foster, &c.), the Progressive Men in the Scottish Establishment (A. Thomson, Chalmers, and E. Irving), and the Representative Men of the Broad Church in England (Arnold, Frederick Robertson, and others).

H. NISBET, PRINTER, TRONGATE, GLASGOW.